Also by V. S. Naipaul

Nonfiction

Fiction

*Published in an omnibus edition entitled *Three Novels*

THE ENIGMA
OF
ARRIVAL

V. S. NAIPAUL

THE ENIGMA OF
ARRIVAL

A NOVEL

ALFRED A. KNOPF   NEW YORK

1987

This is a Borzoi Book
Published by Alfred A. Knopf, Inc.

COPYRIGHT © 1987 BY V. S. NAIPAUL

PORTIONS OF THIS BOOK WERE ORIGINALLY PUBLISHED IN THE NEW YORKER.

LIBRARY OF CONGRESS CATALOGING-IN-PUBLICATION DATA

NAIPAUL, V. S. (VIDIADHAR SURAJPRASAD).
THE ENIGMA OF ARRIVAL.

I. TITLE.
PR9272.9.N32E5   1987   823'.914   86-46149
ISBN 0-394-50971-4

MANUFACTURED IN THE UNITED STATES OF AMERICA

PUBLISHED MARCH 19, 1987
SECOND PRINTING, MAY 1987

IN LOVING MEMORY

OF MY BROTHER

SHIVA NAIPAUL

25 FEBRUARY 1945, PORT OF SPAIN

13 AUGUST 1985, LONDON

CONTENTS

THE ENIGMA
OF
ARRIVAL

JACK'S GARDEN

*F*OR THE first four days it rained. I could hardly see where I was. Then it stopped raining and beyond the lawn and out-buildings in front of my cottage I saw fields with stripped trees on the boundaries of each field; and far away, depending on the light, glints of a little river, glints which sometimes appeared, oddly, to be above the level of the land.

The river was called the Avon; not the one connected with Shake-speare. Later—when the land had more meaning, when it had ab-sorbed more of my life than the tropical street where I had grown up—I was able to think of the flat wet fields with the ditches as "water meadows" or "wet meadows," and the low smooth hills in the back-ground, beyond the river, as "downs." But just then, after the rain, all that I saw—though I had been living in England for twenty years—were flat fields and a narrow river.

It was winter. This idea of winter and snow had always excited me; but in England the word had lost some of its romance for me, because the winters I had found in England had seldom been as ex-treme as I had imagined they would be when I was far away in my tropical island. I had experienced severe weather in other places—in

Spain in January, in a skiing resort near Madrid; in India, in Simla in December, and in the high Himalayas in August. But in England this kind of weather hardly seemed to come. In England I wore the same kind of clothes all through the year; seldom wore a pullover; hardly needed an overcoat.

And though I knew that summers were sunny and that in winter the trees went bare and brushlike, as in the watercolors of Rowland Hilder, the year—so far as vegetation and even temperature went— was a blur to me. It was hard for me to distinguish one section or season from the other; I didn't associate flowers or the foliage of trees with any particular month. And yet I liked to look; I noticed every-thing, and could be moved by the beauty of trees and flowers and early sunny mornings and late light evenings. Winter was to me a time mainly of short days, and of electric lights everywhere at working hours; also a time when snow was a possibility.

If I say it was winter when I arrived at that house in the river val-ley, it is because I remember the mist, the four days of rain and mist that hid my surroundings from me and answered my anxiety at the time, anxiety about my work and this move to a new place, yet an-other of the many moves I had made in England.

It was winter, too, because I was worried about the cost of heating. In the cottage there was only electricity—more expensive than gas or oil. And the cottage was hard to heat. It was long and narrow; it was not far from the water meadows and the river; and the concrete floor was just a foot or so above the ground.

And then one afternoon it began to snow. Snow dusted the lawn in front of my cottage; dusted the bare branches of the trees; outlined disregarded things, outlined the empty, old-looking buildings around the lawn that I hadn't yet paid attention to or fully taken in; so that piece by piece, while I considered the falling snow, a rough picture of my setting built up around me.

Rabbits came out to play on the snow, or to feed. A mother rabbit, hunched, with three or four of her young. They were a different, dirty color on the snow. And this picture of the rabbits, or more particularly their new color, calls up or creates the other details of the winter's day: the late-afternoon snow light; the strange, empty houses around the lawn becoming white and distinct and more important. It also calls up the memory of the forest I thought I saw behind the whitening hedge against which the rabbits fed. The white lawn; the empty houses around it; the hedge to one side of the lawn, the gap in the hedge, a path; the forest beyond. I saw a forest. But it wasn't a forest really; it was only the old orchard at the back of the big house in whose grounds my cottage was.

I saw what I saw very clearly. But I didn't know what I was looking at. I had nothing to fit it into. I was still in a kind of limbo. There were certain things I knew, though. I knew the name of the town I had come to by the train. It was Salisbury. It was almost the first English town I had got to know, the first I had been given some idea of, from the reproduction of the Constable painting of Salisbury Cathedral in my third-standard reader. Far away in my tropical island, before I was ten. A four-color reproduction which I had thought the most beautiful picture I had ever seen. I knew that the house I had come to was in one of the river valleys near Salisbury.

Apart from the romance of the Constable reproduction, the knowledge I brought to my setting was linguistic. I knew that "avon" originally meant only river, just as "hound" originally just meant a dog, any kind of dog. And I knew that both elements of Waldenshaw—the name of the village and the manor in whose grounds I was—I knew that both "walden" and "shaw" meant wood. One further reason why, apart from the fairy-tale feel of the snow and the rabbits, I thought I saw a forest.

I also knew that the house was near Stonehenge. I knew there was a walk which took one near the stone circle; I knew that somewhere high up on this walk there was a viewing point. And when the rain stopped and the mist lifted, after those first four days, I went out one afternoon, looking for the walk and the view.

There was no village to speak of. I was glad of that. I would have been nervous to meet people. After all my time in England I still had that nervousness in a new place, that rawness of response, still felt myself to be in the other man's country, felt my strangeness, my solitude. And every excursion into a new part of the country—what for others might have been an adventure—was for me like a tearing at an old scab.

The narrow public road ran beside the dark, yew-screened grounds of the manor. Just beyond the road and the wire fence and the roadside scrub the down sloped sharply upwards. Stonehenge and the walk lay in that direction. There would have been a lane or path leading off the public road. To find that lane or path, was I to turn left or right? There was no problem, really. You came to a lane if you turned left; you came to another lane if you turned right. Those two lanes met at Jack's cottage, or the old farmyard where Jack's cottage was, in the valley over the hill.

Two ways to the cottage. Different ways: one was very old, and one was new. The old way was longer, flatter; it followed an old, wide, winding riverbed; it would have been used by carts in the old days. The new way—meant for machines—was steeper, up the hill and then directly down again.

You came to the old way if you turned left on the public road. This stretch of road was overhung by beeches. It ran on a ledge in the down just above the river; and then it dropped almost to the level of the river. A little settlement here, just a few houses. I noticed: a small old house of brick and flint with a fine portico; and, on the riverbank, very close to the water, a low, white-walled thatched cottage that was being "done up." (Years later that cottage was still being done up; half-used sacks of cement were still to be seen through the dusty windows.) Here, in this settlement, you turned off into the old way to Jack's cottage.

An asphalt lane led past half a dozen ordinary little houses, two or three of which carried—their only fanciful touch—the elaborate monogram of the owner or builder or designer, with the date, which was, surprisingly, a date from the war: 1944. The asphalt gave out, the narrow lane became rocky; then, entering a valley, became wide, with many flinty wheeled ruts separated by uneven strips of coarse, tufted grass. This valley felt old. To the left the steep slope shut out a further view. This slope was bare, without trees or scrub; below its smooth, thin covering of grass could be seen lines and stripes, like weals, suggesting many consecutive years of tilling a long time ago; suggesting also fortifications. The wide way twisted; the wide valley (possibly an ancient river course) which the way occupied then ran straight and far, bounded in the distance by the beginning of a low down. Jack's cottage and the farmyard were at the end of that straight way, where the way turned.

The other way to the cottage, the shorter, steeper, newer way, up from the main road and then down to the valley and the farmyard, was lined on the northern side with a windbreak, young beech trees protected by taller pines. At the top of the slope there was a modern, metal-walled barn; just a little way down on the other side there was a gap in the windbreak. This was the viewing point for Stonehenge: far away, small, not easy to see, not as easy as the luminous red or orange targets of the army firing ranges. And at the bottom of the slope, down the rocky, uneven lane beside the windbreak, were the derelict farm buildings and the still living row of agricultural cottages, one of which Jack lived in.

The downs all around were flinty and dry, whitish brown, whitish green. But on the wide way at the bottom, around the farm buildings, the ground was muddy and black. The tractor wheels had dug out irregular linear ponds in the black mud.

The first afternoon, when I reached the farm buildings, walking down the steep way, beside the windbreak, I had to ask the way to Stonehenge. From the viewing point at the top, it had seemed clear. But from that point down had risen against down, slope against slope; dips and paths had been hidden; and at the bottom, where mud and long puddles made walking difficult and made the spaces seem bigger, and there appeared to be many paths, some leading off the wide valley way, I was confused. Such a simple inquiry, though, in the emptiness; and I never forgot that on the first day I had asked someone the way.

Was it Jack? I didn't take the person in; I was more concerned with the strangeness of the walk, my own strangeness, and the absurdity of my inquiry.

I was told to go round the farm buildings, to turn to the right, to stick to the wide main way, and to ignore all the tempting dry paths that led off the main way to the woods which lay on the other side, young woods that falsely suggested deep country, the beginning of forest.

So, past the mud around the cottages and the farmyard, past the mess of old timber and tangled old barbed wire and apparently abandoned pieces of farm machinery, I turned right. The wide muddy way became grassy, long wet grass. And soon, when I had left the farm buildings behind and felt myself walking in a wide, empty, old riverbed, the sense of space was overwhelming.

The grassy way, the old riverbed (as I thought), sloped up, so that the eye was led to the middle sky; and on either side were the slopes of the downs, widening out and up against the sky. On one side there were cattle; on the other side, beyond a pasture, a wide empty area, there were young pines, a little forest. The setting felt ancient; the impression was of space, unoccupied land, the beginning of things. There were no houses to be seen, only the wide grassy way, the sky above it, and the wide slopes on either side.

It was possible on this stretch of the walk to hold on to the idea of emptiness. But when I got to the top of the grassy way and was on a level with the barrows and tumuli which dotted the high downs all around, and I looked down at Stonehenge, I saw also the firing ranges of Salisbury Plain and the many little neat houses of West Amesbury. The emptiness, the spaciousness through which I had felt myself walking was as much an illusion as the idea of forest behind the young pines. All around—and not far away—were roads and highways, with brightly colored trucks and cars like toys. Stonehenge, old barrows and tumuli outlined against the sky; the army firing ranges, West Amesbury. The old and the new; and, from a midway or a different time, the farmyard with Jack's cottage at the bottom of the valley.

Many of the farm buildings were no longer used. The barns and pens—red-brick walls, roofs of slate or clay tiles—around the muddy yard were in decay; and only occasionally in the pens were there cattle—sick cattle, enfeebled calves, isolated from the herd. Fallen tiles, holed roofs, rusted corrugated iron, bent metal, a pervading damp, the colors rust and brown and black, with a glittering or dead-green moss on the trampled, dung-softened mud of the pen yard: the isolation of the animals in that setting, like things themselves about to be discarded, was terrible.

Once there were cattle there that had suffered from some malformation. The breeding of these cattle had become so mechanical that the malformation appeared mechanical too, the mistakes of an industrial process. Curious additional lumps of flesh had grown at various places on the animals, as though these animals had been cast in a mold, a mold divided into two sections, and as though, at the joining of the molds, the cattle material, the mixture out of which the cattle were being cast, had leaked; and had hardened, matured into flesh, and had then developed hair with the black-and-white Frisian pattern of the rest of the cattle. There, in the ruined, abandoned, dungy, mossy farmyard, fresh now only with their own dung, they had stood, burdened in this puzzling way, with this extra cattle material hanging down their middles like a bull's dewlaps, like heavy curtains, waiting to be taken off to the slaughterhouse in the town.

Away from the old farm buildings, and down the wide flat way which I thought of as the old road to the farm and Jack's cottage, there were other remnants and ruins, relics of other efforts or lives. At the end of the wide way, to one side of it in tall grass, were flat shallow boxes, painted gray, set down in two rows. I was told later that they were or had been beehives. I was never told who it was who had kept the bees. Was it a farm worker, someone from the cottages, or was it someone more leisured, attempting a little business enterprise and then giving up and forgetting? Abandoned now, unexplained, the gray boxes that were worth no one's while to take away were a little mysterious in the unfenced openness.

On the other side of the wide droveway, its great curve round the farm buildings just beginning here, in the shelter of young trees and scrub there was an old green and yellow and red caravan in good condition, a brightly painted gypsy caravan of the old days (as I thought), looking as if its horses had been unhitched not long before. Another mystery; another carefully made thing abandoned; another piece of the past that no longer had a use but had not been thrown away. Like the antiquated, cumbersome pieces of farm machinery scattered and rusting about the farm buildings.

Midway down the straight wide way, far beyond the beehives and the caravan, was an old hayrick, with bales of hay stacked into a cottage-shaped structure and covered with old black plastic sheeting. The hay had grown old; out of its blackness there were green sprouts; the hay that had been carefully cut one summer and baled and stored was decaying, turning to manure. The hay of the farm was now stored in a modern open shed, a prefabricated structure which carried the printed name of the maker just below the apex of the roof. The shed had been erected just beyond the mess of the old farmyard—as though space would always be available, and nothing old need ever be built over. The hay in this shed was new, with a sweet, warm smell; and the bales unstacked into golden, clean, warm-smelling steps, which made me think of the story about spinning straw into gold and of references in books with European settings to men sleeping on straw in barns. That had never been comprehensible to me in Trinidad, where grass was always freshly cut for cattle, always green, and never browned into hay. Now, in winter, at the bottom of this damp valley: high-stacked golden hay bales, warm golden steps next to rutted black mud.

Not far from the decaying rick shaped like a hut or cottage there were the remains of a true house, a house with walls that might have been of flint and concrete. A simple house, its walls perhaps without foundations, it was now quite exposed. Ruined walls, roofless, around bare earth—no sign of a stone or concrete floor. How damp it felt! All around the plot the boundary trees—sycamore or beech or oak—had grown tall, dwarfing the house. Once they would have been barely noticeable, the trees that, living on while the house had ceased to be, now kept the ground chill and mossy and black and in perpetual shadow. Smaller houses beside the public roads, houses built by squatters in the last century, farm laborers mainly, had established ownership rights for the builders and their descendants. But here, beside the grassy droveway, in the middle of downs and fields and solitude, the owner or the builder of the house had left nothing behind; nothing had been established. Only the trees he had planted had continued to grow.

Perhaps the house had been no more than a shepherd's shelter. But that was only a guess. Shepherd's huts would have been smaller; and the trees around the plot didn't speak of a shepherd's hut, didn't speak of a man lodging there for only a few nights at a time.

Sheep were no longer the main animals of the plain. I saw a sheep-shearing only once. It was done by a big man, an Australian, I was told, and the shearing was done in one of the old buildings—timber walls and a slate roof—at the side of the cottage row in which Jack lived. I saw the shearing by accident; I had heard nothing about it; it just happened at the time of my afternoon walk. But the shearing had clearly been news for some; the farm people and people from else-where as well had gathered to watch. A display of strength and speed, the fleecy animal lifted and shorn (and sometimes cut) at the same time, and then sent off, oddly naked—the ceremony was like something out of an old novel, perhaps by Hardy, or out of a Victorian country diary. And it was as though, then, the firing ranges of Salisbury Plain, and the vapor trails of military aircraft in the sky, and the army houses and the roaring highways didn't lie around us. As though, in that little spot around the farm buildings and Jack's cottage, time had stood still, and things were as they had been, for a little while. But the sheep-shearing was from the past. Like the old farm buildings. Like the caravan that wasn't going to move again. Like the barn where grain was no longer stored.

This barn had a high window with a projecting metal bracket. Per-haps a pulley wheel and a chain or rope had been attached to this metal bracket to lift bales off the carts and wagons and then swing them through the high open window into the barn. There was a similar an-tique fixture in the town of Salisbury, at the upper level of what had been a well-known old grocery shop. It had survived or been allowed to live on as an antique, a trade mark, something suited to an old town careful of its past. But what was an antique in the town was rubbish at the bottom of the hill. It was part of a barn that was crumbling winter by winter—the barn and the other dilapidated farm buildings no doubt allowed to survive because, in this protected area, planning regulations allowed new buildings to go up only where buildings existed.

And just as the modern prefabricated shed had replaced the old rotting hayrick, so—but far away, not a simple addition to the old farm buildings—the true barn was now at the top of the hill, beside the windbreak. It had galvanized tin walls; it would have been rat-proof. There machinery caused everything to go; and the powerful trucks (not nowadays the wagons that might have used the flat drove-way to the old barn at the bottom of the valley) climbed up the rocky lane from the public road and pulled into the concrete yard of the barn, and the spout from the barn poured the dusty grain into the deep trays of the trucks.

The straw was golden, warm; the grain was golden; but the dust that fell all around—on the concrete yard, the rocky lane, the pines and young beeches of the windbreak—the dust that fell after the grain had poured into the trays of the trucks was gray. At the side of the metal-walled barn, and below a metal spout, there was a conical mound of dust that had been winnowed by some mechanical means from the bigger conical mounds of grain in the barn. This dust—the mound firm at the base, wonderfully soft at the top—was very fine and gray, without a speck of gold.

New, this barn, with all its mechanical contrivances. But just next to it, across an unpaved muddy lane, was another ruin: a wartime bunker, a mound planted over with sycamores, for concealment, and with a metal ventilator sticking out oddly now among the trunks of the grown trees. The sycamores would have been planted at least twenty-five years before; but they had been planted close together, and they still looked young.

※　※　※

*J*ACK LIVED among ruins, among superseded things. But that way of looking came to me later, has come to me with greater force now, with the writing. It wasn't the idea that came to me when I first went out walking.

That idea of ruin and dereliction, of out-of-placeness, was something I felt about myself, attached to myself: a man from another hemisphere, another background, coming to rest in middle life in the cottage of a half-neglected estate, an estate full of reminders of its Edwardian past, with few connections with the present. An oddity among the estates and big houses of the valley, and I a further oddity in its grounds. I felt unanchored and strange. Everything I saw in those early days, as I took my surroundings in, everything I saw on my daily walk, beside the windbreak or along the wide grassy way, made that feeling more acute. I felt that my presence in that old valley was part of something like an upheaval, a change in the course of the history of the country.

Jack himself, however, I considered to be part of the view. I saw his life as genuine, rooted, fitting: man fitting the landscape. I saw him as a remnant of the past (the undoing of which my own presence portended). It did not occur to me, when I first went walking and saw only the view, took what I saw as things of that walk, things that one might see in the countryside near Salisbury, immemorial, appropriate things, it did not occur to me that Jack was living in the middle of junk, among the ruins of nearly a century; that the past around his cottage might not have been his past; that he might at some stage have been a newcomer to the valley; that his style of life might have been a matter of choice, a conscious act; that out of the little piece of earth which had come to him with his farm worker's cottage (one of a row of three) he had created a special land for himself, a garden, where (though surrounded by ruins, reminders of vanished lives) he was more than content to live out his life and where, as in a version of a book of hours, he celebrated the seasons.

I saw him as a remnant. Not far away, among the ancient barrows and tumuli, were the firing ranges and army training grounds of Salisbury Plain. There was a story that because of the absence of people in those military areas, because of the purely military uses to which the land had been put for so long, and contrary to what one might expect after the explosions and mock warfare, there survived on the plain some kinds of butterflies that had vanished in more populated parts. And I thought that in some such fashion, in the wide droveway at the bottom of the valley, accidentally preserved from people, traffic, and the military, Jack like the butterflies had survived.

I saw things slowly; they emerged slowly. It was not Jack whom I first noticed on my walks. It was Jack's father-in-law. And it was the father-in-law—rather than Jack—who seemed a figure of literature in that ancient landscape. He seemed a Wordsworthian figure: bent, exaggeratedly bent, going gravely about his peasant tasks, as if in an immense Lake District solitude.

He walked very slowly, the bent old man; he did everything very deliberately. He had worked out his own paths across the downs and he stuck to them. You could follow these paths even across barbed-wire fences, by the blue plastic sacks (originally containing fertilizer) which the old man had rolled around the barbed wire and then tied very tightly with red nylon string, working with a thoroughness that matched his pace and deliberateness to create these safe padded places where he could cross below the barbed wire or climb over it.

The old man first, then. And, after him, the garden, the garden in the midst of superseded things. It was Jack's garden that made me notice Jack—the people in the other cottages I never got to know, couldn't recognize, never knew when they moved in or moved out. But it took some time to see the garden. So many weeks, so many walks between the whitish chalk and flint hills up to the level of the barrows to look down at Stonehenge, so many walks just looking for hares—it took some time before, with the beginning of my new awareness of the seasons, I noticed the garden. Until then it had simply been there, something on the walk, a marker, not to be specially noticed. And yet I loved landscape, trees, flowers, clouds, and was responsive to changes of light and temperature.

I noticed his hedge first of all. It was well clipped, tight in the middle, but ragged in places at ground level. I felt, from the clipping, that the gardener would have liked that hedge to be tight all over, to be as complete as a wall of brick or timber or some kind of man-fashioned material. The hedge marked the boundary between Jack's fruit and flower garden and the droveway, which was very wide here, bare ground around the cottages and the farm buildings, and nearly always soft or muddy. In winter the long puddles reflected the sky between black, tractor-marked mud. For a few days in summer that black mud dried out, turned hard and white and dusty. So for a few days in the summer the hedge that ran the length of the garden that Jack possessed with his cottage was white with chalk dust for a foot or so above the ground; in winter it was spattered with mud, drying out white or gray.

The hedge hid nothing. As you came down the hill with the wind-break you could see it all. The old rust-and-black farm buildings in the background; the gray-plastered cottages in front of them; the ground or gardens in front of the cottages; the emptiness or no-man's land in front of the cottage grounds or gardens. And beside Jack's garden, Jack's hedge: a little wall of mud-spattered green, abrupt in the openness of the droveway, like a vestige, a memory of another kind of house and garden and street, a token of something more complete, more ideal.

Technically, the gardens were at the front of the cottages. In fact, by long use, the back of the cottages had become the front; and the front gardens had really become back gardens. But Jack, with the same instinct that made him grow and carefully clip (and also abruptly end) that hedge beside the droveway, treated his garden like a front garden. A paved path with a border of some sort ran from his "front" door all the way down the middle of his garden. This should have led to a gate, a pavement, a street. There was a gate; but this gate, set in a wide-meshed wire-netting fence, led only to a wire-fenced patch of earth which was forked over every year: it was here that Jack planted out his annuals. In front of this was the empty area, the no-man's land between droveway and the beginning of the cultivated down. Jack's ducks and geese had their sheds in that area, which was messy with dung and feathers. Though they were not penned in, the ducks and geese never strayed far; they just walked back and forth across the droveway.

Hedge, garden, planting-out bed for annuals, a plot for ducks and geese; and beyond that, beyond the ground reserved for the other two cottages, just where the land began to slope up to the farm's machine-cultivated fields, was the area where Jack grew his vegetables.

Every piece of ground was separate. Jack didn't see his setting as a whole. But he saw its component parts very clearly; and everything he tended answered the special idea he had of that thing. The hedge was regularly clipped, the garden was beautiful and clean and full of changing color, and the goose plot was dirty, with roughly built sheds and enamel basins and bowls and discarded earthenware sinks. Like a medieval village in miniature, all the various pieces of the garden Jack had established around the old farm buildings. This was Jack's style, and it was this that suggested to me (falsely, as I got to know soon enough) the remnant of an old peasantry, surviving here like the butterflies among the explosions of Salisbury Plain, surviving somehow industrial revolution, deserted villages, railways, and the establishing of the great agricultural estates in the valley.

So much of this I saw with the literary eye, or with the aid of literature. A stranger here, with the nerves of the stranger, and yet with a knowledge of the language and the history of the language and the writing, I could find a special kind of past in what I saw; with a part of my mind I could admit fantasy.

I heard on the radio one morning that in the days of the Roman Empire geese could be walked to market all the way from the province of Gaul to Rome. After this, the high-headed, dung-dropping geese that strutted across the muddy, rutted way at the bottom of the valley and could be quite aggressive at times—Jack's geese—developed a kind of historical life for me, something that went beyond the idea of medieval peasantry, old English country ways, and the drawings of geese in children's books. And when one year, longing for Shakespeare, longing to be put in touch with the early language, I returned to *King Lear* for the first time for more than twenty years, and read in

Kent's railing speech, "Goose, if I had you upon Sarum Plain, I'd drive ye cackling home to Camelot," the words were quite clear to me. Sarum Plain, Salisbury Plain; Camelot, Winchester—just twenty miles away. And I felt that with the help of Jack's geese—creatures with perhaps an antiquity in the droveway lands that Jack would not have guessed—I had arrived at an understanding of something in *King Lear* which, according to the editor of the text I read, commentators had found obscure.

The solitude of the walk, the emptiness of that stretch of the downs, enabled me to surrender to my way of looking, to indulge my linguistic or historical fantasies; and enabled me, at the same time, to shed the nerves of being a stranger in England. Accident—the shape of the fields, perhaps, the alignment of paths and modern roads, the needs of the military—had isolated this little region; and I had this historical part of England to myself when I went walking.

Daily I walked in the wide grassy way between the flint slopes, past chalk valleys rubbled white and looking sometimes like a Himalayan valley strewn in midsummer with old, gritted snow. Daily I saw the mounds that had been raised so many centuries before. The number of these mounds! They lay all around. From a certain height they were outlined against the sky and looked like pimples on the land. In the beginning I liked to tramp over the mounds that were more or less on my walk. The grass on these mounds was coarse; it was long-bladed, pale in color, and grew in ankle-turning tufts or clumps. The trees, where they existed, were wind-beaten and stunted.

I picked my way up and down and around each mound; I wanted in those early days to leave no accessible mound unlooked at, feeling that if I looked hard enough and long enough I might arrive, not at an understanding of the religious mystery, but at an appreciation of the labor.

Daily I walked in the wide grassy way—perhaps in the old days a processional way. Daily I climbed up from the bottom of the valley to the crest of the way and the view: the stone circles directly ahead, down below, but still far away: gray against green, and sometimes lit up by the sun. Going up the grassy way (and though willing to admit that the true processional path might have been elsewhere) I never ceased to imagine myself a man of those bygone times, climbing up to have this confirmation that all was well with the world.

There was a main road on either side of the Henge. On those two roads trucks and vans and cars were like toys. At the foot of the Henge there was the tourist crowd—not very noticeable, not as noticeable as one might imagine from the fairground atmosphere around the stones when you actually went to them. The tourist crowd, from this distance, was noticeable only because of the red dress or coat that some of the women wore. That color red among the visitors to Stonehenge was something that I never failed to see; always someone in red, among the little figures.

And in spite of that crowd, and the highways, and the artillery ranges (with their fluorescent or semi-luminous targets), my sense of antiquity, my feeling for the age of the earth and the oldness of man's possession of it, was always with me. A vast sacred burial ground, bounded by the sky—of what activity those barrows and tumuli spoke, what numbers, what organization, what busyness in these now virtually empty downs! That sense of antiquity gave another scale to the activities around one. But at the same time—from this height, and with that wide view—there was a feeling of continuity.

So the idea of antiquity, at once diminishing and ennobling the current activities of men, as well as the ideas of literature enveloped this world which—surrounded by highways and army barracks though it was, and with the very clouds in the sky sometimes seeded by the vapor trails of busy military airplanes—came to me as a lucky find of the solitude in which on many afternoons I found myself.

Larkhill was the name of the army artillery school. In my first or second year there was something like a fair or open day there when, in the presence of the families of the soldiers, guns were fired off. But the lark hill I looked for on my walk was the hill with ancient barrows where literally larks bred, and behaved like the larks of poetry. "And drown'd in yonder living blue the lark becomes a sightless song." It was true: the birds rose and rose, in almost vertical flight. I suppose I had heard larks before. But these were the first larks I noticed, the first

I watched and listened to. They were another lucky find of my solitude, another unexpected gift.

And that became my mood. When I grew to see the wild roses and hawthorn on my walk, I didn't see the windbreak they grew beside as a sign of the big landowners who had left their mark on the solitude, had preserved it, had planted the woods in certain places (in imitation, it was said, of the positions at the battle of Trafalgar—or was it Waterloo?), I didn't think of the landowners. My mood was purer: I thought of these single-petaled roses and sweet-smelling blossoms at the side of the road as wild and natural growths.

One autumn day—the days shortening, filling me with thoughts of winter pleasures, fires and evening lights and books—one autumn day I felt something like a craving to read of winter in *Sir Gawain and the Green Knight*, a poem I had read more than twenty years before at Oxford as part of the Middle English course. The hips and the haws beside the windbreak, the red berries of this dead but warm time of year, made me want to read again about the winter journey in that old poem. And I read the poem on the bus back from Salisbury, where I had gone to buy it. So in tune with the landscape had I become, in that solitude, for the first time in England.

Of literature and antiquity and the landscape Jack and his garden and his geese and cottage and his father-in-law seemed emanations.

IT WAS his father-in-law I noticed first. And it was his father-in-law I met first. I met him quite early on, while I was still exploring, and before I had settled on a regular daily route. I walked or picked my way down little-used lateral lanes on the hillsides, lanes deep in mud, or overgrown with tall grass, or overhung with trees. I walked in those early days along lanes or paths I was never to walk along again. And it was on one of those exploratory walks, on a lateral lane linking the steep rocky road beside the windbreak with the wider, flatter way, it was on one of those little-used, half-hidden lanes that I met the father-in-law.

He was fantastically, absurdly bent, as though his back had been created for the carrying of loads. A strange croaking came out of him when he spoke to me. It was amazing that, speaking like that, he should attempt speech with a stranger. But more amazing were his eyes, the eyes of this bent man: they were bright and alive and mischievous. In his cadaverous face, of a curious color, a gray color, a swarthiness which made me think of gypsy origins, in his cadaverous face with a bristle, almost a down, of white on cheek and chin, these eyes were a wonder and a reassurance: that in spite of the accident that had permanently damaged his spine, the personality of the man remained sound.

He croaked. "Dogs? Dogs?" That was what the croaking sounded like. He stopped, raised his head like a turtle. He croaked; he raised a finger of authority. He seemed to say, "Dogs? Dogs?" And it needed only an echoing word from me—"Dogs?"—for him to subside, be again a bent old man minding his own business. His eyes dimmed; his head sank down. "Dogs," he muttered, the word choking in his throat. "Worry pheasants."

Beside the lane, and in the shelter of trees, were hedge-high cages with pheasants. It was new to me, to see that these apparently wild creatures were in fact reared a little like backyard chickens. As it was new to me to understand that the woods all around had been planted, and all the alternating roses and hawthorns beside the windbreak of beech and pine.

In the hidden lane, a little impulse of authority, even bullying, with someone who was a stranger and, in terms of gypsy-ness, twenty times as swarthy. But it was the briefest impulse in the old man; and perhaps it was also a social impulse, a wish to exchange words with someone new, a wish to add one more human being to the tally of human beings he had encountered.

He subsided; the brightness in his eyes went out. And I never heard him speak again.

Our paths never really crossed. I saw him occasionally in the distance. Once I saw him actually with a load of wood on his bent back: Wordsworthian, the subject of a poem Wordsworth might have called

"The Fuel-Gatherer." He walked very slowly; yet in that slowness, that deliberation, there was conviction: he had set himself a task he certainly intended to finish. There was something animal-like about his routine. Like a rat, he seemed to have a "run," though (apart from looking after the pheasants, which might not have been true) it wasn't clear to me what he did on the land.

The droveway, the way along the floor of the ancient river valley, was very wide. When I first went walking it was unfenced. In my first year, or the second, the wide way was narrowed. A barbed-wire fence was put up. It ran down the middle of the way, where the way was long and straight; and those sturdy green fence posts (the thicker ones stoutly buttressed) and the taut lines of barbed wire made me feel, although the life of the valley was just beginning for me, that I was also in a way at the end of the thing I had come upon.

How sad it was to lose that sense of width and space! It caused me pain. But already I had grown to live with the idea that things changed; already I lived with the idea of decay. (I had always lived with this idea. It was like my curse: the idea, which I had had even as a child in Trinidad, that I had come into a world past its peak.) Already I lived with the idea of death, the idea, impossible for a young person to possess, to hold in his heart, that one's time on earth, one's life, was a short thing. These ideas, of a world in decay, a world subject to constant change, and of the shortness of human life, made many things bearable.

Later, even older encroachments were revealed on the droveway. Looking down at Stonehenge one summer, from the hill of larks, I saw, from the change of color in the fields of growing corn beside the droveway, what must have been the ruts of old cart or coach wheels. Because this way had been the old coach or wagon road from Stonehenge to Salisbury, a road that because of mud needed to be much wider than a paved road. Now some of the width of that old road had been incorporated—a long time ago—into fields and was behind barbed-wire fencing.

This fencing-in of a great ancient way, this claiming as private property an ancient wide riverbed, no doubt sacred to the ancient tribes (and at one end of the wide valley, beyond the beehives, the caravan, the old hayrick, and the ruined house with the big sycamores, at that end, below the thin grass on the western bank, there were the marks either of ancient furrows or fortifications), this emphasis on property should have made me think of the present, the great estates by which I was surrounded, the remnant of the estate on which I lived.

I saw the farmer or the farm manager making his rounds in a Land-Rover. I saw the modern grain barn at the top of the hill. I saw the windbreak up and down that hill and saw that it had been recently planted, with the pines growing faster than the beeches they were intended to protect (and already creating something like a strip of woodland, with a true woodland litter of fallen branches and dead wood). I saw the hand of man, but didn't sufficiently take it in, preferring to see what I wanted: the great geography of the plain here, with the downs and the old river valley, far from the course of the present, smaller river. I saw the antiquity; I saw the debris of the old farmyard.

In this way of seeing at that time what I wanted to see I was a little like Jack's father-in-law, who ignored the new fence that cut at many places into segments of his run across the droveway. He ignored the new gates (they were few) and stuck to his run, creating stiles and steps and padded passing-places over and through the barbed wire, working in his old way, rolling blue plastic sacks around the barbed wire and then tying them with spiral after spiral of red-blond raffia or nylon.

The odd zigzag of the old man's run was now revealed, as were its widest limits: from the pheasant cages on the muddy, shaded lane on the far side of the hill with the new barn, down that lane, across the droveway, and all the way up a scrub-bordered field to the old wood on the northern slope. On a field gate there, one day in my first summer, I saw a number of crows spreadeagled and rotting, some recent, some less so, some already reduced to feathery husks. It was strange to link this fierce act with the bent old man, who moved so slowly; but when his mischievous eyes came to mind, his swarthy-white gypsy skin, his strong, sly face, the act fitted.

A whole life, a whole enduring personality, was expressed in that run. And so strong were the reminders of the old man's presence, so much of his spirit appeared to hover over his run, over his stiles and steps and those oddly placed rolled-up plastic sacks, even those he had rolled up and tied long ago and were shredding now, plastic without its shine, blue turning to white, so much did all of this speak of the old man moving slowly back and forth on his own errands, that it was some time before it occurred to me that I had not seen him for a while. And then I understood that what I had been seeing for many weeks past, many months past, were his relics.

He had died. There had been no one to record the fact publicly, to pass the news on. And long afterwards, on the fences growing older themselves, those plastic wraps or pads continued to bleach and shred away. Still with us, like the other debris at the bottom of the valley— the roofless walls of the ruined house, the antiquated farm machinery below the young silver birches, the other machinery and discarded timber and metal below the beech trees at the back of the old farm buildings, the metal bracket in the loading window of the superseded, crumbling barn.

And it was a good while later that I got to know that the old man had lived and died in Jack's house, and that he was Jack's father-in-law.

*B*UT BEFORE I got to know Jack I got to know the farm manager. I suppose (because Jack lived in one of the agricultural cottages attached to the farm) that the farm manager was Jack's boss. I never thought of them in that relationship, though. I thought of them as separate people.

The farm manager made his rounds in a Land-Rover. He had a dog with him, sometimes on the seat beside him, sometimes looking out from the back.

We met on the rocky lane that led up from the bottom of the valley, where the old farm buildings and cottages were, to the new barn at the top of the hill. This was the steepest climb of the walk, and I treated it as the exercise part. It came at the right point, near the end, and it was just long enough and taxing enough to make me feel the muscles of my legs and to set me breathing deeply. It was on this hill that the farm manager stopped one afternoon to speak a friendly word—humorously offering a lift, perhaps, for the last fifty yards. He was a middle-aged man, with glasses.

The lane was narrow; I had on more than one afternoon had to stand aside to let him pass. I had at first seen just the Land-Rover, the vehicle. Then I had seen the man inside, had become familiar with his features, and the contented rather than watchful look of the dog with him. I had assumed that he was the farmer, the owner or lessee of these well-kept acres, and I had accordingly given him a "farmer's walk" when he got out of the Land-Rover at the barn and walked in to see how the grain was drying out or whatever it was he was going to check. I had endowed him with a special kind of authority, a special attitude to the land around us. But then I discovered, from the man himself, that he was not the landowner. And I had to revise my way of looking at him: he was only the farm manager, an employee.

His inspection drives covered part of my walk. The lane beside the windbreak led down to the public road. In the sunken ground across this road was the cow or dairy section of the farm. Behind the cow sheds were the water meadows and, in the distance, the willows and other trees on the riverbank. At the side of the road, at the entrance to this farmyard, there was a wooden platform three or four feet high. On this platform milk churns were placed, for collection by the dairy van. After this, the public road went past a thatched, pink-walled cottage and some plainer houses of flint and brick. Then came the yews and beeches of the manor. This was where my walk ended: a wide entrance in the dark-green gloom, and then the bright lawn in front of my cottage.

This was the part of the public road which, when I had come out onto it after the first four days of rain, had set me a puzzle: whether to turn to the right or the left. Now, if the manager's Land-Rover came from behind and passed me here, I knew where it was going. Past the yews, along the beech-hung road high above the river, and then down to the little settlement at river level where the white-walled thatched cottage was being done up, and where an asphalted lane, progressively more broken, led past a number of small houses, some with raised monograms, to the wide, unpaved droveway.

My feeling for that wide, grassy way had grown. I saw it as the old bed of an ancient river, almost something from another geological age; I saw it as the way down which geese might have once been driven to Camelot-Winchester from Salisbury Plain; I saw it as the old stagecoach road.

But it was near there—the present encroaching all the time on something more than the past, encroaching on antiquity, sacred ground—that among the small houses I had not paid much attention to, in a small, neatly fenced plot with a paved drive and a low little bungalow and an extravagant, overplanted garden, full of tall flowers and dwarf conifers and tall ornamental clumps, it was there, on the paved drive, that I saw the Land-Rover one day and on other days. This, then, was where the manager lived and where his inspection drives ended: a little bit of suburbia at the very edge of antiquity. Yet I had taken the house for granted; in the gradual shaping of the land around me, the neat house had taken longer to come out at me, to be noticed. The antiquity—so much vaguer, so much a matter of conjecture—had made its impression more easily: I was ready for it.

Almost immediately, starting on his farm round, the manager would have driven down the deeply rutted droveway past the almost bare bank welted with ancient furrows. His thoughts no doubt of woods and fields and crops and cattle, seeing different things from those I saw, he would have driven down the straight length of the droveway now bisected by the barbed-wire fence he had himself put up or caused to be put up; past the roofless stone house with the tall sycamores, the old hayrick shaped like a cottage and covered with black plastic sheeting; past the caravan in the shade of the scrub and trees on one side, and the two rows of hives incorporated now into the barbed-wire enclosure on the other side; past the old farm buildings (with the new hay shed, though) and the cottages, one of which was Jack's; past Jack's garden and goose ground, up to the new metal-walled barn.

This was the manager's run, almost circular. It was also Jack's; and it was partly mine.

I had seen Jack at work in his vegetable allotment, the plot beyond the cottage front gardens, at the beginning of the slope towards the farm's cultivated fields. I had noticed the odd elegance of his trimmed, pointed beard. And though, in his allotment, his personality was at once clearer than the personality of the other farm workers (whose personalities were at least half expressed by their tractors or their tractors' tasks, steadily, swath by swath, altering the color or texture of a vast field), Jack had at first been a figure in the landscape to me, no more. As no doubt I also was to him: a stranger, a walker, someone exercising an old public right of way in what was now private land.

But after some time, after many weeks, when he felt perhaps that the effort wouldn't be wasted, he adopted me. And from a great distance, as soon as he saw me, he would boom out a greeting, which came over less as defined words than as a deliberate making of noise in the silence.

I saw him more clearly when he worked in the garden at the front (or back) of his cottage, and most clearly of all when he worked in his wire-fenced bedding-out plot, turning over the soft, dark, much-sifted earth below the old hawthorn tree. That brought back very old memories to me, of Trinidad, of a small house my father had once built on a hill and a garden he had tried to get started in a patch of cleared bush: old memories of dark, wet, warm earth and green things growing, old instincts, old delights. And I had an immense feeling for Jack, for the strength and curious delicacy of his forking-and-sifting gesture, the harmony of hand and foot. I saw too, as the months went by, his especial, exaggerated style with clothes: bare-backed in summer at the first hint of sun, muffled up as soon as the season turned. I grew to see his clothes as emblematic of the particular season: like something from a modern book of hours.

And then one day he, like the farm manager in his Land-Rover, stopped in his car on the steep hill from the farm buildings up beside the windbreak to the barn. Jack and the other cottagers had motorcars; without cars they would not have been able to live easily in those cottages; the cottages were too far from the public road and many miles from shops—I believe that the postman called only once a week.

I had heard the car and stood aside. It was what you had to do on this narrow farm road. (If you wished to hide, you could stand in the windbreak itself, among the beeches and pines, in the shaded litter of fallen branches.) It was from this stepping aside and watching them pass in their cars or tractors that I had got to know the farm workers. And they, after the solitude of their tractor cabs and the downs, were invariably ready for a wave and a smile. It was the limit of communication; there was really nothing to add to the wave, the smile, the human acknowledgment.

So it now turned out with Jack, though this stopping in his own car, in his free time, was special. We looked at each other, examined each other, made noises rather than talked.

I had always noticed his pointed beard. Seeing him from a distance, I had thought of this beard as part of a young man's dash. Seeing him digging, considering his height, the depth of his chest, the sturdiness of his legs, his upright, easy walk, I had thought of him as a young man. But I saw now that his beard was almost gray; he was in his late forties, perhaps.

His eyes were far away. It was his eyes, oddly obstreperous, oddly jumpy, that gave him away, that said he was after all a farm worker, that in another setting, in a more crowded or competitive place, he might have sunk. And the discovery was a little disconcerting, because (after I had got rid of the idea that he was a remnant of an old peasantry) I had found in that beard of his, and in his bearing, his upright, easy, elegant walk, the attributes of a man with a high idea of himself, a man who had out of principle turned away from other styles of life.

We had had little to say, but a neighborliness had been established between us, and it continued to be expressed in his shout from afar.

His garden taught me about the seasons, and I got to know in a new way things I must have seen many times before. I saw the blossom come on his well-pruned apple trees, got to know the color of the blossom, carried it in my mind (and was able therefore always to recall it), attached it to a particular time of year; saw the small fruit form, hang green, grow with the rest of the garden, and then turn color.

I saw the fertility that at first did not seem possible in this chalky, flinty soil which in the summer could show white. In England I was not a gardener and had not taken much interest in the little front gardens I had seen (and saw even now, from the bus into Salisbury). Looking at those gardens, I saw only colors, and was barely able visually to disentangle one plant from another. But afternoon by afternoon I considered Jack's garden, noticing his labor, and looking to see what his labor brought forth.

I saw with the eyes of pleasure. But knowledge came slowly to me. It was not like the almost instinctive knowledge that had come to me as a child of the plants and flowers of Trinidad; it was like learning a second language. If I knew then what I know now I would be able to reconstruct the seasons of Jack's garden or gardens. But I can remember only simple things like the bulbs of spring; the planting out of annuals like marigolds and petunias; the delphiniums and lupines of high summer; and flowers like the gladiolus which, to my delight, flourished in both the climate of England and the tropical climate of Trinidad. There were also the roses trained about tall, stout poles, with hundreds of blooms; and then, on those small apple trees, always pruned down, the wonder of the fruit swelling in the autumn, touched in that cool season with the warmest tints, and looking like the apple trees in a children's book or a schoolbook seen long ago.

At the back of his cottage—the back being where the true front now was, the true entrance from the droveway—there was a greenhouse. It looked like the greenhouses advertised in newspapers and magazines, and might have been bought by mail order. In this greenhouse, resting on a concrete base, oddly level and new and formal in the open littered ground between the old farmyard and the cottages, littered with cottagers' stuff as well as with the farm debris of years, and not far from the ruined old pens where sick cattle and calves were sometimes kept, trampling their own dung into moss-covered black earth, in this greenhouse with its straight lines, new wood, and clear glass, Jack grew the overcultivated flowers and plants of the English greenhouse—the extraordinary fuchsias, for example, which were thought to be so pretty.

So many things to look after! So many different things to grow at different times! Jack, it seemed, was looking for labor, looking for tasks, seeking to keep himself busy. And then it came to me that more than busyness, the filling of the day, was involved, and more than money, the extra money Jack might have made from selling his plants and vegetables. It seemed that in that patch of ground, amid the derelict buildings of a superseded kind of farming (fewer and less efficient machines, many more human hands available in this county of Wiltshire, known in the last century for the poverty of its farm laborers), Jack had found fulfillment.

My wonder at the satisfactions of his life—a man in his own setting, as I thought (to me an especially happy condition), a man in tune with the seasons and his landscape—my wonder turned to envy one Sunday afternoon, when going out after lunch for my walk, I saw Jack's little car bumping about towards his cottage along the wide, rutted droveway, and not doing the more usual thing of coming down the paved lane beside the windbreak. He had been to the pub. His face was inflamed. His shout when he saw me—and he seemed to lean out of the car window—was wonderfully hearty.

Sunday! But why had he chosen to turn off at the grassy droveway? Why hadn't he driven the half a mile or so further up to the more usual way in, easier for his car, the paved (though broken) lane that led straight up the hill to the new barn and then directly down to the cottage? Was it drunkenness? Was it his wish to bang about the droveway? Or was it his fear of the narrow road winding on a ledge above the sharp drop down to the river, with two or three blind corners? It was probably in his own mind his Sunday drive, the climax of the extended pub hour. The pleasures of beer on a Sunday! They were like the pleasures of work in his garden as a free man.

*H*ERE WAS an unchanging world—so it would have seemed to the stranger. So it seemed to me when I first became aware of it: the country life, the slow movement of time, the dead life, the private life, the life lived in houses closed one to the other.

But that idea of an unchanging life was wrong. Change was constant. People died; people grew old; people changed houses; houses came up for sale. That was one kind of change. My own presence in the valley, in the cottage of the manor, was an aspect of another kind of change. The barbed-wire fence down the straight stretch of the droveway—that also was change. Everyone was aging; everything was being renewed or discarded.

Not long after I got to know the manager's run, change began to come to it. The elderly couple in the thatched cottage on the public road, a cottage with a rich rose hedge, left. In their place came strangers, a whole family. Town people, I heard. The man had come to work on the farm as cowman or dairyman. Dairymen—their labor constant and unchanging: seeing a large number of cows through the milking machines twice a day, every day—were the most temperamental of farm workers; some of them were even itinerants, wanderers.

The new dairyman was an ugly man. His wife was also ugly. And there was a pathos about their ugliness. Ugliness had come to ugliness for mutual support; but there had been little comfort as a result.

It was odd about change. There were so few houses in the two settlements that made up the village or hamlet; but because the road was not a place where people walked, because lives were lived so much in houses, because people did their shopping in the towns round about, Salisbury, Amesbury, Wilton, and there was no common or meeting place, and because there was no fixed community, it took time for change, great though it might be, to be noticed. The tall beeches, the oaks and chestnuts, the bends and shadows in the narrow road, the blind curves—the very things that made for country beauty also made for something like secrecy. (It was this feeling, of being private and unobserved, that had made me, at the time of my own arrival, give false replies to questions from people I later knew to be farm workers or council workers. They had been friendly, interested; they wanted to know in which house I was staying. I lied; I made up a house. It didn't occur to me that they would know all the houses.)

I had barely got to know the elderly couple who had lived in the thatched cottage. I knew their cottage better; it had struck me as being picturesque. It was narrow and pink-walled. The thatch was kept in place by wire netting; part of the thatch below the dormer window was brilliant green with moss; and on the ridge of the roof there was the wire-framed figure of a reed or straw pheasant, something I saw (originally a bit of thatcher's fantasy, now a more general decorative feature) on many houses in the locality. With its privet and rose hedge (hundreds of small pink roses), the pink cottage had looked the very pattern of a country cottage.

It was only now, with the departure of the old couple, that I understood that the country-cottage effect of their house, and especially of their hedge and garden, had been their work, their taste, the result of their constant attentions. Very soon now, within months, the garden became ragged. The privet kept its tightness, but the rose hedge, unpruned and untrained, became wild and straggly.

The story about the new family in the cottage—picked up from certain things said by Bray, the car-hire man, their near neighbor; from other things said by the people who looked after the manor; and from words occasionally spoken on the afternoon shopping bus that went to Salisbury—the story was that the new dairyman and his family had had a rough time in a town somewhere, and that they had been "saved" by coming to the valley.

The man was tall, young, with a long head, thin-haired; with a heaviness rather than a coarseness about his features. He had the face of a man who had endured abuse. But it was still a young face. His wife looked aged; whatever it was the family had endured had marked her face. She could have passed as his mother. Where his face and head were long, she was square-faced; and her square face was crushed, wrinkled. She wore rimless glasses (an unexpected attempt at style). She was withdrawn. In time smiles came to her husband's face. But I never saw her smile.

What terrors must there have been in the town for them! How could people like these, without words to put to their emotions and passions, manage? They could, at best, only suffer dumbly. Their pains and humiliations would work themselves out in their characters alone: like evil spirits possessing a body, so that the body itself might appear innocent of what it did.

This couple had two children, boys. The elder had something of his father's abused, put-upon look; but there was about him an added touch of violence, of mischief, of unconscious wickedness. The younger boy was more like his mother. Though he was very small and neat in his schoolboy's gray flannel suit, he already had something of his mother's distant, withdrawn air.

There was a bus that, leaving Salisbury in the early afternoon, served as a school bus for the little towns and villages just to the north. It picked up young children from the infant schools in one direction, and then on the way back it picked up bigger children from the secondary schools. This bus picked up both the dairyman's boys. I sometimes used the bus myself. Life in the valley being what it was, this gave me my closest look at the boys. And I began to feel that though the boys might have been "saved" by the valley, as people said, the ways of the town pressed on them still.

The older children, though noisy, were generally well mannered. It was their custom when the bus was full to stand and offer their seat to an adult; rebellion with them sometimes took the modest form of delaying the gesture. The dairyman's elder son added another tone or mood to the school bus. Noisiness became rowdiness; and one day I saw him not only refusing to stand but also continuing to keep his feet on the seat beside him. He was embarrassed when I got on the bus— I was a neighbor, I knew his house and his parents. But he was also among his friends, and he couldn't let himself down.

The bus dropped us both off in the shade of the great manor yews, near his house and mine.

I said, "Peter."

He stood to attention, like a cadet or a boy in a reformatory, threw back his head, and said, "Sir!" As though expecting at the very least a slap; and at the same time not truly intending apology or respect. In that reaction, which made me nervous, I felt I had a glimpse of his past, and saw his need for aggression, his only form of self-assertion. I didn't know how to go on with him; I didn't particularly want to. I didn't say any more.

He was odd man out on the bus, and like an intruder in the village. In fact, there were no other boys of his age around; people with growing families tended to move out. And though there were a number of young children, the dairyman's younger boy was also a little strange. Among the children from the infant schools on its route, the school bus picked up two or three near idiots. The dairyman's younger son, delicate and small, attached himself to one of these: a fat little boy, thick-featured, with a heavy, round head, a boy dressed in startling colors, bright red sometimes, bright yellow at other times, with pale-blond eyelashes and eyebrows that, oddly, suggested someone dim-sighted. This fat child was restless on the bus. He moved from seat to seat and—as though knowing that the constrictions of school were over—spoke insults casually through his thick wet lips at people on the bus, innocently spoke obscenities, in a tone of voice which permitted one to hear the older person from whom the words had been picked up. This was the friend of the dairyman's younger son.

They were being saved by the job, their life in the valley that so many people wished to live in. But they stood out. And they were wrecking the garden of the pretty pink cottage they had taken over. It wasn't (as with Peter on the bus) a wish to offend; it was ignorance, not knowing, not beginning to imagine that the way they lived at home could be of interest to anyone. Part of their new freedom was the country secrecy, the freedom from observation, which (like me, at the beginning) they thought they had found in the dark empty road and the big empty fields.

Out of that freedom, that new, ignorant pleasure in country life, some curious gypsy or horse-dealing instinct came to the dairyman. He bought a run-down white horse and kept it in a small field beside the public road. The animal was a wretched creature, and was made more wretched now by its solitude; it had soon cropped the grass of its small field right down. It was spiritless, idle; people on the bus commented on its state.

And then something else occurred to make the dairyman talked about. His cows broke loose one evening. They wandered about the road, trampled over fields, a few gardens, and the lawn of the manor, in front of my cottage.

And then one day, again in front of my cottage, down the path on the other side of the lawn, the dairyman led a hairy brown and white pony, thick-legged and thick-necked, to the paddock at the back. And there one afternoon (after schooltime) the dairyman and his son Peter gelded and mutilated the pony and then they led the bleeding animal back past the windows of my cottage to the white wide gate, past the churchyard, to the dark lane below the yews and then to the public road. Did they know what they were doing? Had they been trained? Or had they just been told that the gelding was something they should do?

I never actually heard, but I believe the pony died. It was the cruelty of the man who looked after animals. Not absolute cruelty; more a casualness, the attitude of a man who looked after lesser, dependent creatures, superintending the entire cycle of their lives, capable of tenderness, yet living easily with the knowledge that though a cow might have produced so many calves and given so much milk, it would one day have to be dispatched to the slaughterhouse in a covered trailer.

Cows and grass and trees: pretty country views—they existed all around me. Though I hadn't truly seen those views before or been in their midst, I felt I had always known them. On my afternoon walk on the downs there was sometimes a view on one particular slope of black-and-white cows against the sky. This was like the design on the condensed-milk label I knew as a child in Trinidad, where cows as handsome as those were not to be seen, where there was very little fresh milk and most people used imported condensed milk or pow-dered milk.

Now, not far from that view, there was this intimate act of cruelty. The memory of that mutilated, bleeding pony, still with the bad-tempered toss of its head and mane, being led to the white gate below the yews by the two big-headed men, father and son, was with me for some time.

They had been "saved," that town family. (Was it Bristol they had come from? Or Swindon? How fearful those towns seemed to work-ing people here! And fearful to me, too, though for different reasons.) But their life in the country was not as secret or unobserved as they might have thought. They were more judged now than they had per-haps been in the town. And the feeling began to grow—I heard com-ments on the bus, and more comments were reported to me by the couple who looked after the manor—that it was time for them, so noticeable, causing so many kinds of offense, to leave.

From Bray, the car-hire man, their near neighbor, who liked being odd man out a little himself, I heard the only thing in their favor. Bray came one evening to rescue a starling that had got into the loft of my cottage and couldn't get out again. Bray did the job easily. Then, talk-ing of his neighbors, he said of the dairyman's elder boy, "He's very good with birds, you know."

Bray was holding both his hands around the frightened, glossy, blue-black bird he had brought down; holding both heavy hands to-gether so that the bird rested on his broad fingers and the bird's head protruded from the circle formed by his index fingers and thumbs. The two hands could have crushed the bird with one easy gesture; but only Bray's thumbs moved, stroking the bird's head, slowly, one thumb after the other, until the bird appeared to be looking about itself again. Bray—though he had turned the ground in front of his house into a motor mechanic's yard—was a countryman. His talk about birds and their habits seemed to come from his childhood—almost from an-other age. And I wondered how an understanding of birds, like Bray's understanding, could have come to the dairyman's son.

In place of the white and red-brown pony in the paddock there came a very tall, elegant horse. It was a famous old racehorse, I heard. I don't think its appearance in the paddock had anything to do with the dairyman. Some local landowner—perhaps even the man who, indirectly, was going to get rid of the dairyman—might have been responsible.

The name of the animal and his great fame I didn't know. Nor, from simply looking at him, could I tell his great age. But he was very old; he had only a few months or weeks to live; he had come to the valley to die. He still looked muscular and glossy to me; he was like certain sportsmen or athletes who even in age, when strength and agility have gone, retain something of the elegance of the body they trained for so long.

And hearing about the fame of this animal, his triumphs and great record, I found myself indulging in anthropomorphic questions when I considered him in the paddock. Did he know who he was? Did he know where he was? Did he mind? Did he miss the crowds?

I went one day to the very edge of the manor grounds to look at the horse, past the tall grass, the big spread of stacked-up, wet beech leaves slowly turning to compost, the mossed-over, mildewed apple trees, with a glimpse of the rest of the forested orchard to one side. The old racehorse turned its head towards me in a curious way. And then I saw, with pain and nervousness, that it was blind in its left eye. As I approached, it had had to swivel its head to look at me with its bright and trusting right eye, still to me not at all like an old eye.

How tall he was! And it was only now, close to it, that I saw that its coat had been glossier and more even, that its muscles had been firmer. This animal had grown used to the attentions and kindness of men. It was restful to be close to it. So much more painful, then, to see the blind side of its head. The eye had been taken out altogether and skin had grown over the socket. The skin there was quite whole, so that on the blind side the horse's head was like sculpture.

I had an oblique view from my cottage sitting room of the paddock and the water meadows beyond. The water meadows were now the cows' grazing area, and twice a day the cows came out there after milking, swaying heavily in the wet fields (and sometimes preferring to walk in the ditches). Twice or four times a day, then, calling his cows in or sending them out, the dairyman saw the old horse.

The sight of the horse, noble, famous, partly blind, standing alone, had its effect on him. And he, who had mangled a spirited young pony in the same paddock—he on whom the ax was about to fall: the town from which he had been rescued was the place to which he and his family would soon have to go back—he, whose own life was so full of torment, worked himself up into a state about the abandoned horse (as he saw it), so close to death.

He came to my cottage one Sunday evening. He had never come to the cottage before.

Some friends had called, he said; and they had talked about the horse and the tragedy of its last days. So famous, so pampered, earner once of so much money; and now alone in a small, roughly fenced paddock, waiting for death, without crowds or acclaim. It wasn't fair, the dairyman said. It was terrible for him, seeing that every day.

Who were these friends he had been talking to? What kind of people? Were they his wife's friends as well? Did they come from that "town" where things had gone wrong for the dairyman? Did the friends know that their own friend was about to get the sack, and had they come to commiserate? Or had they just come for the day in the country?

What the dairyman had come to ask, almost in tears at the end of this Sunday afternoon with his friends, was that I should help to "get a book off the ground" about the old racehorse, to do justice to the old animal.

I gave him no encouragement. His sentimentality frightened me. It was the sentimentality of a man who could give himself the best of reasons for doing strange things.

In a short time the horse ceased to be in the paddock. It had died. Like so many deaths here, in this small village, like so many big events, it seemed to happen offstage.

The winter turned unexpectedly mild. The sun came out, a kind of blossom came out.

When I went for my walk I met the dairyman coming down the

39

hill from the barn. He smiled broadly—he had forgotten about the horse. He turned around and waved at the hillside. He said, "May in February!"

He didn't mean the month of May; he meant may, the blossom of the hawthorn. It was the last expression of delight in country things I heard from him. There was an element of acting about it; he was like a man living up to a role that had been given him.

And he was wrong. What had come out at the top of the hill was not the hawthorn, but the blackthorn. At the top of the hill, on a long lateral lane, broken by the paved farm road and the windbreak, there was a line of these trees. (It was on a section of this lane that in my earliest days I had met Jack's father-in-law and exchanged the only words I had ever exchanged with him.) The morning sun struck full on these trees, on the side you saw as you came up the hill from the public road. And in the sudden mildness the trees had turned white with blossom above the black winter mud and the puddles created by the tractor wheels.

THE DAIRYMAN and his family left; unnoticed, quietly. One week they were there, noticeable, in possession of the house and garden; the next week the house felt empty, became more purely a house again, and seemed to be touched again with something of its country-cottage character.

And there were bigger changes. The farm manager retired; he was no longer to be seen making his rounds with his dog in the Land-Rover. The farm passed into new hands. And soon there was new activity: more tractors, more farm machinery, a greater busyness.

The winter that seemed to have retreated so early that year re-turned. At last the true spring came. It touched Jack's garden. But—though all around was activity, on down and droveway and field lane, with tractors of new design and brighter colors—there was no human celebration in Jack's plots of ground, nothing of the rituals I had grown to expect.

The mud-spattered, autumn-clipped hedge burst into life, and the apple trees and the shrubs and the rose bushes; but there was no controlling hand now. No cutting back and tying up; no weeding; nothing done in the greenhouse. No work on the vegetable plot: scattered growths of green there, stray roots and seeds. No turning over of the earth in the bedding-out plot below the old hawthorn tree. Smoke rose from the chimney of Jack's cottage while his garden ran wild. Only the geese and ducks continued to be looked after.

And all around was activity and change. The pink cottage had another couple, young people, in their twenties. The man did not work in the dairy. He was a more general kind of farm worker, and he was like the other workers the new management had brought in. They were young people, these new farm workers, educated up to a point, some of them perhaps with diplomas. They dressed with care; clothes, the new styles in clothes, were important to them. They were not particularly friendly. They might have been reflecting the seriousness and modernity of the new management; or they might have been anxious to make the point that, though they did farm worker's jobs, they were not exactly that kind of person.

The man in the pink cottage had a new or newish car. On fine afternoons his wife sunbathed in the ruined garden, seemingly careless of showing her breasts. She was a short woman with heavy thighs. The contemporary fashions she followed didn't flatter her figure; they made her look heavy, badly proportioned, a little absurd. But one day I saw how the long dresses of an earlier era, with high, narrow waists and full hips, might have been absolutely right for her, would have made her voluptuous. And I felt that this was how she saw herself, immensely desirable; and that this sunbathing in the wreck of the garden, this care of what had at first seemed to me a slack, heavy body, was something she might have thought she owed to her beauty. The new car, her husband's careful clothes—these were further tributes.

New people, young people as well, took over the other two cottages in Jack's row at the bottom of the valley. New brooms down there, in both cottages: they swept clean. They dug up what had been left behind in both gardens, leveled the ground and planted grass.

Jack's garden was wild.

I saw Jack's wife outside the cottage one day. She said, talking of her new neighbors but making no gestures that might have betrayed her, "Have you seen? All lawn, my dear."

The turn of speech, the irony, was a surprise. I had never thought Jack's wife capable of such things; but then I had thought of her—and she seemed to have been content to be regarded—as an appendage of Jack's.

"And the horses," she said.

The people in the middle cottage had a horse.

I said, "How's Jack?"

"He's all right, you know. He's working again."

"There's a lot for him to do in the garden."

She said, "You think so?"

As though I had said something untrue. Why did she want to deny what was so obvious? We were standing outside the garden. Had I mentioned something she felt I shouldn't have mentioned? Was I putting a curse on the sick man?

Because Jack was sick. Though she said he was working again he was not well. And intermittently all that summer, for two or three weeks at a time, even on those sunny days which in previous years he would have celebrated by working bare-backed in his garden, the smoke rose from one of the chimneys of the cottage like a symbol of his sickness, like a sign of the cold he felt, the sick man in his room. While the new farm workers, young men with young wives, drove up and down the big fields in their new tractors, and went out in their new or newish cars after work.

Jack's wife commented gently, ironically, on the changes. But she seemed more and more to accept that Jack's hold on his job, his cottage, and his garden was going, and that her own time there was coming to an end.

His car stopped beside me one day. It was the first time I had seen him since the previous autumn. His face was waxen. I knew the word, from books. But never till now, seeing what it described on a white face, had I truly understood the word. All the brown of Jack's face, all the sun to which he had exposed himself in his garden, had gone. His skin was white and smooth, and it seemed to have the texture and false color of waxen fruit; it was as though a bloom, as on a plum, covered the living skin. His beard was trimmed and neat. Yet even that had a waxen, even waxed, quality. Not many words; quiet words of greeting, friendship, reassurance. His obstreperous eyes were quiet too. Wax. And the smoke came out of his cottage chimney in the autumn and in the winter; and then it stopped.

*T*HE LANE that led up the hill to the new barn and then down to the cottages and old farm buildings, the lane beside the windbreak of beech and pine and the subsidiary hedge of field rose and hawthorn, had grown rough and broken. You could easily have turned your ankle on it. The new farm management began to have that lane mended.

Men and machines came one week, and a level black layer of mixed asphalt and gravel was quickly laid down, in a few days. The black color and the machine finish looked new and unnatural next to the tufted grass of the verges. But the surface that had been so quickly laid down was meant to last: as if in pledge of that, the yellow board of the road makers was set up on the public road, just before the lane, and one end of the board was cut into a directional arrow.

I didn't like the change. I felt it threatened what I had found and what I had just begun to enter. I didn't like the new busyness, the new machines, the machine lopping of the hawthorn and wild rose which left them looking damaged. And I didn't want that new surface on the farm lane to hold.

I looked for cracks and flaws in it and hoped that the little abrasions and water erosions I noticed would spread and make it impossible— fantasy taking over from logic—for the machines to lay down a new asphalt mixture. Of course I knew my fantasy was fantasy: though the farm was set among ruins of many sorts, reminders of the impermanence of men's doings, there was another side to men's work. Men came back, men went on, men did and did again. How small the caravels were that crossed the Atlantic and intruded into the evenness of history on the other side; how few the men in those small vessels, how limited their means; how barely noticed. But they went back. They changed the world in that part forever.

So though the new asphalt layer was crushed here and there into dips by the tractor wheels; and though the rain, running down the hill, sought out every weakness and crack in the dips and dug out minute bits of asphalt from between small stones and then dug more deeply into the loosened surface, and the irregular edge of the surface was undermined by water running down in little channels (miniatures of the larger channels of which our valley was a relic) between the hard black crust and the soft, grass-covered earth, though there were these things that made me feel that the lane might be reduced again to the rocky, uneven condition in which I had first found it, yet the lane was made good, and then made good again, and withstood the winter, which came fiercely that year.

There was a blizzard on Christmas day, with the wind blowing from the northwest. I found, when I went out in the early afternoon, that the snow had been blown into a drift in the windbreak. A bank of snow, then, beside the lane; and in the lee of every tree trunk, every sturdy twig, every obstacle, there was a sharp ridge that indicated the direction of the wind.

The shape and texture of this snow drift reminded me of a climate quite different: of a Trinidad beach where shallow streams—fresh water mingled with salt, salt predominating or lessening according to the tides—ran from tropical woodland to the sea. These streams rose and subsided with the tide. Water flowed now from the sea to the pools of the woodland river, now in the other direction. At every low tide the streams cut fresh channels in the freshly laid sand, created fresh sand cliffs, which then, when the tide began to rise again, fell neatly, segment by clean segment, into the rippled current: a geography lesson in miniature. To me as a child these streams always brought to mind the beginning of the world, the world before men, before the settlement. (Romance and ignorance: for though there were no longer aboriginal people on the island, they had been there for millennia.)

44

So the texture and shapes and patterns of the snow here on the
down in the windbreak and in its lee created, in small, the geography
of great countries. Like the little rivulets that ran between the steep
grass verge and the new asphalt crust of the lane. And this geography
in miniature was set, as I thought, or as I liked to think, in a vaster
geography. The valley of the droveway between the smooth low hills
spoke of vast rivers hundreds of yards across, flowing here in some age
now unimaginably remote: a geography whose scale denied the presence of men. There would have been a brimming river or flow all the
way from Stonehenge (and the plain beyond) to Jack's cottage and
then along the droveway with the beehives and the caravan and stone
shell of a house and farm manager's bungalow and suburban-style
garden; there would have been a river all there, a flat gray flow, de-
bouching into or filling the valley of the present river, a remnant, small-
scale, human, beside which I sometimes walked and where people now
fished for trout, released by keepers. In that vast geography created
by the miniature landscape, and the fantasy of the droveway as river
channel, there was no room for men; that vision was a vision of the
world before men.

Beyond the brow of the hill the wind was keen; shelter was no
longer provided by the hill or the windbreak. A livid gray sky, a gray
but warm dirtiness, hung over the great plain, where the barrows were
like pimples: the stone circles lost in the snow, blurring the view at
the edges, no sight of the colored artillery targets. At the bottom of
the hill, among the farm buildings (made monumental by the snow-
fall), was the dead cottage of Jack: snow lying on the ground about it
(the droveway there normally so muddy and black) like a great clean
thing, like a remaking of the world.

The snow made for hard walking. But weather like this in this
usually mild valley revived in me a wish for extremes, though it was
the cold and the damp and the wet that had carried away Jack. His
damaged lungs, in that damp valley bottom, had denied him warmth
even in the summer. (Something else, of course, if there had been no
cold or damp, would have carried him away.)

On my early walks, after having my fill of the Henge and the barrows, I had looked for hares on one slope. Then, on another hill, at another season I had looked for larks, trying to keep them in sight as they rose and rose, lift upon lift, and watching for them as they dropped down. Now I looked for deer. A family of three had appeared in the valley, coming from no one knew where, and surviving in our well-tilled, well-grazed valley, dangerous over large tracts with military gunfire, crossed at many places by busy highways, surviving among us no one knew how.

They, the deer, had their run too. And it was in the hope of seeing them—in addition to my excitement at the snow and the wind—that I tramped round the farm buildings and up the droveway to the point from which there was a view of the wood and the untilled open slope where the deer sometimes grazed. And unbelievably—my Christmas reward!—they were there, in the snow. Usually, against the wood, the deer were hard to see; lower down, against the chalky green and brown of the bare slope, they were reddish-brown, warm, but they had to be looked for. Now (like the rabbits of my very first week, coming out to feed on the lawn in front of my cottage) the deer were dirty-looking, gray, dark against the snow, easy marks for anyone who wished to knock them off.

I longed for those deer to survive. And they did. Towards the end of the winter I discovered one in the wilderness at the back of my cottage, in the marshland beside the river. He was a young deer and I caught sight of him one morning, all eyes, among the beaten-down brown reeds. And there for many mornings in succession I saw him. I stood on the rotting bridge over the black creek and looked. The secret, then, to see him, to keep him where he was, was to hold his eyes and to be still oneself. As long as you looked, he looked; as soon as you moved or made a gesture he was away, running at first through the reeds and tall grass and then giving the lovely leap that could take him clear over fences and hedges.

The spring came. The new surface of the lane up the hill held. The new life of the farm continued. And for the second year running Jack's cottage and garden were apart from the activity. His death, his funeral—like the death and funeral of his father-in-law some years before—seemed to have happened secretly: one of the effects of the country life, the dark road, the scattered houses, the big views. His vegetable plot, overrun with weeds, was barely noticeable. His fruit and flower garden grew more wild, the hedge and the rose bushes growing out. His greenhouse at the back (really the front) became empty.

So much that had looked traditional, natural, emanations of the landscape, things that country people did—the planting out of annuals, the tending of the geese, the clipping of the hedge, the pruning of the fruit trees—now turned out not to have been traditional or instinctive after all, but to have been part of Jack's way. When he wasn't there to do these things, they weren't done; there was only a ruin. The new people in the other cottages didn't do what he had done. They seemed to have little regard for their bit of cottage land. Or they saw it differently, or they had another idea of their lives.

The first year of Jack's illness Jack's wife had pretended that nothing had changed; that Jack's garden was still a garden. Now she didn't pretend. She was making ready to leave. And she was doing so in a matter-of-fact way. As though, after all, in spite of appearances, in spite of the antique ways of her father, in spite of Jack, little had been invested by her in that cottage, the life attached to it, and those years of the garden.

She now had no connection with the farm or the land. The local council was going to find a house or flat for her on a housing estate in the valley or in one of the nearby towns, Amesbury, Salisbury, Shrewton, Great Wishford, or elsewhere. She would meet more people; she would be nearer the shops. She was looking forward to the move. The "traditional" life, at the bottom of the valley, in the mud and damp around the farm, far from people, where you were shut up for the evening if you didn't have a car, the traditional life hadn't been to her taste.

Still, she thought that Jack had had a good life.

She said, "On the Christmas Eve he got up and went to the pub, you know. He knew he was going to die and he knew it was his last chance."

She spoke quite casually, giving me this news, now more than a year old. She was just making conversation.

She said, "He wanted to be with his friends for the last time."

To be with his friends; to enjoy the last drink; to have the final sweetness of life as he knew it. What an effort it would have taken! To have those blocks of ice for lungs; to be incapable of getting warm; to be fatigued and faint; to want nothing more than to lie down and close one's eyes and sail away into the fantasies that were claiming one. And yet he had roused himself and found the energy to dress and had driven to the pub for the holiday, before his death.

Did he drive along the lane up and down the hill beside the windbreak? Or did he, because it required less judgment, drive along the wide, rutted droveway? That way, along the droveway, would have been more likely to get him to the pub and back. But it would have shaken him up dreadfully—as I had seen him, in another mood, shaken up one spring or summer Sunday afternoon, when his shout had been touched with beer. That final trip to the pub served no cause except that of life; yet he made it appear an act of heroism; poetical.

*A*CROSS THE lawn from my cottage there was a small old flint building. It was covered with ivy, and the ivy was so thick and firm that pigeons roosted in it. The building was square in plan and had a pyramidal roof. This roof appeared to be open at the apex, and above that, on four stilts, was a second, miniature roof of the same pyramidal shape. I was told that the building had been a granary or storehouse and that it was some centuries old. It was not used now; I never saw anyone go into it. It was preserved for its beauty and as something from the past.

Not far from it, and still on the far side of the lawn, was a building that pretended to be a rough old farmhouse. Its walls were made up of bits of brick and stone and flint, the mixture suggesting rubble, peasant pickings. It was about fifty years old and had been put up as one of the ancillary buildings of the manor: a fives court or squash court, but built in this "picturesque" way to suit the setting. Perhaps it had been used as a squash court for some time. But—its "front door" permanently closed, its corrugated-iron roof sagging in places, some of the glass panes of its windows fallen out—it had no function now, had had none for many years. Like the boathouse on the riverbank; like the round, two-story children's house with the conical thatched roof in the overgrown orchard.

The life of the manor had altered; the organization had shrunk. Needs that had once ramified as if to match the resources and organization of the big house had not been permanent. The manor too had its ruins.

Between granary and mock farmhouse, and beyond the manor wall, was the church. To me in the beginning a church was a church, something built in a particular way, with windows of a particular shape: ideas given me by the Victorian Gothic churches I had seen in Trinidad. But I had that village church before my eyes every day; and quite soon—this new world shaping itself about me in my lucky solitude—I saw that the church was restored and architecturally was as artificial as the farmhouse. Once that was seen, it was seen; the church radiated its own mood, the mood of its Victorian-Edwardian restorers. I saw the church not as "church," but as part of the wealth and security of Victorian-Edwardian times. It was like the manor to which my cottage was attached; like many of the other big houses around.

The church stood on a pre-medieval site; that was what was said. But little about the church as it now was had come down from that time. Not a piece of flint; not a slab of dressed stone that framed the Gothic windows. And perhaps not even the faith was old.

Just as it was hard to imagine the lives and religious impulses of the people who had with immense labor turned this plain into a burial ground and preserved its sanctity for centuries, so it was hard, though one stood on the very ground and was exposed to the same weather (but not now the same dawns or sunsets: always the vapor trails of aircraft), to enter into the spirit, the terrors and the need for redemption, of the people who had worshiped a thousand years before in the first Christian church on this site—that lay so close to me, just across the lawn and beyond the play farmhouse.

Play farmhouse, renovated church. Had that been a kind of play, too, the religion of the renovated church? Did the renovators share the old terrors? Or was this faith something quite different, something touched with the sense of history, the assurance of continuity, the sense of something owed to oneself?

When you looked down on the plain from the viewing point in the windbreak on the hill, you could see Stonehenge to the west and the beginnings of the town of Amesbury to the east. The River Avon ran through Amesbury. There were chapels and abbeys here too, beside the river, wide and shallow at this point. Amesbury—now a military town, with little modern houses and shops and garages—was an old place. It was to a nunnery in Amesbury that Guinevere, Arthur's queen, the lover of Lancelot, had retired when the Round Table had vanished from Camelot, all of twenty miles away at Winchester. A sign on the road from Stonehenge, just before you entered Amesbury, celebrated the antiquity of the town: with a coat of arms and a date, A.D. 979.

The historical feeling that had caused that sign to be put up had also brought about the restoration of the chapels and abbeys of Amesbury, as well as of the church that lay across the lawn from my own cottage: history, like religion, or like an extension of religion, as an idea of one's own redemption and glory.

Yet there was an uncelebrated darkness before the foundation of that town of Amesbury in A.D. 979, as recorded by the sign. More than five hundred years before that, the Roman army had left Britain. And Stonehenge had been built and had fallen into ruin, and the vast burial ground had lost its sanctity, long before the Romans had come. So that history here, where there were so many ruins and restorations, seemed to be plateaus of light, with intervening troughs or disappearances into darkness.

We lived still on one such plateau of historical light. Amesbury, founded A.D. 979. History, glory, religion as a wish to do the right thing by oneself—these ideas were still with some people in the valleys round about, though there had been some diminution in personal glory, and the new houses and gardens were like the small change of the great estates of the last century and the beginning of this century. These people—though they had come, many of them, from other places—still had the idea of being successors and inheritors. It was because of this idea of historical inheritance and succession that many new people in our valley went to the restored church. The church had been restored for people like them; it met their needs.

In this they were different from Bray, the car-hire man, who had lived all his life in the valley. Bray never went to the church, and was scornful of the motives of those who did. And the churchgoers were also different from Jack, who had lived the best part of his life in the cottage over the hill and, while he was vigorous, had celebrated the seasons with rituals of his own. On Sundays Jack worked in the morning in his garden, and went to the pub at noon; in the afternoon he worked again in his garden.

*T*HE CHURCH stood on an old site. I could believe that. Beyond the churchyard, and more or less hidden by the church itself, the old flint churchyard wall, and trees on the other side, were the sheds and buildings of the dairy. Did they also stand on an old site? I had no trouble believing that they did. Because the world—in places like this—is never absolutely new; there is always something that has gone before. Shrine or sacred place before church, farm before farm, on the site of an old ford set in a wood, first "walden," then "shaw," then Waldenshaw. A hamlet between the water meadows and the flinty downs; a hamlet, one of many, on the river highway.

New to the valley, overwhelmed by the luck of the near-solitude I had found in this historical part of England, the solitude that had done away with my stranger's nerves, I had seen everything as a kind of perfection, perfectly evolved. But I had hardly begun to look, the land and its life had hardly begun to shape itself about me, when things began to change. And I had fallen back on old ideas, ideas now not so much of decay, as of flux and the constancy of change, to fight the distress I felt at everything—a death, a fence, a departure—that undid or altered or threatened the perfection I had found.

It could have been said that the perfection of the house in whose grounds I lived had been arrived at forty or fifty years before, when the Edwardian house was still fairly new, its family life fuller, when the ancillary buildings had a function and the garden was looked after. But in that perfection, occurring at a time of empire, there would have been no room for me. The builder of the house and the designer of the garden could not have imagined, with their world view, that at a later time someone like me would have been in the grounds, and that I would feel I was having the place—the cottage, the empty picturesque houses around the lawn, the grounds, the wild gardens—at its peak, living in a beauty that hadn't been planned for. I liked the decay, such as it was. It gave me no wish to prune or weed or set right or remake. It couldn't last, clearly. But while it lasted, it was perfection.

To see the possibility, the certainty, of ruin, even at the moment of creation: it was my temperament. Those nerves had been given me as a child in Trinidad partly by our family circumstances: the half-ruined or broken-down houses we lived in, our many moves, our general uncertainty. Possibly, too, this mode of feeling went deeper and was an ancestral inheritance, something that came with the history that had made me: not only India, with its ideas of a world outside men's control, but also the colonial plantations or estates of Trinidad, to which my impoverished Indian ancestors had been transported in the last century—estates of which this Wiltshire estate, where I now lived, had been the apotheosis.

Fifty years ago there would have been no room for me on the estate; even now my presence was a little unlikely. But more than accident had brought me here. Or rather, in the series of accidents that had brought me to the manor cottage, with a view of the restored church, there was a clear historical line. The migration, within the British Empire, from India to Trinidad had given me the English language as my own, and a particular kind of education. This had partly seeded my wish to be a writer in a particular mode, and had committed me to the literary career I had been following in England for twenty years.

The history I carried with me, together with the self-awareness that had come with my education and ambition, had sent me into the world with a sense of glory dead; and in England had given me the rawest stranger's nerves. Now ironically—or aptly—living in the grounds of this shrunken estate, going out for my walks, those nerves were soothed, and in the wild garden and orchard beside the water meadows I found a physical beauty perfectly suited to my temperament and answering, besides, every good idea I could have had, as a child in Trinidad, of the physical aspect of England.

The estate had been enormous, I was told. It had been created in part by the wealth of empire. But then bit by bit it had been alienated. The family in its many branches flourished in other places. Here in the valley there now lived only my landlord—elderly, a bachelor, with people to look after him. Certain physical disabilities had now been added to the malaise which had befallen him years before, a malaise of which I had no precise knowledge, but interpreted as something like acedia, the monk's torpor or disease of the Middle Ages—which was how his great security, his excessive worldly blessings, had taken him. The acedia had turned him into a recluse, accessible only to his intimate friends. So that on the manor itself, as on my walks on the down, I had a kind of solitude.

I felt a great sympathy for my landlord. I felt I could understand his malaise; I saw it as the other side of my own. I did not think of my landlord as a failure. Words like failure and success didn't apply. Only a grand man or a man with a grand idea of his human worth could ignore the high money value of his estate and be content to live in its semi-ruin. My meditations in the manor were not of imperial decline. Rather, I wondered at the historical chain that had brought us together—he in his house, I in his cottage, the wild garden his taste (as I was told) and also mine.

I knew that the life I had in the manor grounds was temporary and couldn't last. The future was so easy to see: a hotel or school or foundation taking over the big house and setting the decayed grounds to rights, grounds where I now walked with such pleasure, and for the first time in my adult life, and more and more as my knowledge increased, felt in tune with the natural world. I dreaded change both here and on the droveway; and that was why, meeting distress halfway, I cultivated old, possibly ancestral ways of feeling, the ways of glory dead, and held on to the idea of a world in flux: the drum of creation in the god's right hand, the flame of destruction in his left.

So for a week or more I balanced between the two things—anxiety, the idea of flux—when I heard, from beyond the churchyard, the sound of a bulldozer or something like it. The noise traveled through the ground, in vibrations; it was not a noise that a window could shut out.

The cow sheds and dairy buildings beyond the churchyard were being pulled down—structures of clay tiles and red brick that had been so much part of the view as I came down the hill at the end of my walk, so natural and right, that I had not paid them too much attention. Now, with the sheds gone, the ground looked naked and ordinary; and the water meadows at the back were exposed, and the trees on the riverbank. The clay tiles from the roofs were stacked up; the roof timbers were stacked up (and how new they looked, though the buildings had seemed to me so old). And then very quickly the open view was blocked out again, with a wide prefabricated shed with slatted timber walls, and with the printed name of the shed makers on a board or metal plate just below the apex of the roof. (A shed like this, but without the slatted walls, had been put up, one or two owners or managers before, at the edge of the old farmyard over the hill, and not far from Jack's cottage, to store hay, to replace the cottage-shaped hayrick covered with black plastic sheeting on the droveway—that hayrick now moldering away, the black plastic itself weathered, without its luster and tension, no longer crackling when it flapped, its texture now rather like the skin of very old people, like a faded rose petal.)

Change! New ideas, new efficiency. Before, on the roadside, at the entrance to the dairy yard, there had been a wooden platform where the milk churns were placed—set at that height to be easily picked up by the milk van or truck. There were to be no churns now. There were to be refrigerated tanks, and milk was to be collected by tanker.

Next to the metal-walled barn at the top of the hill, another prefabricated cow shed was set up; and next to that, a modern milking building. This milking building or milking "parlor" (quaint word) was a mechanical-looking affair. Its concrete floor, set in a sloping field, looked like a concrete platform. It had pipes and meters and gauges; and the men who worked the parlor, who corralled the dung-stained cattle into the pens or channels, had something of the grimness of industrial workers.

They drove up to the milking parlor in brightly colored cars (the colors noticeable up there, against the soft colors of the downs, green and brown and chalk and in the winter the blurred darkness of stripped trees). These cars, when parked, helped to make the milking parlor and the barn and the new prefabricated shed look like a little factory at the top of the hill.

The parlor hissed mechanically, electrically. But the new prefabricated shed gave off a smell of dung. Some of the earth excavated for the foundations of the parlor had been dumped between the parlor and the paved lane; in this area, waste ground, grass grew thick and green, with a scattering of weeds and stray wheat.

The brightly colored cars, the hum and hiss of the milking machine (the cows, even with their dung, reduced to machine-managed objects), the tense young men, conscious of their style, their jeans and shirts, their mustaches and cars—they were all aspects of the new, exaggerated thing that had come upon us.

Twice a day the milk tanker went grinding up the hill, up the resurfaced lane, to empty the refrigerated milk tanks of the new milking parlor. With the farm tractors and the motorcars of the new workers, my walk in the lane beside the windbreak was at times like a walk on a public road; I had to watch for traffic.

On the public road, the thatched cottage with the pink walls and the straw pheasant on the ridge of the roof lost a little more of its first character. So pretty, so like a postcard, when I had first seen it, so like something one had always known, with its rose hedge and its small, polished windows. The dairyman would have loved it too, I am certain; but, like me at the beginning, he would have seen its beauty as a natural attribute of the country setting; and he had lived in the house as he might have lived in a house in the town from which he had come, without any feeling that anything was owed to the house in which he and his family lived; having all his life considered houses, even those in which he lived, as belonging to other people. Basins and pots and pans and bits of paper and tins and empty boxes had been left out in the garden; and some of those things had stayed there even after the dairyman and his family had gone.

Now part of the hedge and the wire fence were taken down, so that the car of the new couple could be parked off the public road. The car was important to the new people, more important than the house. They were young people, without children; and they handled the house in a new way. It was a place of shelter, no more: temporary shelter for a temporary job. The wife sunbathed in the front garden whenever she could; and perhaps this was why the front door was often open. That open front door was very unsettling.

The house as a place of shelter, not as a place to which you could transfer (or risk transferring) emotion or hopes—this attitude of the new couple to the thatched house seemed to match the more general new attitude to the land. The land, for the new workers, was merely a thing to be worked. And with their machines they worked it as though they intended to turn all the irregularities of nature into straight lines or graded curves.

One day I saw a heavy, wide roller being pulled by a tractor through a field of young grass, already fairly tall though, and succulent-looking. The roller appeared to be breaking the stalks of the grass and creating, as if spectrally, the effect of a striped, two-toned lawn. What was the point of that? The young man I asked seemed bemused. Perhaps he hadn't understood what I had said. He mumbled something which I couldn't understand—all his style breaking down at this moment of speech (and making me think back to the strangled speech, like gruff throat noises, of Jack's father-in-law: "Dogs? Dogs. Worry pheasants"). Even when what the young man said was made clear to me, it didn't make sense. The stalks were being crushed, he said, to encourage stronger growth.

Another man said, on another day, that the point of the roller was to press down the "Wiltshire flints" into the ground, so that when the time came the grass could be cut without damage to the cutting machine. "One Wiltshire flint," he said—and the flints of Wiltshire and of the downs of my daily walk were given an importance and malignity I had never attached to them—"could do thousands of pounds' worth of damage to one of these machines."

One new machine in particular I noticed. It made great rolls out of hay, great Swiss rolls of hay, as it were. These rolls, too big to be lifted or unrolled by a man, were manhandled by another impressive machine, a machine with iron grapples like giant scorpion's tails. A store of these rolls—in two layers, like a store of hay against some epic winter—was established far from the old farm buildings, in an unfenced, flint-rubbled valley off the droveway, just below the hill with the larks and the barrows, and from the top of which you had a sudden, near view of Stonehenge.

So there were three stores of hay at different places: the Swiss rolls here, the golden rectangular-sided bales in the new hay shed at the edge of the old farmyard, and the bales, also rectangular-sided, in the rotting hayrick halfway down the straight stretch of the droveway. What was the point of the Swiss rolls? Was there an advantage over the traditional bales? I never knew until years later, when this section of my life was closed. The bales, tightly banded by the baling machines, had to be broken into by hand and then spread out for cattle. The big rolls had simply to be unrolled; a machine did the job in minutes.

Such refinement! But perhaps the scale—for farming—was wrong. Perhaps time should never be as valuable as that, day after day. Perhaps when routines became as tight as that, they could too easily go awry. One broken link—and human ventures were always liable to error—could throw the entire operation out of true.

Everything the new farm did was big. A very big silage pit

was excavated at the bottom of the hill just across the lane from the windbreak, and not far from the cottages. There was only one old-fashioned aspect to that silage pit. It was covered by black plastic sheeting, and the things used to keep the plastic sheeting tight and in place were the things that in my experience had always been used for that purpose: old tires. They were bought in enormous numbers. Scores and scores of them must have been used; and scores and scores of them were about at the bottom of the valley, in the droveway, just across from what used to be Jack's goose ground.

Those tires, and the deep new silage pit with its braced-up wall of timber planks, and the banks of rubble from the digging for the pit, and the dark-brown silage additive trickling out at the bottom, gave a touch of the rubbish tip to that part of the droveway where, when Jack lived, geese and ducks wandered about.

With the old farm workers the first caution with strangers, the sizing up, was followed by a dumb friendliness, the country sociableness of people who spent hours alone in the fields in their tractors. The new workers, who were like city people in the country, city people in a larger workplace, didn't have that kind of friendliness. They hadn't come to the valley to stay. They saw themselves as people with a new kind of job and skill; they were almost migrant agricultural workers; they were people on the move. Quite a few came and went.

I never got a smile from any of the people who moved into Jack's house after Jack's wife had left. She had said of the first lot of her new neighbors that they were "snobbish" people, who were interested in lawns and horses rather than old-fashioned cottage gardens. After some comings and goings, people who fitted that description settled in Jack's cottage.

His greenhouse, the one bought as it seemed from a catalog and once green with hanging plants, was empty, its glass murky with dust and rain, its timber frame weathered. One day it was taken down, revealing the concrete foundation or floor. The elaborate garden, with all its time-eating chores, was flattened. What was left didn't need much attention. No bedding out plants now; no forking over of the ground below the hawthorn tree; no delphiniums in the summer. The garden was flattened, all but two or three rose bushes and two or three apple trees which Jack had pruned in such a way that they bunched out at the top from a thick straight trunk. And the ground was grassed over. The hedge, once tight at the top, mud-spattered and ragged at the bottom, a half or quarter barrier between garden and rutted farm road, the hedge began to grow out into trees.

Now more than ever the cottages appeared to have neither front nor back, and to stand in a kind of waste ground. It matched the people and their attitude to the place. It matched the new way of farming, logic taken to extremes, the earth stripped finally of its sanctity—the way the pink thatched cottage on the public road, once pretty with its rose hedge, had been stripped of its atmosphere of home by the people who looked to it only for shelter.

But that might have been only my way of looking. I had known —for a short time—the straight stretch of the droveway open and unfenced. It had been fenced down the middle in my first year and had remained fenced; but I carried that earlier picture. I had arrived at my feeling for the seasons by looking at Jack's garden, adding events on the river and the manor riverbank to what I saw in his garden. But there were other ways of looking. Jack himself, giving the attention he gave to a meaningless hedge—a hedge that ran down the length of his garden and then abruptly stopped—saw something else, certainly.

And perhaps the young children of the new people in Jack's cottage saw differently. They went to a junior school in Salisbury. The afternoon bus, bringing them back, set them down on the public road; their mother picked them up in her car. Often on my afternoon walk I had to stand aside on the paved lane to allow the mother's car to pass. She never acknowledged my stepping aside; she behaved as though the lane were a public road and her car had the right of way. And I also never took in or properly noticed what she was like. Her personality was expressed for me only in the color and shape of her car, speeding up or down the hill, going to get her children, or coming back with them.

I doubt whether any children in those farm cottages had been met like that off the school bus. What pictures of their time at the bottom of the valley—brief though that time was to be—would remain for them! What immense views, what a memory of emptiness, down the vast droveway and over the flinty slopes of the downs!

At the foot of the paved lane down the hill, across from the silage pit, there was a narrow, little-used track, overgrown, hardly showing as a track, that ran along a dip in the downs to a small abandoned farm building, weathered, not very noticeable, something perhaps from the last century. In that lane one Saturday afternoon, when they were free from school and the bus, I saw the children from Jack's old cottage playing. Like prehistorical children, in a great solitude. But they were among the leftover tires of the silage pit (certain ones had been turned into their toys, their pretend paddling rafts); and the whitening banks and mounds of excavated rubble sprouting scattered weeds, pale green with bright yellow flowers; and concrete blocks left over from the building.

*F*RIENDSHIP HAS its odd ways. I had thought of the couple who looked after the manor, Mr. and Mrs. Phillips, people in their forties, as stern and self-sufficient, locked away and content in their manor job, and having a private and much less stern leisure life with old friends in a town somewhere. But then they developed a local friendship, and for some time I felt this friendship threatened my own life in the manor grounds.

Across the lawn from my cottage, against the "farmhouse" wall of the squash court—not farmhouse, not squash court—against that wall with its studied mixture of flint, red brickbats and bits of stone, there grew three old pear trees. They had been carefully pruned and trained at one time; and even now the main branches, still pinned to the wall, created a formal effect, making the trees look like large candelabra. The seasons dressed these branches in different ways; and the view from my cottage was always rich. The trees bore fruit. Always a surprise; always seemingly sudden. But to me they were not fruit to eat, and only partly because the fruit belonged to the manor: they were part of the picture.

In the great days of the manor sixteen gardeners looked after the grounds and the orchard and the walled vegetable garden. So I was told. Sixteen! How could anyone not running a plant nursery find sixteen gardeners nowadays or pay their wages? How different the hamlets and villages round about must have been then, how many working people in little houses!

The cottage where I lived had once been the garden office. Now I, who did nothing in the grounds, lived there. And there was only one gardener. He had a system. He used a hover-mower to cut the lawns, at the back and side of the manor and in front of my cottage, two or three times in the summer, after a very low cut in the early spring. In the early spring he also laid down weed killer on the drive and the old graveled path around the cottage lawn and on all those paths that had not been surrendered to grass. Once a year, in late August, he cut the tall grass and stalky weeds in the old orchard, where in the hollow knots of untended trees nestlings cheeped in the spring, and the trees themselves grew on, flowering at the correct time, bearing fruit, dropping fruit, attracting wasps. In the autumn he had a great leaf gathering. But his main work for much of the year was on the vegetable and flower garden, separated from the path at the back of my cottage by a high wall. The system worked. The garden had its wild parts; the water meadows were marsh; but elsewhere the gardener's attentions, slight but regular and with method, suggested a controlling hand.

The gardener's name was Pitton. I called him Mr. Pitton at the start, and called him that to the very end.

It was Pitton who one year, talking of the pear trees on the farmhouse wall, gave me a new determinative use of the preposition "in." The pears were ripe. The birds were pecking at them. I mentioned it to Pitton, thinking that with all the things he had do he mightn't have noticed. But he said he had noticed; the pears were very much on his mind; he intended any day now "to pick them in." To pick the pears *in*—I liked that *in*. I played with it, repeated it; and though I don't believe I heard Pitton use the word in that way again, I associated it with him.

Then (as the reader will learn about in more detail in a later place in this book) Pitton had to go. The manor couldn't afford him. And there were no more regular gardeners, where there had been sixteen. No one to look after the vegetables in the walled garden or cut the grass or weed-kill the drive and paths or pick the pears in or keep the branches of the pear trees pinned to the squash-court wall.

The wind tore the upper branches of one tree free of the wall. The main trunk sagged forward, leaving a ghostlike outline in green-black on the wall; the branches drooped; the tree seemed about to break. But it didn't. The tree flowered; and at the foot of the wall in the summer, beside the path Pitton had once weed-killed, there grew up tall weeds that might have been chosen for their picturesque effect: shades of green, different degrees of transparency, different sizes of leaf. Above that, delicate white pear blossom turned to heavy fruit, at last. The birds became interested. No one now to pick the pears in, officially.

But then one Sunday, from my bedroom window, I saw a curiously dressed man looking at the pear trees, assessing them, and then, tentatively, picking the pears on the lower branches.

Strange people came into the manor grounds at various times. Pitton, when he had been there, had let in certain people. The Phillipses, the couple in the manor, had their own friends and visitors; and there were certain odd-job people they employed. And very occasionally there were people connected with my landlord. The curiously dressed man was unusual. But I had no means of knowing whether he was a marauder, someone simply picking the pears; or whether he was someone who had authority, and was picking them *in*, for the use of the manor or people of whom the manor approved.

He was curiously dressed. In army camouflage clothes, trousers, tunic, round-brimmed hat. The clothes didn't look like army surplus, or at any rate the stuff in the windows of the surplus stores. There was a quality of dash and swash in the cut, the camouflage pattern, and the muted colors; and, curiously, with the dressiness there was an element almost of disguise, which made the man seem dangerous, like an intruder.

As he looked at the trees, and with his tentative hands tugged at the lower pears, he turned from time to time to one side (his face still hidden by the camouflage collar and hat), in the direction of the manor courtyard, like a man nervous of being observed. But then, getting out the ladder from the garden shed next to the squash court, the shed that had been Pitton's, placing the ladder against the wall, starting from the top and working methodically, carefully down, leaving nothing for the birds, bucket by bucket the man in army clothes picked the pears. And it became clear that he was picking them *in*, and that he was picking the pears of the old trees in because he had the blessing of Mr. and Mrs. Phillips in the manor.

He had looked shifty at the beginning, uncertain, as though expecting someone to appear behind him. The person he must have been looking for appeared while he was on the ladder; because then, like a man apparently satisfied, he had concentrated on the pears.

The person who had appeared was a girl or, rather, a young woman; and she was half familiar to me. She walked on the lawn, and directly in front of my windows. The Phillipses never walked in front of my windows; they allowed me my privacy in the openness of the lawn; they were careful to walk on the far path, beside the squash court and the pear trees. This woman was going nowhere; she had come from the manor for a saunter on the lawn. She was short and heavy-hipped; her tight jeans emphasized the slowness and smallness of her steps. She was like someone who had been granted the freedom of the grounds and was at that moment beginning to taste the new freedom.

She too was unusually dressed. The extravagance was in her top: a shirt with the tails knotted in front, just below her breasts, leaving her midriff bare—not quite suitable at that time of year.

She had been half familiar to me. Now I knew her. She was the woman I had seen sunbathing in the ruined garden of the thatched cottage. I had associated her so much with her cottage and garden and car and open front door that this sight of her in another, more open setting, and so close to me, was like the sight of a new person. And the man in army camouflage on the ladder was her farm-worker husband.

Here, on a Sunday afternoon, they were in the manor grounds; she strolling about the lawn, her hips tight in hard jeans folding horizontally, and almost in a straight line, into alternate lateral peaks; her husband picking pears, ripe fruit from old trees that might have been planted against the wall by the person who had designed the wall, trees once carefully tended and still, after years of neglect, showing signs of that early care.

They, the woman with the midriff and the man in the army-style camouflage, must have attracted the Phillipses in some way. Perhaps the women had got on; perhaps the men had got on; perhaps—the Phillipses were ten to fifteen years older—there might have been a cross-attraction of some sort. The woman with the midriff would have been important to the relationship; at any rate, the relationship between the four couldn't have existed without her support or encouragement.

Already, and mainly from glimpses I had had of her in her ruined garden, lying on a cheap aluminum-framed easy chair, I had wondered about this woman. She had given me the impression of being at the center of passion, the cause of pain; a woman whose beauty caused pain to the man who at that moment was permitted to possess her; a woman who knew this.

That impression, arrived at from a distance, was added to now by the clearer and fuller sight I had of her on the lawn. To the narrow waist, the full hips, the firm thighs and upper arms, the breasts, flesh without muscle, half revealed, half flattened by her sunbathinglike top, to this voluptuousness were now added the stare (rather than the fire) in her unsteady light eyes, the greediness expressed by her mouth with its seemingly swollen lower lip, and by the distinct spaces between her top front teeth. Her sexuality was precious to her, more precious than anything else.

And here she was, in the grounds of the manor. And she was like someone in her own park, as though, just a few steps away from the clutter and constriction of the thatched cottage that had come with her husband's agricultural job (and which she couldn't therefore see as a real house), she had found a resort more suited to her style.

She walked slowly up and down the lawn, as though making herself familiar with a new pleasure. And the man in the army camouflage stood on the ladder and picked the pears, keeping his back to her, not turning round to look for her, as though he was now content, with his wife being where she was, with him.

Perhaps they and the Phillipses had come together as "town" people, working in the country but separate from the life of country people. Town people, but servants, all four, with their special style and pride, sharing now the grounds and privileges of the manor, offering and returning hospitality.

I couldn't tell who out of the four was benefiting most from the relationship. The person with most at stake was Les, the farm worker, who spent hours away from his wife, in his own solitude, in his tractor cab, seeing the tedium of a particular job physically expressed in the extent of a great down, perhaps without trees or windbreak, moving slowly back and forth, his thoughts no doubt often going back to the woman in the thatched cottage.

The grandeur of the manor, the grounds, the gardens, the river—these were like things he could present her with now, another side of what was to be found in the country, some little reward for the desolation of her life in that valley which others thought beautiful, and in that thatched cottage which others thought picturesque, but was picturesque only to people with another kind of life, different resources, another idea of what was owed them.

I was nervous of Brenda. She had no great regard for me. She had her own idea of what was to be respected; and the way I lived—a middle-aged man in a small cottage—and the work I did (if she had found out) didn't fit into that idea. In this she was different from the Phillipses, who saw me as "artistic," a version of their employer, and had always been protective. There was a difference of generations here.

But it was this difference that (over and above common interests) lay at the heart of the relationship between the four: the older people glamoured by the style and boldness of the younger.

Brenda was being groomed to serve in the manor when the Phillipses were on holiday or wished to take a day off. They had been looking for some time for a suitable person, someone compatible as well, a friend, yet someone who would not be a threat. And the prospect of a part-time light job in the manor for Brenda, the prospect of having the run of the little wild estate, the gardens, the orchard, the riverbank walks, this bound the younger people to the Phillipses.

And that took some understanding, that people like Brenda and Les, who were so passionate, so concerned with their individuality, their style, the quality of their skin and hair, it took some understanding that people who were so proud and flaunting in one way should be prepared in another corner of their hearts or souls or minds to go down several notches and be servants. They were servants, all four. Within that condition (which should have neutered them) all their passions were played out. But that might have been my own special prejudice, my own raw nerves. I came from a colony, once a plantation society, where servitude was a more desperate condition.

Les was under pressure. From his work on the farm, and his uncertainty about what was going to happen with that very big venture; if it failed, he would have to move on, find another position. From his obsession with Brenda, whose beauty so obviously tormented him: possession of the woman not enough, constantly reminding him of what he might lose. And pressure, too, from his increasingly dependent relationship with the Phillipses.

He wished to keep the footing he had obtained in the manor; he wished Brenda—to whom it mattered—to continue to enjoy the freedom of the grounds. To do so he had to put himself in some ways in the power of the Phillipses; had to some extent, after the servitude of his own job, to serve them.

He cut the grass on the various lawns, a big job. He made himself busy on Saturdays and Sundays with his hammer and saw, mending bridges over the creeks (black with rotting leaves) in the water meadows, keeping a path clear to the riverbank. He even tried to revive some of the vegetable plots of the walled garden—between the paths, a wilderness of weeds in the old sifted earth, many times forked over and fertilized, but the garden as a whole still showing a fair amount of its original design and (like the pear trees) preserving after many years of care something of its formality, even with the wire netting and coops and rough carpentry and basins, all the abandoned intentions of the various odd-job people who had worked in the garden and grounds after Pitton had left.

Les worked on the vegetable plots in the evenings, after his work on the farm. Energy! But this late work on the vegetables became an irritation to me. He used the sprinkler then; and the flow of water there set up a high-pitched vibration in the old metal pipes that ran through my own cottage; so that my cottage hissed and hummed while the sprinkler played.

Pitton and his successors had used the garden hose or sprinkler during the day; but the noise then had been muffled by the noises of the day. In the silence of the evening—the old silence of the country (even with the electric-light glow in the sky of the towns all around), a silence so pure that the trains going in and out of Salisbury station six or seven miles away could be heard sometimes when I went out of my cottage door—in the evening those hissing pipes could be clearly heard, and couldn't be ignored.

I did something I hadn't done before. I telephoned Mrs. Phillips at the manor to complain. I was expecting her to be combative, and protective towards her friends. To my surprise she made no fuss. She accepted what I said about the peculiar nuisance of the hissing pipes in the evening, and said she would go and turn the sprinkler off herself. She did that; and the abrupt silence in the cottage—coming at first like a ringing in the ears or the head, a noise of cicadas—was like a blessing.

What accidents had given me my life in the cottage! What accidents protected it! How little it would have taken to alter the whole feel of the place, and to drive me away! A disturbance like the sprinkler late in the evening; or Brenda walking too often outside my window; or too many strangers making free of the lawn outside; or too many parties and visitors in the servants' quarters of the manor.

Mrs. Phillips had been cooperative. But I expected after this that there would be a certain awkwardness with her, and a more pronounced awkwardness—long building up—with Brenda and Les. And such was my mood, my acceptance of the inevitability of change, my idea that things lasted for their season, such was the effect of my training myself to say, "Well, at least I have had this for a year," and, "At least I have had this for two years," that I was half prepared to feel that my life on the estate had changed for good.

But there was no awkwardness with Mrs. Phillips or Mr. Phillips. And no awkwardness at all with Les. In fact, Les, with whom I had so far had little to do, made a friendly move towards me. And he did so the very next day.

At the time when the sprinkler might have been turned on—and from my kitchen door I might have seen the arc or fan of the parallel water jets, hypnotically appearing and disappearing, waxing and waning against the late southern sky, above the high wall of the vegetable garden, the wall that ran beside the little lane at the back of my cottage—at that time he knocked at my kitchen door. Technically, it was a back door; but it was the only door I used to go in and out of my cottage.

I saw him through the high glass panes in the door. He was bareheaded when I opened. His camouflage hat (a relic of the camouflage outfit) was in one hand, and he was offering some vegetables in a basin. The gesture, of offering, was graceful, classical; and he was smiling. The picture remained with me: the lean, sunken-cheeked, tanned face; the hat held in one hand, the two hands together holding the basin with the vegetables; the smile.

Yet what was also noticeable about him was his lack of beauty. And this was now noticeable because I had expected a man of good looks, from his physique, the way he carried himself, his clothes. His chin was heavy; his teeth were bad: they mocked his smile; his skin was marked. And yet he had worked hard at his looks. His hair was stylishly cut, soft, freshly washed. I understood now why he always wore unusual or elegant hats. They helped; from a distance he looked good in hats. I understood also a little of the anxiety I had sensed in him about Brenda; as well as a little more of Brenda's manner, the manner of a woman who was still owed a lot.

When the Phillipses went on their holiday, Brenda took over at the manor. She moved into the Phillipses' quarters. Les stayed on in the thatched cottage.

I had to be away for a few days at this time. On the morning after I got back I went to the manor to get my letters. My letters were kept there when I was away; that was the arrangement with the Phillipses.

I rang at the kitchen door in the manor courtyard. I heard music inside. Brenda was a long time coming.

She would have been deep in the Phillipses' quarters. They had elegant rooms. They had a sitting room with a stone terrace leading out onto the back lawn, which had been laid out fifty or more years before and had big trees and flower beds and old rose bushes and old pieces of garden statuary: in the distance, the marsh of the water meadows, the river, and the meadows and the down on the other bank. To this, on the stone terrace just outside, the Phillipses had added bird tables and pendant seed bells, at which tits and other birds pecked.

Brenda was carefully got up. Jeans and blouse; her full lips painted, something done to her eyelashes, emphasizing the stare of her unsettling blue eyes; her appearance at the same time suggesting an immense idleness in the Phillipses' quarters. Servant and not servant; and now not particularly attentive to me. She said she had seen no letters.

At her back was the big kitchen of the manor, which (from what they told me) the Phillipses had done up or caused to be done up. A warm, inviting kitchen, with a big stove and many cupboards; thick walls, small windows set in deep embrasures, the electric lights on; a feeling of space and protection, of doors opening into corridors and big room standing beside big room.

Shortly after she came back Mrs. Phillips telephoned me to say that there were many letters for me at the manor. When I went to her kitchen to get them I told her that Brenda had told me there were none.

Mrs. Phillips didn't seem displeased to hear this. No explanation, no comment; just a hint of a nod. She was like someone digesting a piece of news, adding it to what she already possessed.

And I felt that Mrs. Phillips had changed her mind about Brenda; that once again—as had happened with other people she had tried out as her holiday replacement—Mrs. Phillips had found a reason for recoiling from having a stranger in her kitchen and rooms. Brenda might have been the central person at the beginning of the relationship between the four. But now Mrs. Phillips was more important.

I was not surprised then when Brenda stopped appearing in the manor. But I was not prepared for the news Mrs. Phillips gave one day.

"She's run off to Italy with Michael Allen," she said.

Michael Allen was a central heating contractor. He was a young man with a newish business. He had profited from the old-fashioned ways of the older central heating and plumbing firms, used to dealing with big houses, used to being well thought of, but burdened by the expensive town-center premises and large staffs of older days.

I had got to know Michael Allen after he had come to the manor to do something about a boiler that had exploded. I asked him about the hissing pipes in my cottage. He said in his brisk way that the only cure for that as well as for other things in the manor was to scrap the entire plumbing system, all those antiquated metal pipes. I remembered his confidence, the way he walked, the way he came into my cottage: he actually had a little strut. He was a country fellow and a great boaster. In the short time we spoke he boasted about many things; he asked me nothing about myself. He employed six people, he said; he intended to retire when he was forty.

In a bigger town, in London, say, people like Michael Allen do not really have personalities: their personalities seldom make an impression and do not matter. They or their employees come out of the streets, do their jobs, and return to the streets. They disappear; they are hardly their names; they are more their telephone numbers and their bills. In a place like the valley the entry of the same kind of person into your house is more of a social occasion. He comes with more readable attributes and many more points of contact: his village or small town, his neighbors sometimes, his education, his background, the houses and people he has served, and the services and shops he in his turn shares with you.

Michael Allen boasted. He saw himself as a man of energy and ambition, and for this reason untouched by the recession other people complained about. He saw himself as adventurous, several cuts above the general run of people who didn't have the courage or the spirit to go into business on their own and were content to be employed by others. His looks were passable; he had a mustache, of the current fashion. But after that meeting I remembered more his absurd pride and boastfulness, and the strutting, almost hands-in-pockets way he came into the cottage, as though he were doing it and me a favor.

I saw his van sometimes in Salisbury. Once or twice I saw him and his van outside the Safeway supermarket. Michael didn't like that: being seen using his van as a car. I saw his van outside Brenda and Leslie's cottage, and in the courtyard of the manor. But that wasn't surprising. I was used to seeing his van (as well as the vans of certain local builders) up and down the valley; certain tradesmen were never idle.

But Italy! What old-fashioned idea of romance had sent Michael and Brenda there? What film or television show? Or was it, more simply, that Michael had been there on a package holiday and felt safer with what he knew? But wasn't that going abroad itself a sign of the brevity of the passion? How could Michael give up his six employees, his local reputation, his van with his name painted on the sides and the back? How long before he wished to return, not only to that fame and career, but also to his old life?

And so it happened.

Brenda reappeared. Not in the manor. That interlude was over. Even before Brenda had gone away Les had stopped coming to the manor, had given up the vegetable garden, the hammering on weekends, the doing of odd jobs about the grounds. All that effort to put things right, all that effort of heart and hand, had gone to waste; the manor had swallowed it up. Waste; but the manor had given things in return, had given pleasure, had given Les for many weeks the freedom of its wild grounds. Just as, before Les and Brenda had come to the thatched cottage, the country life and its seeming secrecy had given the dairyman from the town some genuine new idea of the beauty of the days.

Now the manor was in the past, and Les had retreated to his thatched cottage—never romantic to him, and now no doubt the wretchedest of places for him; had retreated to the solitude and noise of his tractor cab, going up and down the immense slopes of the downs, considering earth and dust, now black, now brown, now white, and the physical desolation of his fields. I had seen him at one of his best moments: appearing at the door with his vegetables, offering them with that classical gesture, and a smile of pure goodwill, the smile of a man receiving at that time a little love from the person he loved, and passing a bit of it back to the people around him.

For Brenda that return, not just from Italy, but from Italy to the cottage, must have been awful. After half queening it in the grounds of the manor, and queening it for a full fortnight in the quarters of the Phillipses, with that grand view from the sitting room of the lawn and statues and old trees and the river. She had asked for so much from her beauty; so much, and then she had asked so much again.

Mrs. Phillips said of Brenda, "Michael kicked her out." And that was all.

Michael! The use of the first name pointed to some new attachment on Mrs. Phillips's part, some new—or old—sympathy, something born of that "town" life—pub, club or hotel bar—which at one time might have involved them all, Mr. and Mrs. Phillips, Brenda and Les, and Michael Allen.

It was a good thing that the autumn was well advanced. No question now of Brenda's having to show herself to anybody, to prove that she was unabashed and that life was going on. She could close her front door and stay indoors; just as Les could take out his tractor and hide behind the tinted plastic of his cab.

The farming organization that had brought these town people to the valley (and had in their own way remade parts of the valley) was fading, for reasons I didn't know. With such ventures it was as with the military exercises on the ground or in the air that were so often with us: one saw a great deal, but understood little.

Les was looking, it was said, for another job. Three or four times I saw Brenda and Les on the road in their little dark-red motorcar. They had taken down part of the fence and the hedge to make a space for that car in the garden. And the thatched cottage had indeed been no more than temporary shelter. To have invested more in it emotionally would have been a waste, more of a waste than Les's evening and weekend work in the manor grounds.

The first time I saw them in their car after they had stopped coming to the manor there was some kind of half recognition from Les. From Brenda there was none. Perhaps there had been some trouble with Mrs. Phillips over my letters—the letters being put forward by her as a cause—and I had not been forgiven. On the later occasions I saw them there was nothing at all. Our brief acquaintance was over.

There was a van that I also saw, the van of Michael Allen, going importantly about on its central heating business. Country-town success! Michael had given me a glimpse of that side of things here. But Italy! Who would have associated romance with that van and the name painted on the sides and the back of the van, painted in three places. Whenever I saw the van I thought of Mrs. Phillips's words: "Michael kicked her out." How hard it must have been for Les and Brenda to live with those words, which others must also have heard!

The days shortened. The way below the yews from the public road to the manor drive and to my cottage, that way was so dark at four in the afternoon that when I went shopping in Salisbury on the mid-afternoon bus I needed to take a flashlight for the short walk back from the bus stop.

Country darkness! Big things could happen almost secretly. And one such thing happened in the thatched cottage with the straw pheasant on the roof.

It was Mrs. Phillips who gave me the news.

She said, two days after the event, "Brenda's dead."

She added, and it seemed calmly, "Les murdered her."

"Murdered," the formal word, rather than "killed." We use formal words, even empty words, when events are big.

I thought of the way they had both appeared on the lawn during the pear picking—two birds in bright plumage. I thought of the face of the satisfied lover offering me the vegetables at the kitchen door, the gift of the happy man. Then I thought of Italy and the Michael Allen van going about its money-making business, spreading the name around—while Les was running about in his red car looking for a new job.

So hard to contemplate, the physical act, the setting, the finality, the body, just a few hundred yards away. I thought of the least intrusive question I might ask. "Where did he kill her?"

"Right in that cottage. On Saturday night."

Saturday night! Was it a night of drink and temper? It wasn't what I associated with them.

Mrs. Phillips said: "She taunted him."

And "taunted" I felt to be a technical word, as technical as "murdered." It had sexual connotations. She, the Italian runaway, had done the sexual taunting. She had not come back abashed. She had done the taunting, the goading. How often, to punish someone for her Italian failure, she must have "taunted" him! And it was hard not to feel that she didn't have some idea of what she was provoking. And how, having started on the job of destruction—he had used a kitchen knife—having started on that, from which very quickly there was no turning back, however much in a corner of his mind he might have been wishing it all undone, healed again, how he must have struck, until the madness and the life was over! All in that little thatched cottage with the ruined garden.

Worker bees work till they die. When they die other bees clear the hive, get rid of the bodies. Because bees work and are clean. And so, without disturbance, without many people knowing, even people on the bus, the cottage was cleansed and cleared of its once precious life, its once precious passions.

She "taunted" him—it was the verdict. And all hearts were with the living, the survivor, the man; as, had it occurred the other way, they would have been with the woman. The police were discreet, hardly seen, almost as secretive as the event itself. More information was to be had from the local weekly paper than from immediate neighbors. They had seen very little, and didn't want to blame one partner more than the other: everyone drawn close at this moment to Brenda and Les, seeking to remember them, and responding to this very near event almost as to a family tragedy.

One local formality remained. Brenda's "things" had to be collected. And some weeks later, before the winter turned to spring with the gales of spring, Brenda's sister came to collect Brenda's things from the unoccupied cottage, where there was no longer a dark-red motorcar.

Collecting the dead person's things: it was like something from the old world—an aspect of the idea of sanctity, an aspect of decent burial, the honoring of the dead—and it seemed to call for some ritual. But there was none. The coming for the dead woman's things was matter-of-fact. I wouldn't have known about it if I wasn't in the kitchen of the manor, settling some little bill with Mrs. Phillips, when Brenda's sister came to call.

Mrs. Phillips knew Brenda's sister. It was another indication of the Phillipses' "town" life, their life outside the manor and the village. Mrs. Phillips became much graver when Brenda's sister said what she had come for. I was moved myself. And we all went, after introductions, to Mrs. Phillips's sitting room with its view of the down and the river, the water meadows and the big aspens of the garden, the old stone terrace, the urns, the moss, the mottled stone, the seed bells for the birds, the lines of washing—the mixture of big-house garden and backyard domesticity which I had seen (through rain and mist) on my first day in the grounds when, hardly knowing where I was or understanding what I saw, I had called on the Phillipses. Thereafter I had seen that view only at Christmastime (those years when I was not abroad), when I called on the Phillipses to give them my presents.

Brenda's sister was not immediately like Brenda. She was older, fatter. There was a quality in the fatness, the puffiness, which suggested illness, a clinical condition, rather than grossness. Brenda's heaviness, in hips and thighs, had been different; it had suggested someone spoilt, someone who felt that her beauty entitled her to luxurious sensations and felt at the same time that her beauty could support a certain amount of self-indulgence. But then I began to see Brenda's full lips and wild eyes in her sister's face, saw those features lost or altered in puffy flesh; saw, too, the smoothness of skin and purity of complexion which would have given the girl, when she was a girl, a high idea of herself and her potential, but which was now part of the breathy wreck she had become. Things had not gone well for these sisters; in different ways their gift of beauty had turned out to be a torment for them.

Brenda's sister lived in a small, newish town to the south, between Salisbury and Bournemouth, not town, not country, not the sort of desolate place she had thought she would end up in.

In the Phillipses' sitting room it was for a while as though Brenda's sister's call was a purely social one. But then she seemed suddenly to remember what had brought her.

She said, "You want to save everything. And then you want to throw everything away." Her voice broke; her eyes went watery. "She left so little. Her clothes." She tried to smile. "She was so particular about her clothes. But what can I do about her clothes?"

No ill will, no anger, no wish for revenge.

She said, "She was too much for him. He couldn't handle her."

Mrs. Phillips allowed Brenda's sister to talk on.

Brenda's sister said, "She even thought he was queer. Did you know that? She told me he washed his hair every morning. Not in the evening after work, because he didn't want to sleep on it when it was wet. But in the morning. He is like my son Raymond. I hope nobody thinks he is queer because he does that. Raymond does it for the girls at his school."

I had always assumed it was Brenda who had encouraged Les to dress up, and had thought that she had chosen things for him. This news about the washing of the hair suggested a lonelier and more desperate man.

Brenda's sister said, "She expected so much from her life. My mother drilled it into us how much she suffered before the war, living in a little army house, hoping for great things to happen to my father. And that was all that ever happened to us. We lived in a little army house."

The story she told us was that her father, a simple serviceman with some factory experience, had had a fleeting moment of inspiration early in the war. He had hit on a new way of mounting guns in the tail of an airplane; and from being a simple serviceman he had been taken up by the authorities for a few months. He was not alone, though; there were many others like him, men with ideas.

"Always he was on his way to Ministry of Defence. Ministry of Defence, Ministry of Defence, I heard those words all the time. When I see the advertisements in the paper today and see the same words, it brings it back."

I didn't think she was romancing. Her use of the words "Ministry of Defence" without the definite article—the *the* that the average person would have wanted to add—was convincing; it suggested that she knew the words as well as she had said.

But nothing had happened to her father. Guns were changed; aircraft were modified or replaced; and the serviceman had become ordinary again. But his daughters had inherited through their mother a dream of glory together with a general pessimism, a wishing to hope and a nervousness about hoping. It made for temperament, frustration, self-destructiveness. It is as if we all carry in our makeup the effects of accidents that have befallen our ancestors, as if we are in many ways programmed before we are born, our lives half outlined for us.

Brenda's sister said, "I can't talk. I didn't do so well myself."

She had married a builder who—when she had at last got out into the world, got away from the little army house—had seemed to her immensely prosperous and stylish; but had then seemed less so; had fallen on hard times, had done even worse when, trying to change his luck, he had set up in business in Germany; and had then been unfaithful with a younger woman, as glamoured by his manner as Brenda's sister once had been. He had finally left home, left his wife and child.

An old story—that was what Brenda's sister said; and that was the way she told it, playing down the drama. "As usual, Muggins was the last to know." All her care now was for her son; he was her sole interest; she had narrowed herself down to that.

So, though she didn't make the point, there was a pattern to her life. Her father had been replaced by her husband, and her husband by her son. Her life had repeated; she had lived the same life or versions of the same life. Or, looking at it another way, almost as soon as it had begun, her life of choice and passion had ended—as it had ended for her father, her mother, and possibly for generations of her ancestors.

All Brenda's sister's talk of herself came out without prompting; and her hysteria became noticeable. So it was possible, after her early calmness, even formality, in Mrs. Phillips's sitting room, with the grand view, to see Brenda's sister as an ill person, someone more marked than Brenda had been by their family past, the past that had really been the absence of a great event. And it was possible at the same time to see in her not only more and more reminders of Brenda's looks, but also something—like another side—of Brenda's passions. Such varied passions, so many roots, so little understood, even by the people who had become victims of those passions.

Then the hysterical woman with the still smooth skin, the still unblotched color, remembered her social graces. The call was over. She had to do what she had come to do: collect the things of her sister, who had left so little behind.

We left the sitting room. A corridor; thick walls, stone mullions in the window; a door to the big kitchen. And there at the portico Mrs. Phillips said good-bye.

When we were out of the manor courtyard and on the rough, stony drive, Brenda's sister said—and it was sudden after her apparent trustingness in the sitting room—"I don't think I will ever forgive Mrs. Phillips."

She was distressed. I began to walk with her to the road. As we walked below the yews she told me of Brenda's flight to Italy.

Michael Allen had gone by air. Brenda had gone by train. During that journey—hearing so little English, talking so little to people— she had thought a lot about what she was doing and she had become afraid. By the time she reached Rome she had decided not to go to Michael. She thought she would go and stay at a hotel and get a message to Leslie, even send for him. She had a little money, enough for a few days. She booked into a hotel near the railway station. There was no telephone at home, in the thatched cottage. So she had telephoned the manor and asked for a message to be passed on to Leslie.

Nothing had happened; no word came from Leslie. Then, swallowing her pride (because there had been some quarrel between them), Brenda had telephoned the people in Jack's old cottage—the woman who drove fast up the hill in her motorcar to collect her children from the school bus every weekday afternoon and had never smiled at me; the woman who had leveled Jack's garden. But still no message came from Leslie. By this time Brenda's money had run out. She had then done what she had decided not to do. She had gone after all to Michael Allen and had been with him until, as we had all been told, he had kicked her out.

She had come back aggrieved, angry, in a mood to taunt the man she regarded or pretended to regard as a queer, not fully a man. She felt mocked by the romantic impulse that had thrilled and sustained her for a while in the hotel near the railway station in Rome: the girl in need, the girl in danger, the lover eager at the other end. Leslie should have done everything, sold everything, to go to her. But there had been no word from Leslie.

Brenda's sister said, "Mrs. Phillips never passed the message to Leslie. She did it four or five days later, when Brenda had left the hotel and was with Michael. She said she forgot. She said other things came up. She said she didn't think it was all that important. But I think it was deliberate."

From the woman who lived in Jack's old house Brenda's sister said she didn't expect anything. But this story gave a new character to the woman—and the shape and color of her car—racing up the hill to meet her young children off the afternoon school bus.

One day, late in the summer, walking past the old farm buildings and what had been Jack's cottage and garden—the junk and ruins which had formed no part of Jack's vision of a world ever renewed, ruins to which now, across the droveway, was added a burning pit in the chalk for industrial-looking rubbish, the fire of which occasionally singed the silver birches planted years before to screen the old patch of waste ground—one day, walking past the farm and its spreading litter and on up to where the Swiss rolls of hay had been stacked and were already going black and brilliant green with new shoots of grass, I heard the sound of a great fire behind the young wood—and that wood was no longer so young.

I heard the sound behind the trees; saw the smoke and, between the black of the tree trunks, the flames in the field beyond, the heat waves distorting the view like a pane of old-fashioned glass; felt the heat; and then very quickly was engulfed by the noise, rising fast to an amazing crepitation. And I thought of another sound I had heard more than twenty-five years before in the highlands of northeastern South America: the sound of a big waterfall. Water, fire—in great disturbance they made the same sound. And fleetingly to me, walking on the downs in that overpowering noise, it seemed that all matter was one.

On the way back—the fire quickly burnt away, finished, ashes in the field behind the wood—on the way back from my walk, then and afterwards, the thick patch of moss below the dormer window on the thatched roof of the empty house, a green that was shining, unnatural, that green, once part of the beauty of thatch, seemed to stand for more than vegetable matter.

So quiet the thatched house now; so ruined the little garden once neat with its hedge, scores of small roses in the summer.

And so quiet, over the hill on the other side, at the bottom of the valley, where an old, grassed-over field track led to a small abandoned farm building, all black and rust in a little dip in the land, so quiet when I saw them on a Saturday or Sunday afternoon, in the silence of the empty downs: the children from what had been Jack's cottage, playing amid the rubble (whitening, sprouting a few weeds with yellow flowers) and the tires of the silage pit.

*A*ND THERE, perhaps, Jack's vision of the valley as a whole place would continue; a vision without the decadence that was in my eye; a vision of childhood that would expand in the adult mind.

There were others who saw the valley and droveway as a place without decay. Walking one day past the old farm buildings, past the fresh litter below the birch trees, the fire in the chalk pit, turning up towards the new wood, I saw a figure in the distance.

I was used to solitude on the walk. The sight of a person in the distance like this, with the prospect of an encounter ten or fifteen minutes ahead, could spoil all the intervening walk and the walk back as well (because the person encountered would be likely to be walking back himself, usually to a parked car at the far end of the droveway, where it met one of the highways). I preferred therefore, if I saw a person approaching, to give up the walk and turn back.

This time, however, I didn't. The person I was walking towards turned out to be a middle-aged woman. She was quite small. In the distance, and especially when seen against the sky, she had seemed physically imposing; people stood out in the emptiness. Her greeting just before we crossed was easy, open; we stopped and spoke. She was a working woman from Shrewton. When she lived at Amesbury, she said, she had regularly done the walk we were both now doing. She had come out now to look for the deer. So we had that in common as well. She said she had worked out the circuit of the deer; she knew roughly where they crossed the public road. And it was extraordinary, the survival of the family of deer in a piece of land bounded on three sides by busy highways and on one of those sides in addition by the army firing ranges.

No decay in that woman's eye. Downs, walks, deer: the wonder of the natural world as available as it had always been.

And no decay in the eye of the old farm manager either. I saw him one day on a horse on the rising stretch of the droveway between the wood on one side and a treeless field or pasture on the other, before the hill with the larks and the barrows on the brow of the hill. In the old days he had seldom come so far on his inspection tours in his Land-Rover. But now he was retired and could roam; and he was on a horse, a further sign of leisure.

It was a big horse, of a beautiful color, white or gray spotted or spattered with red-brown. It was a difficult horse, he said. It was the gift of his daughter, who had married and gone to live in Gloucestershire. And that was what his talk was about: his daughter (so good with horses) and her gift of the horse (no trouble to her, that animal).

His suburban house at the very edge of the antique droveway; his neat garden; his daughter grown up and gone away; and now the empty days. How quickly his time had passed! How quickly a man's time passed! So quickly, in fact, that it was possible within a normal span to witness, to comprehend, two or three active life cycles in succession.

That wasn't what I thought about when I met him. When I met him on the horse that he was finding so difficult—he dismounted, with some relief, to talk to me—I thought at first only that it was true what some people said: that people who retired after active or physically energetic lives aged fast. He had aged; he had become bent; his walk was stiff (the walk in which, when I had first seen him and thought him to be an exemplar of the farmer "type," I had seen a "farmer's walk").

The other thought, about the shortness of a man's active cycle, his doing period, came to me afterwards, when I had left the manor and my cottage, when that section of my life had closed, and I had begun to feel, myself, that energy and action were things no longer absolutely at my command, that everyone had been given his particular measure of energy, and that when it was used up it was used up. These thoughts came to me not many years after I had seen the manager on his difficult horse, and seen the gap between us in age and energy and expectations. But middle age or the decline associated with it comes abruptly to some people; and middle age had come as abruptly to me as old age appeared to me then to have come to the old manager.

I would have liked to hear the old manager say something about the new farm people. I would have then said—more in tribute to him as someone from my past, than because I understood what I saw of the farming around me—how much I preferred his way. But he wasn't interested. So the solidarity went unexpressed. And it was just as well. Because eventually, mysteriously (at least to me), the new venture failed, after two harsh, dry summers, summers so harsh that the old mock orange shrub outside my cottage died.

During one of those droughts I heard talk—on the bus, and from Bray, the car-hire man—that water wasn't to be brought to the cattle, but that the cattle were to be transported to where there was water, transported perhaps to Wales! Such was the scale and style and reputation of the new venture. I don't know whether anything like that happened, or whether it was just excited local exaggeration. Soon, however, it didn't matter. The venture failed. And even this failure— large as it was, affecting so many people, affecting the eventual appearance of so many acres—seemed to happen quietly.

It was some time before I knew that there had been failure. The machines were there; the cows were there; the men were up and down in their cars; the big trucks came to take away the grain from the metal-walled barn. But then gradually the failure, the withdrawal at the center, began to show.

The prefabricated cow shed next to the barn was opened, front and back, and cleared of its dung and straw; and it remained open and clean (though stained) and empty: the stalls, the concrete floor with its canals, the slatted timber of the walls striping the sunlight, radiating it at many angles, and giving the shed an internal glow. The new milking building or parlor was taken down. So newly put up, its concrete platform—all that remained—still so new and raw-looking on the hillside. It was like Jack's greenhouse; that, too, had left only a concrete floor.

Again, here, building had been on too big a scale, a scale too big for men. Needs had been exaggerated, had ramified, and had left a ruin. An empty cow shed that might eventually be taken down and sold elsewhere; a milking machine that no doubt had already been sold, leaving only a concrete floor. So small in the openness now, that floor, where the milking machines had hummed and hissed and dials had kept check of this and that; while the dung-stained cows, corralled into their iron-railed passages at particular times, had waited with a curious stillness to give milk to the machines, after being walked up the hill to the cowman's shouts (the only human remnant of the milking ritual).

The cows themselves eventually disappeared. Some would have been sold; but whether sold or not, what would have happened to them would have been what always happened to cows when their time was judged to have come: batches of them were regularly taken off in covered vans to the slaughterhouse.

I had seen the cows on the hillsides against the sky, heads down, grazing, or looking with timorous interest at the passing man. And they had seemed like the cows in the drawing on the label of the condensed-milk tins I knew in Trinidad as a child: something to me as a result at the very heart of romance, a child's fantasy of the beautiful other place, something which, when I saw it on the downs, was like something I had always known. I had seen the big eyes, the occasional mild stampede of the herd as, within their pasture, they had followed the walking man, thinking he had brought them something tasty or was to lead them to something they had been trained to like. I had seen the big, wet, black noses, the fly-repellent in the metal sachets clipped to the ears, which they flapped like heavy fans. One sees what one sees. Harder to imagine, unreal, what one doesn't see.

It had taken me some time to see that though milk came from cows that had dropped calves, no calf was to be seen, except very sick ones: little, seemingly fluid sacks of black and white or brown and white on straw, creatures still seeming fresh from the womb. And no cow with its calf. No lowing herd winding o'er the lea here, as in Gray's

"Elegy"; no "sober" herd lowing to meet their young at evening's close, as in "The Deserted Village."

Pictures of especial beauty at one time, those lines of poetry, matching the idea of the cows on the condensed-milk label. Especial beauty, because (though I knew that "sober" well—lovely, apt word—and knew the ritual of bedding down cattle for the night) we had no herds like that on my island. We didn't have the climate, the pasture; the island had been developed for the cultivation of sugar-cane. But there were cattle. Some members of my family, like other country people, kept cows, one or two, for milk, for love, for religion.

We were at the very end of the old Aryan cow worship, the worship of the cow that gave milk, without which men's life would have been harder and in some climates and lands impossible. This worship was something our grandfathers had brought with them from peasant India; when I was a child, we still honored the idea for its own sake, as well as for its link with the immemorial past. Among us, the new milk from a cow that had just calved was almost holy. A special sweet was made from this very rich milk and sent by the cow's owner to friends and relations, sent in very small portions, like a consecrated offering from a religious rite.

Our few cows (perhaps like Gray's or Goldsmith's herds) were poor things compared with the healthy, big animals on the downs. But these animals on the downs, even with their beauty, were without the sanctity, the constant attention of men, which as a child I thought cows craved. These cows in railed pastures or meadows had numbers scored into their rumps. No sanctity at birth, and none at death; just the covered van. And sometimes, as once in the derelict, mossy yard at the back of Jack's cottage, there were reminders of assisted insemination or gestation going wrong: when for some days, isolated from the animals that had all come out well, oddly made cattle were penned up there, with that extra bit of flesh and hair (with the black and white Frisian pattern) hanging down their middle, as of cow material that had leaked through the two halves of the cow mold.

And now, with the disappearance of the cattle, there came to the old and new lanes and ways of the downs around the farm (whose life might have seemed to the visitor unchanging and ritualized) a moment of stasis, suspense. There had been great activity; now there were more ruins than ever.

The manor in whose grounds I lived, so many of its rooms shut up; the gardens of the manor; the forested orchard; the children's house there, with the conical thatched roof, the thatch rotting, the thick stack of the damp reeds slipping out of the wire netting in one place, creating the effect at the bottom of a diagonal slicing of the reeds; the squash court that was not squash court or farmhouse; the old granary with the double pyramidal roof.

Beyond the renovated church, the old farm buildings had been taken down and replaced by the prefabricated shed, which was now empty; with the round convex silver mirrors at the entrance to the cow yard as reminders of the traffic that had once been. The pink house with the green-stained thatched roof and the shredding straw pheasant on the roof; its garden now a piece of waste ground. The new barn and the new half-slatted cow shed at the top of the hill with the windbreak of pine and beech, trees which had grown so much since I had first seen them. At the bottom of that hill, the silage pit with the thick timber-plank walls against the excavated hillside, the timber planks stained with creosote; the tires all around, bought in such number from people who dealt in such things, tires worn smooth from many miles on many roads; and the rubble of the excavation, hummocked and chalky white and full of grass and weeds.

And these were set among older ruins. The small old farm building, perhaps from the last century, far to the right at the end of the overgrown track at the foot of the hill; and all the many farm buildings, old or very old, at the back of Jack's cottage. Along the droveway: the beehives; the house-shaped old rick; the old stone house, ruined walls alone, surrounded by trees which, tall and overhanging the ruin when I had first seen them, were now ten years older: vegetable nature moving on, stone immovable.

And in the walk in the other direction, away from the old Land-Rover run of the old manager: the great Swiss rolls of hay still stacked in the space between the wood—how grown!—and the hill of larks, with the ancient barrows at the top, part of the pimpling of the downs as seen against the sky: those rolls of hay now as black and as earthlike as the older bales that, at the other end of the droveway, had indeed, below their tattered plastic sheeting, turned to earth. Grass to hay to earth.

M Y OWN time here was coming to an end, my time in the manor cottage and in that particular part of the valley, my second childhood of seeing and learning, my second life, so far away from my first.

I had tried almost from the beginning to make myself ready for this end. After the glory and surprise of the first spring on the riverbanks—the new reeds, the water clearing to crystal ("freshing out," as I learned to say), but this water green and dark with olive-blue suggestions and with illusory depth where it reflected the thick, succulent growth on the banks, and especially below trees—after that first spring I would say: "At least I had a spring here." And then I said: "At least I had a spring and summer here." And: "At least I've had a year here." And so it went on, as the years passed. Until time began to telescope, and experience itself began to change: the new season not truly new any more, bringing less of new experience than reminders of the old. One had begun to stack away the years, to count them, to take pleasure in the counting, accumulation.

One autumn afternoon I had a slight choking fit as I walked past Jack's old cottage and the derelict old farmyard. The fit passed by the time I had got round the corner, cleared the farmyard, and left behind the old metal and tangled wire and timber junk below the beeches. (Not the birches near the fire pit; they were on the other side of the way. These beeches were at the edge of the farmyard, big trees now in their prime, their lowest branches very low, providing a wonderful, rich, enclosing shade in the summer that made me think of George Borrow and his wanderings in *The Romany Rye* and *Lavengro*.) Past the beeches and the farm, in the familiar solitude of the grassy way, I began to breathe easily again. Some irritation, something in the air around the farmyard, some passing allergy, I thought, and did nothing about it when I went home. That evening the fit returned. It was like a continuation of the moment near Jack's cottage; but this time it stayed with me, and within two or three hours I was seriously ill.

This was the illness that did away with whatever remained of youthfulness in me (and much had remained), diminished my energy, and pushed me week by week, during my convalescence, month by month, into middle age.

It was the end, for me, of the manor cottage as well. The downs, the uplands, the river and its banks—the geography here was simple. Water drained off the downs to the river. After rain, on the paved lane beside the windbreak, there were the little pebbled rivulets I had minutely observed running between the asphalt edge and the grass verge, down to the public road and then, over the road surface or through culverts, towards the river. Little rivulets like that, but charged with beech mast, now fresh, now old, ran past my kitchen door after rain; and left little tide wracks, almost, of beech-mast debris all down the path. My cottage was cold. The solid stone and flint walls which I loved—for the warm color of the stone especially—kept in this cold. The beech trees that embowered it also kept out the sun. Even in summer it never got warm; even during the summer drought that killed the old mock orange shrub I needed heat at night.

The beauty of the place, the great love I had grown to feel for it, greater than for any other place I had known, had kept me there too long. My health had suffered. But I couldn't say then, and can't say now, that I minded. There is some kind of exchange always. For me, for the writer's gift and freedom, the labor and disappointments of the writing life, and the being away from my home; for that loss, for having no place of my own, this gift of the second life in Wiltshire, the second, happier childhood as it were, the second arrival (but with an adult's perception) at a knowledge of natural things, together with the fulfillment of the child's dream of the safe house in the wood. But there was the cold of the cottage, and the damp and mist of the glorious riverbank; and the illnesses that come to people who have developed or inherited weak lungs.

It was some time before I went walking again. I was working on a big book. At a certain stage in that kind of labor, energy becomes one: mental energy, physical energy, the use of one depleting the other. And when I was sufficiently recovered, most of my energy went on my book.

I was also, sadly, preparing to leave. Just a few miles away, on a dry down, I was converting two derelict agricultural cottages into a house. The cottages had been built eighty years or so before on the site of an old agricultural hamlet with a very old name. The old hamlet had disappeared; nothing remained of it except a few level areas, little green platforms or terraces, close to one another, in certain meadows. During my own building work, old brick walls and brick foundations from the last century and the black earth of old latrines were dug up where—with smooth green slopes all around—I had been expecting only chalk.

The walls and foundations of workers' houses: generations of agricultural workers had lived on the site. And even in the pair of cottages I was renovating, the cottages that had been built early in the century over the foundations and debris of the old hamlet, many generations of workers, or many different people, had lived. Now I, an outsider, was altering the appearance of the land a little, doing what I had been aware of others doing, creating a potential ruin.

(And later, after I had moved there, when old people came to look at the cottages where they had lived or visited, I felt ashamed. And once—when a very old lady, not far from death, was brought by her grandson to look at the cottage where as a girl she had lived for a summer with her shepherd grandfather, and was so bewildered by the changed cottage she found that she thought she had come to the wrong place—once I pretended I didn't live there.)

I should have made a clean break, gone elsewhere. But having cut myself off from my first life, and having had, unexpectedly, and twenty years after that earlier casting off, the good fortune to have found a second life, I was unwilling to move too far. I wanted to stay with what I had found. I wanted to recreate, so far as it was possible, what I had found in the manor cottage.

One day, perhaps nine or ten months after I had fallen ill, I went on my old walk. New associations now, to add to the old. And, as if to match my mood, I saw, almost as soon as I began to go down the hill beside the windbreak, a greater change at the bottom of the valley than any I had known.

What had been the row of three farm cottages, one of which had been Jack's, was being converted into one big house. The basic work had been done. The three cottages, or so it appeared from the outside, had been turned into a large living room; new spaces or rooms had been added to this big central room. The roof of the house was being put on: new, red-blond rafters. The design of the house was not elegant. But it was going to be roomy and comfortable; and every window would give a staggering green view, of the droveway, or the slopes of the downs, the woods of birch and beech, or the lines of blackthorn and hawthorn along the lateral field lanes.

Most of the old farm buildings had gone. But some at the back were still there, among them the old barn with the high loading window and the projecting metal bracket where a pulley and cable would once have helped to lift sacks or bales from loaded wagons and swing them into place inside.

The builders were working on the roof, hanging slates fast. The van with the builder's name was on the droveway, where once Jack's geese had roamed. There was a radio playing loudly somewhere in the unfinished, hollow, reverberating building. The builders, town people, were more unwelcoming than the town farm workers had been.

How exposed a house looks when it becomes a site for builders, how stripped of sanctity, when a room, once intimate, becomes mere space! Jack's cottage (whose interior I had never seen until now) had been reduced—without side wall or middle flooring—to pure builder's space, and at this stage of building was still pure space, like the space within the ruined stone-walled house with the big sycamores further along the droveway. Somewhere in that space Jack had made his bravest decision, to leave his deathbed for the last Christmas season with his friends, in the so ordinary public house not far from the end of the droveway. And that was the space to which—with what illness, delirium, resignation, or perhaps reconciliation—he had returned to die.

I saw this new building going up in summer, in white chalk dust. But in winter, as I knew, the site had been one of mud and water, settling at the bottom of the valley, mud and water many inches deep. That was the source of the damp that had given Jack his bronchitis and his pneumonia. But now that wet and damp had been dealt with. All the ground that had been Jack's garden and goose ground, and the gardens or grassed-over areas of the other cottages, all that had been concreted over, to create a forecourt for the big house.

At the back, the concrete floor of Jack's greenhouse was not to be seen; the area had been incorporated into the new living space of the big house.

So at last, just as the house was cleansed of Jack's life and death, so the ground he had tended finally disappeared. But surely below all that concrete over his garden some seed, some root, would survive; and one day perhaps, when the concrete was taken up (as surely one day it would be taken up, since few dwelling places are eternal), one day perhaps some memory of Jack, preserved in some shrub or flower or vine, would come to life again.

With that building of a big house where once, perhaps for centuries, had stood the cottages or dwellings of farm or country laborers, a cycle had been completed.

Once there would have been many hamlets, settlements of farm workers and shepherds, near the fording places along the river. These hamlets had dwindled; they had dwindled fast with the coming of machinery. Fewer hands had been needed; and then, when sheep stopped being kept, even shepherds were not needed.

The garden of the manor, the forested orchard, lay partly on the site of one vanished hamlet. Such building-over would have occurred many times before. The duplicate name of the hamlet or village, Waldenshaw—the same word (for forest or wood) in two tribal languages, both long since absorbed into other languages—the very name

spoke of invaders from across the sea and of ancient wars and dis-
possessions here, along the picturesque river and the wet meadows.

This history had repeated, had radiated outwards, as it were: much
of the wealth for the Victorian-Edwardian manor, its gardens and ancillary buildings, had come from the empire, ventures abroad. Once
the manor estate had covered many of the acres of my afternoon walks.
But its glory had lasted one generation. The family had moved elsewhere; the estate had become the manor and grounds alone; it had
shed its farms and land. Others had taken over those acres, built new
big houses in villages or on the sites of hamlets once full of working
people. And now the last of the peasant or farm cottages along the
droveway had been taken over. What had once been judged a situation suitable only for agricultural cottages—next to a farm, far from
roads and services—had become desirable. The farm had gone; the
very distance from the public road was a blessing. And so, the quality
or attributes of the site changing, the past had been abolished.

I had lived, very soon after coming to the valley, with the idea of
change, of the imminent dissolution of the perfection I had found. It
had given a poignancy to the beauty I had experienced, the passing
of the seasons. I had promised myself again and again, every spring,
every autumn, to get a camera (or at least to relearn how to use the
one I owned) to record the droveway and the ruined house below the
sycamores and the gypsy caravan and the farm buildings and Jack's
cottage and garden and goose ground. But I had never once taken a
camera on my walks; and perhaps because I had no physical record
of these things, they had an added poignancy, since they very soon
began to exist only in my head.

I had thought that because of my insecure past—peasant India,
colonial Trinidad, my own family circumstances, the colonial smallness that didn't consort with the grandeur of my ambition, my up-
rooting of myself for a writing career, my coming to England with so
little, and the very little I still had to fall back on—I had thought that
because of this I had been given an especially tender or raw sense of
an unaccommodating world.

I had seen Jack as solid, rooted in his earth. But I had also seen him as something from the past, a remnant, something that would be swept away before my camera would get the pictures. My ideas about Jack were wrong. He was not exactly a remnant; he had created his own life, his own world, almost his own continent. But the world about him, which he so enjoyed and used, was too precious not to be used by others. And it was only when he had gone, when the town workers who had replaced him had gone, it was only then that I saw how tenuous, really, the hold of all of these people had been on the land they worked or lived in.

Jack himself had disregarded the tenuousness of his hold on the land, just as, not seeing what others saw, he had created a garden on the edge of a swamp and a ruined farmyard; had responded to and found glory in the seasons. All around him was ruin; and all around, in a deeper way, was change, and a reminder of the brevity of the cycles of growth and creation. But he had sensed that life and man were the true mysteries; and he had asserted the primacy of these with something like religion. The bravest and most religious thing about his life was his way of dying: the way he had asserted, at the very end, the primacy not of what was beyond life, but life itself.

*M*Y TIME was over in the valley, that particular, rhythmical time of manor cottage and grounds and the special signs there of the seasons, and walks on the downs and the riverbank. And I felt like that—that the second life I had been granted had ended—though I did not move far. The cottages I had been renovating were on the same bus route, the bus that made fewer trips, with fewer passengers, for more and more money.

One day a middle-aged woman spoke to me. Some of the people on the bus spoke to me; some, even after twelve years, never did. I did not recognize the woman who spoke to me.

She said, "Jack. Jack's wife."

And then I remembered her face and the cadaverous, wicked-eyed face of her father.

She spoke of Jack, always, in this distant way, as though speaking of another person altogether, someone she had known rather than lived with.

She said, "It's the hair you didn't recognize."

She fingered her hair. It was short.

She said, "Jack liked it long. He liked me to wear it in a bun."

This was something new about Jack. From a distance, his own beard, and his upright posture, had made him look like a romantic, something like an early socialist (in my fantasy); and perhaps he had copied the beard from an older person. Perhaps he had, after all, self-consciously lived out a certain kind of life. Perhaps in his own way he had been a tyrant, imposing, in addition to the long hair and the bun, a style and way of life that had been irksome to his wife.

She lived now in a small settlement of council houses in a small town in another valley. She liked the area, her house, her neighbors. She found it strange—no more than that—that a big house should have been put up where she had lived for all those years. She said, "Isn't it funny what they do?"

For her, Jack's wife, the move away from the cottage had been good. She saw her life as a small success story. Father a forester, a gamekeeper of sorts; Jack the farm worker, the gardener; and now she half a townswoman.

One cycle for me, in my cottage, in the grounds of the manor; another cycle on the farm, among the farm buildings; another cycle in the life of Jack's wife.

THE JOURNEY

*T*o WRITE about Jack and his cottage and his garden it was necessary for me to have lived a second life in the valley and to have had a second awakening to the natural world there. But a version of that story—a version—came to me just days after I came to the valley, to the cottage in the manor grounds.

The cottage at that time still had the books and some of the furniture of the people who had been there before. Among the books was one that was very small, a paperback booklet, smaller in format than the average small paperback and with only a few pages. The booklet, from a series called the Little Library of Art, was about the early paintings of Giorgio de Chirico. There were about a dozen reproductions of his early surrealist paintings. Technically, in these very small reproductions, the paintings did not seem interesting; they seemed flat, facile. And their content was not profound either: arbitrary assemblages, in semi-classical, semi-modern settings, of unrelated motifs—aqueducts, trains, arcades, gloves, fruit, statues—with an occasional applied touch of easy mystery: in one painting, for instance, an overlarge shadow of a hidden figure approaching from round a corner.

But among these paintings there was one which, perhaps because of its title, caught my attention: *The Enigma of Arrival*. I felt that in an indirect, poetical way the title referred to something in my own experience; and later I was to learn that the titles of these surrealist paintings of Chirico's hadn't been given by the painter, but by the poet Apollinaire, who died young in 1918, from influenza following a war wound, to the great grief of Picasso and others.

What was interesting about the painting itself, *The Enigma of Arrival*, was that—again perhaps because of the title—it changed in my memory. The original (or the reproduction in the Little Library of Art booklet) was always a surprise. A classical scene, Mediterranean, ancient-Roman—or so I saw it. A wharf; in the background, beyond walls and gateways (like cutouts), there is the top of the mast of an antique vessel; on an otherwise deserted street in the foreground there are two figures, both muffled, one perhaps the person who has arrived, the other perhaps a native of the port. The scene is of desolation and mystery: it speaks of the mystery of arrival. It spoke to me of that, as it had spoken to Apollinaire.

And in the winter gray of the manor grounds in Wiltshire, in those first four days of mist and rain, when so little was clear to me, an idea—floating lightly above the book I was working on—came to me of a story I might one day write about that scene in the Chirico picture.

My story was to be set in classical times, in the Mediterranean. My narrator would write plainly, without any attempt at period style or historical explanation of his period. He would arrive—for a reason I had yet to work out—at that classical port with the walls and gateways like cutouts. He would walk past that muffled figure on the quayside. He would move from that silence and desolation, that blankness, to a gateway or door. He would enter there and be swallowed by the life and noise of a crowded city (I imagined something like an Indian bazaar scene). The mission he had come on—family business, study, religious initiation—would give him encounters and adventures. He would enter interiors, of houses and temples. Gradually there would come to him a feeling that he was getting nowhere; he would lose his sense of mission; he would begin to know only that he was lost. His feeling of adventure would give way to panic. He would want to escape, to get back to the quayside and his ship. But he wouldn't know how. I imagined some religious ritual in which, led on by kindly people, he would unwittingly take part and find himself the intended victim. At the moment of crisis he would come upon a door, open it, and find himself back on the quayside of arrival. He has been saved; the world is as he remembered it. Only one thing is missing now. Above the cutout walls and buildings there is no mast, no sail. The antique ship has gone. The traveler has lived out his life.

I didn't think of this as an historical story, but more as a free ride of the imagination. There was to be no research. I would take pointers from Virgil perhaps for the sea and travel and the seasons, from the Gospels and the Acts of the Apostles for the feel of the municipal or provincial organization of the Roman Empire; I would get moods and the idea of ancient religion from Apuleius; Horace and Martial and Petronius would give me hints for social settings.

The idea of living in my imagination in that classical Roman world was attractive to me. A beautiful, clear, dangerous world, far removed from the setting in which I had found myself; the story, more a mood than a story, so different from the book on which I was working. A taxing book: it had been occupying me for eight or nine months and I still hadn't completed a draft.

At the center of the book I was writing was a story set in an African country, once a colony, with white and Asian settlers, and now independent. It was the story of a day-long journey made in a car by two white people at a time of tribal war, suddenly coming, suddenly overwhelming colonial order and simplicity. Africa had given both those white people a chance, made them bigger, brought out their potential; now, when they were no longer so young, it was consuming them. It was a violent book—not violent in its incidents, but in its emotions.

It was a book about fear. All the jokes were silenced by this fear. And the mist that hung over the valley where I was writing; the darkness that came early; the absence of knowledge of where I was—all this uncertainty emanating from the valley I transferred to my Africa. And it did not occur to me that the story of *The Enigma of Arrival*—a sunlit sea journey ending in a dangerous classical city—which had come to me as a kind of release from the creative rigors and the darkness of my own African story, it did not occur to me that that Mediterranean story was really no more than a version of the story I was already writing.

Nor did it occur to me that it was also an attempt to find a story for, to give coherence to, a dream or nightmare which for a year or so had been unsettling me. In this dream there occurred always, at a critical moment in the dream narrative, what I can only describe as an explosion in my head. It was how every dream ended, with this explosion that threw me flat on my back, in the presence of people, in a street, a crowded room, or wherever, threw me into this degraded posture in the midst of standing people, threw me into the posture of sleep in which I found myself when I awakened. The explosion was so loud, so reverberating and slow in my head that I felt, with the part of my brain that miraculously could still think and draw conclusions, that I couldn't possibly survive, that I was in fact dying, that the explosion this time, in this dream, regardless of the other dreams that had revealed themselves at the end as dreams, would kill, that I was consciously living through, or witnessing, my own death. And when I awoke my head felt queer, shaken up, exhausted; as though some discharge in my brain had in fact occurred.

This dream or nightmare or internal dramatization—perhaps a momentary turbulence in my brain had created the split-second tableau of the street, the café, the party, the bus, where I collapsed in the presence of people—had been with me for a year or more. It was a dream that had been brought on by intellectual fatigue and something like grief.

I had written a lot, done work of much difficulty; had worked under pressure more or less since my schooldays. Before the writing, there had been the learning; writing had come to me slowly. Before that, there had been Oxford; and before that, the school in Trinidad where I had worked for the Oxford scholarship. There had been a long preparation for the writing career! And then I discovered that to be a writer was not (as I had imagined) a state—of competence, or achievement, or fame, or content—at which one arrived and where one stayed. There was a special anguish attached to the career: whatever the labor of any piece of writing, whatever its creative challenges and satisfactions, time had always taken me away from it. And, with time passing, I felt mocked by what I had already done; it seemed to belong to a time of vigor, now past for good. Emptiness, restlessness built up again; and it was necessary once more, out of my internal resources alone, to start on another book, to commit myself to that consuming process again.

I had finally been undermined. My spirit had broken; and that breaking of the spirit had occurred not long before I had come to the valley. For two years I had worked on an historical book about the region where I had been born. The book had grown; and since (beyond a certain length) a big book is harder to write, more exhausting, than a shorter one, I had resisted its growth. But then I had become excited by the story it told. The historian seeks to abstract principles from human events. My approach was the other; for the two years that I lived among the documents I sought to reconstruct the human story as best I could.

It was a labor. Ten or twelve documents—called up from memory, almost like personal memories—might provide the details for a fairly short and simple paragraph of narrative. But I was supported by my story, the themes it touched on: discovery, the New World, the dispeopling of the discovered islands; slavery, the creation of the plantation colony; the coming of the idea of revolution; the chaos after revolutions in societies so created.

A great packed education those two years had been. And I had such faith in what I was writing, such faith in the grandeur of my story, that I thought it would find the readers that my books of the previous twelve years had not found. And I behaved foolishly. Without waiting for that response, I dismantled the little life I had created for myself in England and prepared to leave, to be a free man.

For years, in that far-off island whose human history I had been discovering and writing about, I had dreamed of coming to England. But my life in England had been savorless, and much of it mean. I had taken to England all the rawness of my colonial's nerves, and those nerves had more or less remained, nerves which in the beginning were in a good part also the nerves of youth and inexperience, physical and sexual inadequacy, and of undeveloped talent. And just as once at home I had dreamed of being in England, so for years in England I had dreamed of leaving England. Now, eighteen years after my first arrival, it seemed to me that the time had come. I dismantled the life I had bit by bit established, and prepared to go. The house I had bought and renovated in stages I sold; and my furniture and books and papers went to the warehouse.

The calamity occurred four months later. The book in which I had placed such faith, the book which had exhausted me so much, could not please the publisher who had commissioned it. We had misunderstood one another. He knew only my name; he did not know the nature of my work. And I had misunderstood his interest in me. He had approached me as a serious writer, but he had wanted only a book for tourists, something much simpler than the book I had written; something at once more romantic and less romantic; at once more human and less human. So I found myself up in the air. And I had to return to England.

That journey back—from the island and continent I had gone to see with my new vision, the corner of the New World I had just written about, from there to the United States and Canada, and then to England—that journey back to England so mimicked and parodied the journey of nineteen years before, the journey of the young man, the boy almost, who had journeyed to England to be a writer, in a country where the calling had some meaning, that I couldn't but be aware of all the cruel ironies.

It was out of this grief, too deep for tears or rage—grief that began partly to be expressed in the dream of the exploding head—that I began to write my African story, which had come to me as a wisp of an idea in Africa three or four years before.

The African fear with which as a writer I was living day after day; the unknown Wiltshire; the cruelty of this return to England, the dread of a second failure; the mental fatigue. All of this, rolled into one, was what lay on the spirit of the man who went on the walks down to

Jack's cottage and past it. Not an observer merely, a man removed; but a man played on, worked on, by many things.

And it was out of that burden of emotion that there had come to the writer, as release, as an idyll, the ship story, the antique quayside story, suggested by *The Enigma of Arrival*; an idea that came innocently, without the writer's suspecting how much of his life, how many aspects of his life, that remote story (still just an idea for a story) carried. But that is why certain stories or incidents suggest themselves to writers, or make an impression on them; that is why writers can appear to have obsessions.

I WENT for my walks every afternoon. I finished my book. The panic of its composition didn't repeat in the revision. I was beginning to heal. And more than heal. For me, a miracle had occurred in this valley and in the grounds of the manor where my cottage was. In that unlikely setting, in the ancient heart of England, a place where I was truly an alien, I found I was given a second chance, a new life, richer and fuller than any I had had anywhere else. And in that place, where at the beginning I had looked only for remoteness and a place to hide, I did some of my best work. I traveled; I wrote. I ventured out, brought back experiences to my cottage; and wrote. The years passed. I healed. The life around me changed. I changed.

And then one afternoon came that choking fit as I was walking past Jack's old cottage—Jack himself long dead. A few hours later came the serious illness which that choking fit had presaged. And when after some months I recovered, I found myself a middle-aged man. Work became harder for me. I discovered in myself an unwillingness to undertake new labor; I wished to be free of labor.

And whereas when I came to the valley my dream was the dream provoked by fatigue and unhappiness—the dream of the exploding head, the certainty of death—now it was the idea of death itself that came to me in my sleep. Death not as a tableau or a story, as in the earlier dream; but death, the end of things, as a gloom that got at a man, sought out his heart, when he was at his weakest, while he slept. This idea of death, death the nullifier of human life and endeavor, to which morning after morning I awakened, so enervated me that it sometimes took me all day, all the hours of daylight, to see the world as real again, to become a man again, a doer.

The dream of exhaustion once; now the debilitation brought on by involuntary thoughts of the final emptiness. This too was something that happened to the man who went walking, witness of people and events in the valley.

It was as though the calling, the writer's vocation, was one that could never offer me anything but momentary fulfillment. So that again, years after I had seen the Chirico picture and the idea for the story had come to me, again, in my own life, was another version of the story of *The Enigma of Arrival*.

*A*ND INDEED there had been a journey long before—the journey that had seeded all the others, and had indirectly fed that fantasy of the classical world. There had been a journey; and a ship.

This journey began some days before my eighteenth birthday. It was the journey which—for a year—I feared I would never be allowed to make. So that even before the journey I lived with anxiety about it. It was the journey that took me from my island, Trinidad, off the northern coast of Venezuela, to England.

There had, first, been an airplane, a small one of the period, narrow, with a narrow aisle, and flying low. This had given me my first revelation: the landscape of my childhood seen from the air, and from not too high up. At ground level so poor to me, so messy, so full of huts and gutters and bare front yards and straggly hibiscus hedges and shabby backyards: views from the roadside. From the air, though, a landscape of logic and larger pattern; the straight lines and regularity and woven, carpetlike texture of sugarcane fields, so extensive from up there, leaving so little room for people, except at the very edges; the large, unknown area of swampland, curiously still, the clumps of mangrove and brilliant-green swamp trees casting black shadows on the milky-green water; the forested peaks and dips and valleys of the mountain range; a landscape of clear pattern and contours, absorbing all the roadside messiness, a pattern of dark green and dark brown, like camouflage, like a landscape in a book, like the landscape of a real country. So that at the moment of takeoff almost, the moment of departure, the landscape of my childhood was like something which I had missed, something I had never seen.

Minutes later, the sea. It was wrinkled, as in the fragment of the poem by Tennyson. It glinted in the sun; it was gray and silver rather than blue; and, again as in the fragment by Tennyson, it did crawl. So that again the world in which I had lived all my life so far was a world I had never seen.

And then the little airplane rose just above the clouds and flew like that, just above the clouds, until we reached Puerto Rico. I had heard about the beauty of the clouds seen from the top from someone who had traveled to Jamaica, perhaps in an even smaller airplane, five years before. So this was a beauty and an experience which I was ready for, and was overwhelmed by. Always, above the cloud, the sun! So solid the cloud, so pure. I could only look and look; truly to possess that beauty, to feel that one had come to the end of that particular experience, was impossible. To see what so few men had seen! Always there, the thing seen, the world above the clouds, even when unperceived; up there (as, down below, sometimes at sunset) one's mind could travel back—and forward—aeons.

We droned on to Puerto Rico. It was late afternoon. Another country, already, after only a few hours. Travel! Another language; people of mixed race, mulattoes, but subtly different from the mixed people of my own place.

There was a Negro in the hangar. (Or so the place seemed to me; there was no airport terminal to speak of; air travel, though a luxury, still had in those days a rough-and-ready side.) The Negro was from the little airplane. I asked him whether he was from Trinidad. Of course he was. I knew that. I had seen him in the plane. But I asked him. Why? Friendship? I didn't need that. I noted the falsity in my behavior. In the hangar or shed there was a man from another plane, or waiting for another plane, who was reading that day's edition of *The New York Times*. This large world had always existed outside my little island—like the sun above the clouds, always there, even when unperceived. And this large world was now within reach!

For eight hours—or was it thirteen?—we drove on in a dark sky to New York. Hours away from the life of my island, where nothing had savor, and even the light had a life-killing quality (as I thought), I lived—like any peasant coming for the first time to a capital city— in a world of marvels. I had always known that this world existed; but to find it available to me only for the price of a fare was nonetheless staggering. With the marvels, however, there went, as in a fairy story, a feeling of menace. As the little plane droned and droned through the night the idea of New York became frightening. Not the city so much as the moment of arrival: I couldn't visualize that moment. It was the first traveler's panic I had experienced.

The passenger beside me was an Englishwoman. She had a child with her. I saw them only in that way: an Englishwoman and a child. I had no means of placing them.

I wrote my diary. I had bought, for that purpose, a cheap little lined pad with a front cover that held envelopes in a pocket. I also had an "indelible" mauve pencil, of the sort that serious people—especially officials, in Trinidad—used in those days. When you licked the pencil the color became bright; dry, the color was dull. I had bought the pad and the pencil because I was traveling to become a writer, and I had to start.

I asked the stewardess to sharpen my pencil. I did so partly to taste the luxuriousness of air travel. The plane was small, but it offered many little services, or so the airline advertisements said. This request to the stewardess was in the nature of a challenge; and to my amazement the stewardess, white and American and to me radiant and beautiful and adult, took my request seriously, brought the pencil back beautifully sharpened, and called me, two weeks away from being eighteen, sir.

So I wrote my diary. But it left out many of the things that were worth noting down, many of the things which, some years later, I would have thought much more important than the things I did note down. The diary I wrote in the airplane left out the great family farewell at the airport in Trinidad, the airport building like a little timber house with a little garden at the edge of the asphalt runway.

That family farewell was the last of the big Hindu or Asiatic occasions in which I took part—those farewells (from another era, another continent, another kind of travel, when a traveler might indeed never return, as many of us, or our grandfathers, had never returned to India) for which people left their work, gave up a day's earnings, and traveled long distances to say good-bye. And not really to say good-bye, more to show themselves, to be present at a big clan occasion, to assert their membership of the clan; in spite of the fact (or because of the fact) that there were now such differences between various branches of the extended family, and conversation was already touched with condescension or social nervousness on one side or the other.

I did not note down that occasion in my writer's diary with the indelible pencil sharpened by the elegant Pan American World Airways stewardess in the little airplane. And one reason was that the occasion was too separate from the setting in which I wrote, the setting of magic and wonder. Another was that the occasion, that ceremonial farewell with stiff little groups of people hanging about the wooden building at the edge of the runway, did not fit into my idea of a writer's diary or the writer's experience I was preparing myself for.

Nor did I write about—something I would certainly have written about, not many years later, when I had begun to work towards some understanding of the nature of my experience—the cousin and his advice at the airport.

This cousin was a half-witted or certainly dim-witted fellow who had developed a little paunch at the age of fifteen or so, had kept it ever since, and had in some bizarre way—without any knowledge of grammar or feeling for the English language or any other language—made himself a journalist. He had no goodwill towards me. Perhaps he even had ill will; perhaps he would have easily—not out of any positive malice, but halfheartedly, as befitted his character, and out of a simple principle of family hate—done the equivalent of sticking pins in my effigy.

But he was moved by the occasion, or felt he had to act up to it. And at that crowded farewell at the airport, where a few people (some of whom I didn't know) were even managing to cry, this cousin came up to me and, as though passing on a secret handed to him, a journalist, from the highest quarters, from the airport manager, from the director of Pan American World Airways, or from God himself, whispered: "Sit at the back of the airplane. It's safer there." (Travel was still an adventure, by sea or by air. And it may be that what my cousin said about sitting at the back of the airplane was right. Perhaps, though—and more likely—his advice was based on the child's comic-strip idea of the airplane crash, the plane diving down, crashing on its nose.)

I didn't write about this cousin and his advice in my airplane diary, because—like the family send-off, the remnant of peasant Asia in my life—the frivolous advice did not seem to me suitable to the work, which was about a more epic vision of the world and about a more epic kind of personal adventure. Perhaps it never even occurred to me to write about the farewell or the cousin's advice; there was no question of rejecting the themes.

But though personal adventure was my theme, I was in no position to write about something more important, the change in my personality that travel and solitude had already begun to bring about. The intimations of this alteration were very slight. In five years I was to see very clearly that the family farewell and my cousin's advice were "material." But it was to be many years after that before the alterations in my personality, or the slight intimations I was beginning to have about those alterations, intimations that were minute fractions of that first day's adventure, were to acquire their proper proportions.

There had been the Negro in the hangar or airport shed in Puerto Rico where, after many hours, and in the late afternoon, our little airplane had made its first halt. Already the light had changed; the world had changed. The world had ceased to be colonial, for me; people had already altered their value, even this Negro. He was bound for Harlem. At home, among his fellows, just a few hours before, he was a man to be envied, his journey indescribably glamorous; now he was a Negro, in a straw-colored jacket obviously not his own, too tight across his weight lifter's shoulder (weight lifting was a craze among us). Now, in that jacket (at home, the badge of the traveler to the temperate north), he was bluffing it out, insisting on his respectability, on not being an American Negro, on not being fazed by the airplane and by the white people.

He was not an educated man, not someone I would have sought out at home. Yet already I had sought him out and even claimed kinship with him. Why? I felt the gestures of friendship to be false even as I made them. In his tight, respectable jacket, he was cool with me; and I was half glad he was, because friendship, chat, with him wasn't what I wanted. But I had made the gestures. If I had been asked whether I was feeling solitary, vulnerable, I would have said that the opposite was true, that I was in a state of great excitement, that I was loving everything; that everything I had seen so far in the second half of that great day was new and wonderful.

He was cool, the Trinidad man, buttoned up, his eyes quiet, no shine to his color, which had rather a mat or dead quality that spoke of tension. I let him be. I stayed by myself. The light yellowed, darkened. Then we were airborne again.

The little airplane droned on and on. The repetitiveness of this form of travel was an unexpected revelation. So that though the journey was the fastest I had ever made, and though I knew that compared with a ship's journey it was extraordinarily short, yet it was neither exaggerated nor pretentious to feel that it was "boring."

There were the woman and her child beside me. The woman was English, as I have said. I had never met an Englishwoman of her age before—had indeed met only one Englishwoman—and had no means of reading her character or intelligence or education. I was not interested in children; was not interested in women with children. Yet towards this woman—much taken up with her child—I found myself making overtures of friendship.

I was carrying some bananas to New York. They were in a paper bag, perhaps on the floor. Some remnant of old peasant travel, with food for the journey; some genuine Hindu distrust of the food that might be offered by the airplane and then by the hotel in New York. The bananas were smelling now; in the warm plane they were ripening by the hour. I offered the woman a banana. Did she take it for her child? I cannot remember. The fact was, I made the offer. Though, really, I didn't want this woman's friendship or conversation, and was not interested in the child.

Was there some fear of travel, in spite of my longing for the day, and in spite of my genuine excitement? Was this reaching out to people a response to solitude—since for the first time in my life I was solitary? Was it the fear of New York? Certainly. The city, my behavior there at the moment of arrival, my inability to visualize the physical details of arrival, how and where I was going to spend the night—these were developing anxieties as we flew on and on.

I witnessed this change in my personality; but, not even aware of it as a theme, wrote nothing of it in my diary. So that between the man writing the diary and the traveler there was already a gap, already a gap between the man and the writer.

Man and writer were the same person. But that is a writer's greatest discovery. It took time—and how much writing!—to arrive at that synthesis.

On that day, the first of adventure and freedom and travel and discovery, man and writer were united in their eagerness for experience. But the nature of the experiences of the day encouraged a separation of the two elements in my personality. The writer, or the boy traveling to be a writer, was educated; he had had a formal school education; he had a high idea of the nobility of the calling to which he was traveling to dedicate himself. But the man, of whom the writer was just a part (if a major, impelling part), the man was in the profoundest way—as a social being—untutored.

He was close to the village ways of his Asian-Indian community. He had an instinctive understanding of and sympathy for its rituals, like the farewell at the airport that morning. He was close to the ways of that community, which was separated from peasant India only by two or three generations in a plantation colony of the New World. Yet there was another side to the man: he did not really participate in the life or rituals of that community. It wasn't only that he was educated in the formal way of a school education; he was also skeptical. Unhappy in his extended family, he was distrustful of larger, communal groupings.

But that half-Indian world, that world removed in time and space from India, and mysterious to the man, its language not even half understood, its religion and religious rites not grasped, that half-Indian world was the social world the man knew. It was all that he had outside school and the life of the imagination fed by books and the cinema. That village world had given him its prejudices and passions; he was interested in, had been passionate about, the politics of India before and after independence. Yet he knew little about his community in Trinidad; he thought that because he belonged to it he understood it; he thought that the life of the community was like an extension of the life of his family. And he knew nothing of other communities. He had only the prejudices of his time, in that colonial, racially mixed setting. He was profoundly ignorant. He hadn't been to a restaurant, hated the idea of eating food from foreign hands. Yet at the same time he had dreamed of fulfillment in a foreign country.

He looked for adventure. On this first day he found it. But he also came face to face with his ignorance. This ignorance undermined, mocked the writer, or the ambition of the writer, made nonsense of the personality the writer wished to assume—elegant, knowing, unsurprised. (Like Somerset Maugham. Or—a truer comparison—like the Trinidad Negro with the tight borrowed jacket in the hangar or shed at Puerto Rico, on his way to Harlem and quite another idea of glamour.)

So my memories of my arrival late at night in New York are vague. I think back hard now, and certain details become clearer: a very bright building, dazzling lights, a little crowd in a small space, a woman official with a very sharp "American" accent calling out the names of certain passengers.

There was a letter for me. A man from the British Consulate should have met me. But the plane had been so delayed he had gone home, leaving this letter, which gave me only the name of the hotel he had booked me into. He should have protected me. He left me at the mercy of the taxi driver who took me into the city. The driver cheated me, charged too much; and then, seeing how easily I acquiesced, he stripped me of the few remaining dollars I had on me (I had a few more, very few, hidden in my suitcase) by claiming them as a tip. I felt this humiliation so keenly that memory blurred it soon; and then eradicated it for many years.

I preferred to remember the taxi driver as being talkative, because that was the way taxi drivers were. I worked hard at remembering what he had said. ("We sold the Japs all our scrap metal and they shot it right back at us.") And I remembered the Negro (he must have occurred in the hotel) who talked like a Negro in a book or film ("Dis city never sleeps" or "Dis city sho don' sleep, man") and whom I couldn't tip because I had no money on me.

The talkative taxi driver, the quaintly spoken Negro—I cherished them because I felt I knew them, because I felt they were confirming so much of what I had read, were confirming so much of my advance information. They reassured me that I was indeed traveling, and was already in New York. And in their familiar aspect they were material, suitable for the writer. But the humiliation connected with each (the driver's theft, my inability to tip the Negro, who was expecting me to play a character role too and give him a tip) got in the way; and they were edited out of my memory for twenty years. They were certainly edited out of the diary which I wrote with indelible pencil (already a little blunt) that evening in the hotel (on the hotel paper, for the extra drama).

A family farewell in the morning, thousands of miles away: a farewell to my past, my colonial past and peasant-Asiatic past. Immediately, then, the exaltation: the glimpse of the fields and the mountains which I had never seen; the rippled or wrinkled sea crawling; then the clouds from above; and thoughts of the beginning of the world, thoughts of time without beginning or end; the intense experience of beauty. A faint panic, then; even an acted panic; then a dwindling of the sense of the self. A suppressed, half true, but also half intensely true, diary being written in a small dark room of the Hotel Wellington in New York. And already a feeling of being lost, of truth not fully faced, of a world whose great size I had seized being made at night very small for me again.

I had come to New York with some bananas. I had eaten some on the plane and left the others behind, guiltily but correctly (they would almost certainly have been taken from me by the authorities). I had also been given a roasted chicken or half a roasted chicken: my family's peasant, Indian, Hindu fear about my food, about pollution, and this was an attempt to stay it, if only for that day. But I had no knife, no fork, no plate, and didn't know that these things might have been got from the hotel; wouldn't have known how to set about asking, especially at that very late hour.

I ate over the wastepaper basket, aware as I did so of the smell, the oil, the excess at the end of a long day. In my diary I had written of the biggest things, the things that befitted a writer. But the writer of the diary was ending his day like a peasant, like a man reverting to his origins, eating secretively in a dark room, and then wondering how to hide the high-smelling evidence of his meal. I dumped it all in the wastepaper basket. After this I needed a bath or a shower.

The shower was in my own room: a luxury. I had dreaded having to use a communal one. One tap was marked HOT. Such a refinement I had never seen before. In Trinidad, in our great heat, we had always bathed or showered in water of normal temperature, the water of the tap. A hot shower! I was expecting something tepid, like the warm bathwater (in buckets) that my mother prepared for me (mixed with aromatic and medicinal neem leaves) on certain important days. The hot water of the Hotel Wellington shower wasn't like that. Hot was hot. Barely avoiding a scalding, I ducked out of the shower cubicle.

So the great day ended. And then—it was my special gift, and remained so for nearly twenty years, helping me through many crises—I fell asleep as soon as I got into bed and didn't wake up again until I had slept out all my sleep.

My memory retains nothing of the hotel room in daylight, nothing of the room in which I awakened. Perhaps, then, some embarrassment obliterated the memory. Less than twenty-four hours out of my own place, the humiliations had begun to bank up: to my own developed sense of the self was now added another sense of the self, a rawness of nerves and sensibility against which from now on for many years all my impressions, even the most exalted, were to be set. As were the impressions of the morning, the ones that remained with me, impressions that (after the humiliations of the previous evening, the humiliations of arrival) resumed the romance.

The newsstand downstairs, in the lobby of the Wellington, was part of this romance: a little shop, in the building where one lived: it was quite new to me, quite enchanting. I bought a packet of cigarettes from the man who was selling, a tall, gray-haired man, as well dressed and formal and educated, I thought, as a teacher. (Not like the Indian shopkeepers of our country villages, men who kept themselves deliberately dirty and ragged, the dirtier the better, to avoid hubris, to deter jealousy and the evil eye. Not like the Chinese in their "parlors," who wore sleeveless vests and khaki shorts and wooden clogs, stayed indoors all the time, and in spite of their wizened, famine-stricken, opiumden appearance, fathered child after child on happy black concubines or blank-faced, flat-chested Chinese wives.)

From the tall gray-haired man I bought a packet of Old Golds. I had no palate in tobacco, couldn't tell the difference between brands, and went mainly by things like names. In Trinidad only locally made or English cigarettes were sold in the shops; American cigarettes were available, informally and in quantity, because of the American bases, but they were never sold in the shops; and this ability to buy a packet of American cigarettes, from the whole range of American names, was wonderful. As was the price, fifteen cents, and the book of matches that came with it. Largesse!

The sensuousness of those soft American cigarette packets! The cellophane, the name of the brand, the paper of the packet outlining the shapes of the cigarettes: the thin red paper ribbon at the top of the packet which enabled you to undo the cellophane: the delicious smell.

Cigarettes had always been for me an aesthetic experience. The flavor of burning tobacco I had never cared for; so the smoking addiction, when it came, had been severe. And if I had stopped smoking many times already at home, it was because I had for many months during the past worrying year been denying myself things, at one stage even (secretly) denying myself food, out of a wish not to lose my scholarship, the scholarship that was to take me to England and Oxford, which was not a wish so much to go to Oxford as a wish to get out of Trinidad and see the great world and make myself a writer. Such passion, such longing had gone into this journey, which was less than a day old!

From the teacherlike gray-haired man at the newsstand I also bought a copy of *The New York Times*, the previous day's issue of which I had seen the previous day at Puerto Rico. I was interested in newspapers and knew this paper to be one of the foremost in the world. But to read a newspaper for the first time is like coming into a film that has been on for an hour. Newspapers are like serials. To understand them you have to take knowledge to them; the knowledge that serves best is the knowledge provided by the newspaper itself. It made me feel a stranger, that paper. But on the front page, at the bottom, there was a story to which I could respond, because it dealt with an experience I was sharing. The story was about the weather. Apparently it was unseasonably cool and gray for the end of July, so unseasonable that it was worth a story.

Without the paper I would not have known that the weather was unseasonable. But I did not need the paper to make me see the enchantment of the light. The light indoors in the hotel was like the light outdoors. The outdoor light was magical. I thought it was created by the tall buildings, which, with some shame, I stopped to look up at, to get their size. Light indoors flowed into light outdoors: the light here was one. In Trinidad, from seven or eight in the morning to five in the afternoon, the heat was great; to be out of doors was to be stung, to feel the heat and discomfort. This gray sky and gray light, light without glare, suggested a canopied, protected world: no need, going outside, to brace oneself for heat and dazzle. And the city of protected-feeling streets and tall buildings was curiously softly colored. I hadn't expected that, hadn't seen that in photographs or read about it. The colors of the New York streets would have appeared to me, in Trinidad, as "dead" colors, the colors of dead things, dried grass, dead vegetation, earth, sand, a dead world—hardly colors at all.

I went walking. In my memory there is only one walk. But I believe now that there would have been two, with a taxi ride in between (to check up on the sailing time for the ship that was to take me away that afternoon). Without the money in the suitcase I would have been penniless; so at least that precaution had served.

I saw a cinema advertising *Marius* with Raimu. The advertisement was in movable letters. I had never seen a French film in my life. But I knew much about French cinema. I had read about it, and I had even in some way studied it, in case a question came up in a French cultural "general" paper. So much of my education had been like that, abstract, a test of memory: like a man, denied the chance of visiting famous cities, learning their street maps instead. So much of my education had been like that: monkish, medieval, learning quite separate from everyday things.

Marius, Raimu. One name was like an anagram of the other, bar the *s* (my monkish way of observing, studying, committing to memory). And if it had been afternoon, and if I didn't have a ship to take, I would have gone, for at home that was where, imaginatively, I lived most profoundly: in the cinema. Really—over and above that quirk of literary ambition—there was a great simplicity to my character. I knew very little about the agricultural colony in the New World where I was born. And of my Asiatic-Hindu community, a transplanted peasant community, I knew only my extended family. All my life, from the moment I had become self-aware, had been devoted to study, study of the abstract sort I have tried to give some idea of. And then this idea of abstract study had been converted into an idea of a literary life in another country. That had committed me to further, more desperate, more consuming study; had committed me to further withdrawal. My real life, my literary life, was to be elsewhere. In the meantime, at home, I lived imaginatively in the cinema, a foretaste of that life abroad.

On Saturday afternoons, after the special holiday shows which began at one thirty (and which we simply called "one thirty" rather in the way other people might speak of matinees), it was painful, after the dark cinema and the remote realms where one had been living for three hours or so, to come out into the very bright colors of one's own world.

But I had not seen any French films. They had never been shown in Trinidad. And perhaps, like British films, if they had been shown they would have found no audience, being of a particular country, local, not universal like the Hollywood pictures, which could quicken the imaginations of remote people. I knew French films from books, especially Roger Manvell's *Film*. I knew all the still photographs in that book. His reverential text, and the enthusiasm that had been given me at school for France as the country of civilization, made me see extraordinary virtue in those strongly lighted, poorly reproduced small photographs.

And now, less than a day into my great adventure, seeing the name *Marius* and its near anagram Raimu on the cinema board, I felt I was close to something that was mine by right (by education, vocation, training, yearning, sacrifice)—like *The New York Times* itself, which yet (when bought by me) didn't hold me, being like a crossword puzzle I could only partly fill in.

And a similar feeling of being let down by what should have been mine by right came when I found and went into a bookshop. Great cities possessed bookshops—just as they had cinemas which showed French films. Colonial towns or settlements like my own didn't have bookshops. In the old colonial main square in Port of Spain—antique roofs and awnings of corrugated iron, once painted red or in alternate stripes of white and red; old carpentry, fretted gables with finials, decorative Victorian ironwork; architecture that spoke to me of our remoteness from the ports where that timber and decorative ironwork and corrugated iron were shipped—in the old colonial square there were emporia that sold schoolbooks and perhaps children's books and coloring books, and had perhaps as well a short shelf or two of Penguin books, a few copies of a few titles, and a few of the Collins Classics (looking like Bibles): emporia as dull as the emporia of those days could be, suggesting warehouses for a colonial population, where absolutely necessary goods (with a few specialist lines, like mosquito nets and the Collins Classics) were imported and stored in as unattractive and practical a way as possible.

And here, in the city of New York, was a bookshop. A place I should have entered as though I had journeyed to enter it. I loved books, I was a reader—it was my reputation at home. But the books I knew or knew about were few. There were the books in my father's bookcase: classics from the Everyman series, religious books, books about Hinduism and India. These last were bought from a trader in Indian goods in a petty commercial street in Port of Spain, and bought, most of them, as a gesture of Indian nationalism; few of them were read by my father, and none by me. There were the books I had studied at school; there were the books I saw in the Central Library. Really, though, I knew only the classical or established names, the French, Spanish, and English books I had studied at school, and the very famous names my father had introduced me to.

To enter this New York bookshop was to find myself among unhallowed names. I was traveling to be a writer, but this world of modern writing and publishing I had walked into was not something I was in touch with. And among all these unfamiliar, unhallowed names, I looked for the familiar, the classics, the uniform series, the very things I had looked at (with a feeling of deprivation and being far away) in the dark colonial emporia of Port of Spain, among the reams of paper and the stacks of exercise books, next to wholesalers of various kinds of imported goods (cloth and coal pots), all in a warm smell of spices and damp raw sugar and various cooking oils from the wholesale grocers of South Quay, where there were donkey carts and horse carts and pushcarts among the motor trucks.

This was an American shop, not one with English stock, the stock I was more familiar with. I settled then for the Modern Library series, and bought *South Wind*. This had been recommended to me by an English teacher who knew of my writing ambitions. I had despaired of finding this book in the emporia of Trinidad. Here, part of the great wealth of New York, was the book, immediately available. I paid one twenty-eight, and the assistant, who must have been eight or ten years older than me, called me sir.

South Wind! But it remained unread. My first attempt to read it was like all the attempts I made later: it showed me that—like the books of Aldous Huxley and D. H. Lawrence and certain other contemporary writers whose names had come to me through my father or through teachers at school—this book, with a young man called Denis and a bishop, and an island called Nepenthe, was alien, far from anything in my experience, and beyond my comprehension. But the alienness of a book, though it might keep me from reading it (I never read beyond the first chapter of *South Wind*), did not prevent me from admiring it. The very alienness, the inaccessibility, was like a promise of romance—a reward, some way in the future, for making myself a writer.

So much of my education had been abstract that I could live like this and think and feel like this. I had, for instance, studied classical French drama without having any idea of the country or the court that had produced this drama; without having the capacity to grasp the historical reality of France, and in fact quietly (in my own mind) rejecting as a fairy story all that I was told in introductions or textbooks about kings and ministers and mistresses and religious wars. These things were too removed from my experience and I could not grasp them; I knew only my island and my community and the ways of our colony. I had prepared essays on French and Soviet cinema simply by reading books and articles. I had learnt the great names of art and architecture in the same way.

So, though now in New York I was a free man, and this was the first book I was buying in a great city, and the occasion was therefore important, historical for me, romantic, I took to it the abstract attitudes of my school education: the bright boy, the scholarship boy, not acting now for his teachers or family, but acting only for himself.

Yet, with the humiliations of my first twenty-four hours of travel, my first twenty-four hours in the great world, with my increasing sense of my solitude in this world, I was aware (not having a home audience now, not having any audience at all) that I felt no joy. The young man in the shop called me sir and that was unexpected and nice. But I felt a fraud; I felt pushed down into a part of myself where I had never been.

Less than twenty-four hours had passed since the magical vision of landscape, sugarcane fields and forested hills and valleys; and the crawling sea; and the clouds lit from above by the sun. But already I could feel the two sides of myself separating one from the other, the man from the writer. Already I felt a twinge of doubt about myself: perhaps the writer was only a man with an abstract education, a capacity for concentration, and a capacity for learning things by heart. And I had worked so hard for this day and this adventure! With the new silence of my solitude, this solitude something I had never anticipated as part of the great adventure, I watched the two sides of myself separate and dwindle even on this first day.

And that afternoon in New York, from a pier whose number I carried for many years in my head, but which I have now forgotten, a number not associated with romance but with humiliation and uncertainty, there began a journey on a ship of some days. Port of Spain to Puerto Rico to New York, by air. New York to Southampton, by ship.

*T*HAT JOURNEY by ship was for a long time—many weeks, many months: a long time to a boy of eighteen—my most precious piece of writer's material. Or so I saw it. And for a long time, in a boardinghouse in Earl's Court in London, in the dreariness of my college room in Oxford, and in the greater dreariness of a bed-sitting-room in the holidays, using my indelible pencil or my Waterman pen or the very old typewriter I had bought in London for ten pounds, more than a week's allowance for me (expensive, but new typewriters at that time, the war not being long over, were still not easily available), I wrote and cherished a piece I called "Gala Night."

It was my first piece of writing based on metropolitan material. It was wise; it suggested experience and the traveler. "Gala Night"—it might have been written by a man who had seen many gala nights.

Knowing what it was doing, knowing the value of names, it played easily with great names—New York, the Atlantic, the S.S. *Columbia*, United States Lines, Southampton (especially beautiful, as a name, this last).

The gala night that provided the material for this piece of descriptive writing—it was not a story—took place on shipboard on our last full day on the Atlantic. In the morning we were to call at Cobh in Ireland; then we were to dock at Southampton in the afternoon. Most of the passengers were to get off at Southampton; the others would get off the next morning at Le Havre. The gala night was a dance after dinner in one of the lounges of the tourist class. And it was disturbing to me to see—as from a distance, and as though I were studying a kind of animal life, since no shipboard romance had come to me—how the sexual impulse, like drink, clouded and distorted people I knew, men and women. To me, a lover of women but quite virginal at that time, the distortion in the women I had got to know was especially unsettling.

There was a dainty girl who had spoken to me of poetry. How strange to see her now in the company of a man of no particular education or quality, and to see her moist-eyed, as though worked upon by forces outside her control. There was no recognition of me now in her eyes. And how distant, earnest, and preoccupied hitherto friendly men became, how impatient of conversation with me, conversation they had at other times welcomed. There was a man from San Francisco, an Armenian; he had fought in Europe during the war, and we had talked of the war and the soldier's life. He had told me that the only true war film he had seen was *A Walk in the Sun*. His thoughts were now elsewhere.

Part of the trouble was that the gala night was also an occasion of drinking; and I at that time didn't drink at all. To win my scholarship, I had punished myself with study; and because I wished things to go well for me, I was full of ascetic self-castigations.

In what I wrote I was recording my ignorance and innocence, my deprivations (of which the asceticism was a disingenuous sign) and frustration. But "Gala Night," in the intention of the eighteen-year-old boy who was doing the writing, was knowing and unillusioned. So that in the writing, as well as in the man, there was a fracture. To a truly knowing person the piece would have given itself away in more than one place.

I concentrated towards the end of the piece on the figure of the ship's night watchman. He was standing outside the lounge where the dancing was taking place, and he had begun to address the disconsolate and unlucky men standing outside with him, men to whom, even on this wanton occasion, when dainty girls went dreamy and wild, no shipboard romance had come. He was as divided as I was, and perhaps the other men who were listening to him. There was a sourness in their silence. He, the night watchman, was lively; he spoke as a man who had seen it all. He was a heavily built man in his forties; in the lecturing posture he had settled into, his hands, stretched out on either side of him, grasped the handrail against which he was leaning. He paused between sentences, to allow the wickedness he was describing to sink in; looking at no one in particular, he pressed his lips together; and then, as if talking to himself, he started again.

People changed after three days on a ship, he said. Faithful wives and girl friends became faithless. Always, after three days. Men became violent and were ready to fight over women, even men with young and loving wives to whom they had just said good-bye. He said (or in many versions of "Gala Night" I made him say): "I have seen a captain make to kill a guy in this here place."

"Make to," "kill," "guy," "this here place"—in addition to what he was saying, his lack of illusion about men and women (comforting in one way, that lack of illusion and the fierce judgment it implied, but also very painful, this account of a near-universal wantonness that was nevertheless denied us), the night watchman talked like someone in a film. And that was why, as material, he was so precious to me. That was why the hard indelible pencil traced again and again, in those faint letters (which would brighten and turn purple when dampened), the words he spoke.

In "Gala Night" I looked for metropolitan material; I stuck to peo-

ple who seemed to me to have this quality. There was a man, originally from the Middle East but now in spite of his Muslim name entirely
American, who said he was an entertainer. He spoke familiarly of famous stars, stars whose films I had seen; and it never occurred to me
to wonder why this entertainer was traveling tourist. He read me some
of his material, after the usual three days. "Material"—that was what
he called it, and the short and simple jokes were typed. That was impressive and strange and "American" to me: that such trivial "material" should be typed, should be given that formality. As impressive
as that was his way of talking of his time in animated cartoons. They
made many cartoons at the same time, he said. "We make them and
we can them." "Can"—I was entranced by the word, so knowing, so
casual, so professional. Just as his "material" became part of mine, so
his language became part of my material as well. So that I was having
it both ways with him: making use as a writer of his metropolitan
knowingness, appropriating it, yet keeping myself at a distance from
him (not on the ship, only in "Gala Night"), as though he, being only
an entertainer (traveling tourist) and dubiously American, was a kind
of buffoon (the kind of buffoon such a person should be, in writing
of the sort I was aiming at) and as though I—now adrift, supported
only by the abstractions of my colonial education—stood on firmer
ground than he.

Two Salvation Army girls were also among my material. They
were traveling to a conference somewhere in Europe; but they were
ready to flirt. This flirtatiousness in religious girls struck me as strange;
with my deprivations, I saw oddity where there was none. And there
was a young man from the South. He shared the entertainer's cabin.
He was heavy and pockmarked and he wore glasses. In "Gala Night"
he appeared—and the scene was written so often by me that in my
imagination he remains forever—in undershirt and underpants, sitting on the upper bunk, in the dim top light, peeling and eating an
orange, and talking about girls, perhaps the Salvation Army girls.

He said, looking down at his orange, "I'm a plodder. I know what
I want and I go get it—see?"

That was material for me: I could show the world—writing like that, observing things like that—that I knew the world. I could say in effect: "I, too, have seen this. And I, too, can write about it."

But there was another memory, disconnected from the first. In some versions of "Gala Night" I used it. In other versions I left it out.

The young Southerner was talking about "colored people." He said, "Nowadays they want to get in your bed and sleep with you."

I was taken aback by that, and then amazed: that he, so full of racial feeling, could talk to me like that, as though he didn't see me racially. But that topic of race—though it was good, familiar material, and could prove my knowledge of the world—formed no part of "Gala Night." It was too close to my disturbance, my vulnerability, the separation of my two selves. That was not the kind of personality the writer wished to assume; that was not the material he dealt in.

So that, though traveling to write, concentrating on my experience, eager for experience, I was shutting myself off from it, editing it out of my memory. Editing out the airport taxi driver who had overcharged me—the humiliation had been too great; editing out the Negro at the hotel.

Nor, as a writer, could I acknowledge the other, hideous anxiety of my day in New York. The journey in a liner across the Atlantic should have been pure romance; the going aboard the ship that afternoon in New York should have been pure romance. But romance was in only one part of my mind; there was something else in another part of my mind. I was nervous about sharing a cabin. For months I had worried about that aspect of my journey across the Atlantic. I feared being put with aggressive or disagreeable or sexually unbalanced people. I was small and felt my physical weakness. I feared being assaulted; I feared attracting someone's malevolence.

That had been a great anxiety for me. But when I went aboard the ship it had been miraculously resolved. Yet I could not, in "Gala Night," wishing to be the kind of writer I wanted to be, write about that.

The British vice-consul in New York had booked a passage for someone who, when he went aboard the ship at the pier in New York, was clearly seen not to be English and was a puzzle to the purser. I remember it only now—so successful was "Gala Night" in cutting out the memory. Only now, laying aside the material of "Gala Night," I remember having to stand about for some hours while they decided where to put me. I would have been unplaced, would have been standing about, worried about my few pieces of luggage, even while the ship was leaving the pier. My sight of the New York harbor and the famous skyline would have been tainted by that standing about. And then someone took a decision, and the issue was wonderfully resolved.

I was given a cabin absolutely to myself in a higher class. And I was given a key to open the door that separated that class from the tourist class, where I was to continue to live and eat during the day. This was a wonderful piece of luck. Immediately, much of my anxiety left me. I thought it a very good omen for the future. I thought (still with the fear of sharing cabins, compartments, and hotel bathrooms) that I would be blessed with what I thought of then as "traveler's luck."

But that night, when I was asleep, there was a commotion that awakened me. The top light of the cabin was put on. There were voices. I knew then, I knew, what was about to happen. Someone was going to be put with me. Someone else from "tourist" was going to be given a key to the door—which for some hours that evening I had thought of as a very private possession, almost a secret—that separated the classes. And the top light, put on just like that, and the raised voices, were so inconsiderate. I closed my eyes. Like a child. Like someone practicing magic. If I pretended to be asleep, if I pretended to know nothing, then nothing might happen; and the people who had come in might all just go away.

But there was trouble. The man who had been brought in was making trouble. He was rejecting the cabin. His voice was rising. He said, "It's because I'm colored you're putting me here with him."

Colored! So he was a Negro. So this was a little ghetto privilege I had been given. But I didn't want the Negro or anybody else to be with me. Especially I didn't want the Negro to be with me, for the very reasons the Negro had given.

And he wasn't to be with me. The top light went out; the cabin door closed; the people who had come in went out. And the Negro was no doubt taken back past the barrier door to tourist class and fitted into some crowded three- or four-berth cabin, but with white people. Satisfactory to him, the black man; but at what price, at what cost in strain and tension for the days of the journey across the great Atlantic. Frightening, that glimpse of another man's deprivation and drive. Yet I was also ashamed that they had brought the Negro to my cabin. I was ashamed that, with all my aspirations, and all that I had put into this adventure, this was all that people saw in me—so far from the way I thought of myself, so far from what I wanted for myself. And it was shame, too, that made me keep my eyes closed while they were in the cabin.

He, the black man, sought me out the next morning in the lounge of the tourist class, to apologize. He was tall, slender, well dressed, with a suggestion of boniness and sharpness below his fine, thin summer suiting: bony knees, sharp shins. He was well spoken, quieter with me than he had been in the cabin. He had thought that the people from the purser's office were genuinely offering him a better and less crowded cabin when they led him beyond the tourist door. But when he saw me he changed his mind. He knew that I had become the nucleus of a little ghetto; he knew the Americans, he said. What else did he tell me? What else was there to him apart from his racial passion? Was he so restricted? I remember nothing else. I remember no other meeting with him.

A woman—young, but older than my eighteen—told me more about him one day on deck: he clearly had made an impression on some of the passengers. He was fatigued by American prejudice, the woman said; and she spoke of him with understanding and also a kind of admiration. He was going to live in Germany, she said. His wife was German; they had met when he was serving with the army in Germany; he had grown to like the German people. Strange pilgrimage!

In Puerto Rico there had been the Trinidad Negro in a tight jacket on his way to Harlem. Here was a man from Harlem or black America on his way to Germany. In each there were aspects of myself. But, with my Asiatic background, I resisted the comparison; and I was traveling to be a writer. It was too frightening to accept the other thing, to face the other thing; it was to be diminished as man and writer. Racial diminution formed no part of the material of the kind of writer I was setting out to be. Thinking of myself as a writer, I was hiding my experience from myself; hiding myself from my experience. And even when I became a writer I was without the means, for many years, to cope with that disturbance.

I wrote on with my indelible pencil. I noted dialogue. My "I" was aloof, a man who took notes, and knew.

Night and day a man stood in the bow of the ship, scanning the gray sea ahead. And when finally I landed at Southampton I had for a short while the pleasing sensation that the ground moved below my feet the way the ship had moved for five days.

I had arrived in England. I had made the journey by ship. The passenger terminal was new. Southampton, of the pretty name, had been much bombed during the war. The new terminal looked to the future; but passenger liners were soon to be things of the past.

*A*FTER THE gray of the Atlantic, there was color. Bright color seen from the train that went to London. Late afternoon light. An extended dusk: new, enchanting to someone used to the more or less equal division of day and night in the tropics. Light, dusk, at an hour which would have been night at home.

But it was night when we arrived at Waterloo station. I liked the size, the many platforms, the big, high roof. I liked the lights. Used at home to public places—or those I knew, schools, stores, offices— working only in natural light, I liked this excitement of a railway station busy at night, and brightly lit up. I saw the station people, working in electric light, and the travelers as dramatic figures. The station lights gave a suggestion (such as the New York streets had already given me) of a canopied world, a vast home interior.

After five days on the liner, I wanted to go out. I wanted especially to go to a cinema. I had heard that in London the cinemas ran continuously; at home I was used to shows at fixed times. The idea of the continuous show—as the metropolitan way of doing things, with all that it implied of a great busy populace—was very attractive. But even for London, even for the metropolitan populace of London, it was too late. I went directly to the boardinghouse in Earl's Court, where a room had been reserved for me for the two months or so before I went to Oxford.

It was a small room, long and narrow, made dark by dark bulky furniture; and bare otherwise, with nothing on the walls. As bare as my cabin on the *Columbia*; barer than the room I had had in the Hotel Wellington for that night in New York. My heart contracted. But there was one part of me that rejoiced at the view from the window, some floors up, of the bright orange street lights and the effect of the lights on the trees.

After the warm, rubbery smell of the ship, the smell of the air conditioning in enclosed cabins and corridors, there were new smells in the morning. A cloying smell of milk—fresh milk was rare to me: we used Klim powdered milk and condensed milk. That thick, sweet smell of milk was mixed with the smell of soot; and that smell was overlaid with the airless cockroachy smell of old dirt. Those were the morning smells.

The garden or yard or plot of ground at the back of the house ran to a high wall. Behind that high wall was the underground railway station. Romance! The sound of trains there all the time, and from very early in the morning! Speaking directly to me now of what the Negro in the New York hotel had spoken: the city that never slept.

The bathrooms and lavatories were at the end of the landing on each floor. Or perhaps on every other floor—because, as I was going down, there came up a young man of Asia, small and small-boned, with a pale-yellow complexion, with glasses, and an elaborate Asiatic dressing gown that was too big for him in the arms; the wide embroidered cuffs hid his hands. He gave out a tinkling "Goo-ood morning!" and hurried past me. Was he Siamese, Burmese, Chinese? He looked forlorn, far from home—as yet, still full of my London wonder, my own success in having arrived in the city, I did not make the same judgment about myself.

I was going down to the dining room, in the basement. The boardinghouse offered bed and breakfast, and I was going down to the breakfast. The dining room, at the front of the house, sheltered from the noise of the underground trains, subject only to the vibration, had two or three people. It had many straight-backed brown chairs; the walls were as blank as the walls of my room. The milk-and-soot smell was strong here. It was morning, light outside, but a weak electric bulb was on; the wall was yellowish, shiny. Wall, light, smell—they were all parts of the wonderful London morning. As was my sight of the steep narrow steps going up to the street, the rails, the pavement. I had never been in a basement before. It was not a style of building we had at home; but I had read of basements in books; and this room with an electric light burning on a bright sunny day seemed to me romantic. I was like a man entering the world of a novel, a book; entering the real world.

I went and looked around the upper floor afterwards, or that part of it that was open to guests. The front room was full of chairs, straight-backed chairs and fat low upholstered chairs, and the walls were as bare as the walls everywhere else. This was the lounge (I had been told that downstairs); but the air was so still, such a sooty old smell came off the dark carpet and the tall old curtains, that I felt the room wasn't used. I felt the house was no longer being used as the builder or first owner had intended. I felt that at one time, perhaps before the war, it had been a private house; and (though knowing nothing about London houses) I felt it had come down in the world. Such was my tenderness towards London, or my idea of London. And I felt, as I saw more and more of my fellow lodgers—Europeans from the Continent and North Africa, Asiatics, some English people from the provinces, simple people in cheap lodgings—that we were all in a way campers in the big house.

And coming back night after night—after my tourist excursions through London—to this bare house, I was infected by its mood. I took this mood to what I saw. I had no eye for architecture; there had been nothing at home to train my eye. In London I saw pavements, shops, shop blinds (almost every other one stenciled at the bottom *J. Dean, Maker, Putney*), shop signs, undifferentiated buildings. On my tourist excursions I went looking for size. It was one of the things I had traveled to find, coming from my small island. I found size, power, in the area around Holborn Viaduct, the Embankment, Trafalgar Square. And after this grandeur there was the boardinghouse in Earl's Court. So I grew to feel that the grandeur belonged to the past; that I had come to England at the wrong time; that I had come too late to find the England, the heart of empire, which (like a provincial, from a far corner of the empire) I had created in my fantasy.

Such a big judgment about a city I had just arrived in! But that way of feeling was something I carried within myself. The older people in our Asian-Indian community in Trinidad—especially the poor ones, who could never manage English or get used to the strange races—looked back to an India that became more and more golden in their memory. They were living in Trinidad and were going to die there; but for them it was the wrong place. Something of that feeling was passed down to me. I didn't look back to India, couldn't do so; my ambition caused me to look ahead and outwards, to England; but it led to a similar feeling of wrongness. In Trinidad, feeling myself far away, I had held myself back, as it were, for life at the center of things. And there were aspects of the physical setting of my childhood which positively encouraged that mood of waiting and withdrawal.

We lived, in Trinidad, among advertisements for things that were no longer made or, because of the war and the difficulties of transport, had ceased to be available. (The advertisements in American magazines, for Chris Craft and Statler Hotels and things like that, belonged to another, impossibly remote world.) Many of the advertisements in Trinidad were for old-fashioned remedies and "tonics." They were on tin, these advertisements, and enameled. They were used as decorations in shops and, having no relation to the goods offered for sale, they grew to be regarded as emblems of the shopkeeper's trade. Later, during the war, when the shanty settlement began to grow in the

swampland to the east of Port of Spain, these enameled tin advertisements were used sometimes as building material.

So I was used to living in a world where the signs were without
meaning, or without the meaning intended by their makers. It was of
a piece with the abstract, arbitrary nature of my education, like my
ability to "study" French or Russian cinema without seeing a film, an
ability which was, as I have said, like a man trying to get to know a
city from its street map alone.

What was true of Trinidad seemed to be true of other places as
well. In the book sections of some of the colonial emporia of Port of
Spain there would be a shelf or two of the cheap wartime Penguin
paperbacks (narrow margins, crudely stapled, with the staples rusting
quickly in our damp climate, but with a wonderful color, texture, and
smell to the paper). It never struck me as odd that at the back of those
wartime Penguins there should sometimes be advertisements for certain British things—chocolates, shoes, shaving cream—that had never
been available in Trinidad and were now (because of the war, as the
advertisements said) no longer being made; such advertisements being
put in by the former manufacturers only to keep their brand names
alive during the war, and in the hope that the war would turn out well.
These advertisements—for things doubly and trebly removed from
possibility—never struck me as odd; they came to me as an aspect of
the romance of the world I was working towards, a promise within
the promise, and intensely romantic.

So I was ready to imagine that the world in which I found myself
in London was something less than the perfect world I had striven
towards. As a child in Trinidad I had put this world at a far distance,
in London perhaps. In London now I was able to put this perfect world
at another time, an earlier time. The mental or emotional processes
were the same.

In the underground stations there were still old-fashioned, heavy
vending machines with raised metal letters. No sweets, no chocolates
came from them now. But for ten years or so no one had bothered to
take them away; they were like things in a house that had broken down

or been superseded, but remained unthrown away. Two doors away from my boardinghouse in Earl's Court there was a bomb site, a gap in the road, with neat rubble where the basement should have been, the dining room of a house like the one in which I lived. Such sites were all over the city. I saw them in the beginning; then I stopped seeing them. Paternoster Row, at the side of St. Paul's Cathedral, hardly existed; but the name still appeared on the title page of books as the London address of many publishers.

My tramps about London were ignorant and joyless. I had expected the great city to leap out at me and possess me; I had longed so much to be in it. And soon, within a week or less, I was very lonely. If I had been less lonely, if I had had the equivalent of my shipboard life, I might have felt differently about London and the boardinghouse. But I was solitary, and didn't have the means of finding the kind of society I had had for the five days of the Atlantic crossing.

There was the British Council. They ran a meeting place for foreign students like me. But there one evening, the first time I went, I found myself, in conversation with a bored girl, turning to the subject of physical pain, a fearful obsession of mine, made more fearful with the war (and one further explanation of the austerities I practiced at various times). I began to talk of torture, and persevered, though knowing it to be wrong to do so; and was so alarmed by this further distortion of myself (more distorted than my behavior during the flight to New York, first with the Negro in Puerto Rico, then with the Englishwoman in the seat beside me) that I never went to that British Council place again, for shame.

I had only the boardinghouse and that curious, mixed, silent company of English people, Europeans in limbo, and a few Asiatic students to whom English was difficult. And perhaps that boardinghouse life might have meant more to me if I were better read in contemporary English books, if, for example, I had read *Hangover Square*, which was set in the very area just eleven years or so before. A book like that would have peopled the area and made it romantic and given me, always needing these proofs from books, some sharper sense of myself.

But in spite of my education, I was under-read. What did I know of London? There was an essay by Charles Lamb—in a schoolbook —about going to the theater. There were two or three lovely sentences—in another schoolbook—about the Embankment, from "Lord Arthur Savile's Crime." But Sherlock Holmes's Baker Street was just its name; and the London references in Somerset Maugham and Waugh and others didn't create pictures in the mind, because they assumed too much knowledge in the reader. The London I knew or imaginatively possessed was the London I had got from Dickens. It was Dickens—and his illustrators—who gave me the illusion of knowing the city. I was therefore, without knowing it, like the Russians I was to hear about (and marvel at) who still believed in the reality of Dickens's London.

Years later, looking at Dickens during a time when I was writing hard myself, I felt I understood a little more about Dickens's unique power as a describer of London, and his difference from all other writers about London. I felt that when as a child far away I read the early Dickens and was able with him to enter the dark city of London, it was partly because I was taking my own simplicity to his, fitting my own fantasies to his. The city of one hundred and thirty years before must have been almost as strange to him as it was to me; and it was his genius to describe it, when he was an adult, as a child might have described it. Not displaying architectural knowledge or taste; not using technical words; using only simple words like "old-fashioned" to describe whole streets; using no words that might disturb or unsettle an unskilled or unknowledgeable reader. Using no words to unsettle a child far away, in the tropics, where the roofs were of corrugated iron and the gables were done in fretwork, and there were jalousied windows hinged at the top to keep out the rain while letting in light and air. Using, Dickens, only simple words, simple concepts, to create simple volumes and surfaces and lights and shadows: creating thereby a city or fantasy which everyone could reconstruct out of his own materials, using the things he knew to recreate the described things he didn't know.

To Dickens, this enriching of one's own surroundings by fantasy was one of the good things about fiction. And it was apt that Dickens's childlike vision should have given me, with my own child's ideas, my abstract education and my very simple idea of my vocation, an illusion of complete knowledge of the city where I expected this vocation to flower. (Leaving room at the same time, fantasies being what they are, for other, late-nineteenth-century ideas of size and imperial grandeur, which neither Buckingham Palace nor Westminister nor Whitehall gave me, but which I got from Paddington and Waterloo stations and from Holborn Viaduct and the Embankment, great Victorian engineering works.)

I had come to London as to a place I knew very well. I found a city that was strange and unknown—in its style of houses, and even in the names of its districts; as strange as my boardinghouse, which was quite unexpected; a city as strange and unread-about as the Englishness of *South Wind*, which I had bought in New York for the sake of its culture. The disturbance in me, faced with this strangeness, was very great, many times more diminishing than the disturbance I had felt in New York when I had entered, as though entering something that was mine by right, the bookshop which had turned out to have very little for me after all.

And something else occurred in those very early days, the first days of arrival. I lost a faculty that had been part of me and precious to me for years. I lost the gift of fantasy, the dream of the future, the far-off place where I was going. At home I had lived most intensely in the cinema, where, before the fixed-hour shows, the cinema boys, to shut out daylight or electric street light, closed the double doors all around and untied the long cords that kept the high wooden windows open. In those dark halls I had dreamt of a life elsewhere. Now, in the place that for all those years had been the "elsewhere," no further dream was possible. And while on my very first night in London I had wanted to go to the cinema for the sake of those continuous shows I had heard about, to me the very essence of metropolitan busyness, very soon now the idea of the cinema, the idea of entering a dark hall to watch a moving film became oppressive to me.

I had thought of the cinema pleasure as a foretaste of my adult life. Now, with all kinds of shame in many recesses of my mind, I felt it to be fantasy. I hadn't read *Hangover Square*, didn't even know of it as a book; but I had seen the film. Its Hollywood London had merged in my mind (perhaps because of the associations of the titles) into the London of *The Lodger*. Now I knew that London to be fantasy, worthless to me. And the cinema pleasure, that had gone so deep into me and had in the barren years of abstract study given me such support, that cinema pleasure was now cut away as with a knife. And when, ten or twelve years later, I did return to the cinema, the Hollywood I had known was dead, the extraordinary circumstances in which it had flourished no longer existing; American films had become as self-regardingly local as the French or English; and there was as much distance between a film and me as between a book or a painting and me. Fantasy was no longer possible. I went to the cinema not as a dreamer or a fantast but as a critic.

I had little to record. My trampings about London didn't produce adventures, didn't sharpen my eye for buildings or people. My life was restricted to the Earl's Court boardinghouse. There was a special kind of life there. But I failed to see it. Because, ironically, though feeling myself already drying up, I continued to think of myself as a writer and, as a writer, was still looking for suitable metropolitan material.

Metropolitan—what did I mean by that? I had only a vague idea. I meant material which would enable me to compete with or match certain writers. And I also meant material that would enable me to display a particular kind of writing personality: J. R. Ackerley of *Hindoo Holiday*, perhaps, making notes under a dinner table in India; Somerset Maugham, aloof everywhere, unsurprised, immensely knowing; Aldous Huxley, so full of all kinds of knowledge and also so sexually knowing; Evelyn Waugh, so elegant so naturally. Wishing to be that kind of writer, I didn't see material in the campers in the big Earl's Court house.

❊　❊　❊

ONE SUNDAY, not long after I had come to London, I was invited to lunch by the Hardings. Mr. Harding was the manager of the boardinghouse, but I had seen almost nothing of him or his wife. I had seen more of Angela, whose last name I seldom used and in the end forgot. Angela was Italian, from the south of the country. She was in her mid or late twenties, but I couldn't really tell: she was older than me, ten years at least, and I saw her as very mature. She had spent all the war in Italy and had somehow fetched up—like many of her friends—in London.

Angela had a room in the house and some kind of position, but I wasn't sure what the position was. She sometimes was in the dining room in the basement, serving the breakfasts; and sometimes she was there in the evening. She also worked on some evenings as a waitress in the Italian restaurant, the Venezia or some such name, not far from Earl's Court station; she served the two-and-six or three-and-six dinners. I had the dinner there a few times. It gave me an indescribable pleasure to be in a restaurant where I knew the waitress, even though I didn't understand the menu and didn't particularly like the food.

Angela was the first woman outside my family I had got to know. There was an easiness about her from the start. I found her very attractive and—still a virgin myself—was half in love with her. This acquaintance with Angela gave me, fleetingly, a little metropolitan excitement, told me I was far from home and in a great city in Europe. The boardinghouse; the underground railway at the back of the house, and the entrance to the many-platformed station just around the corner; the Italian restaurant, the waitress one knew. I liked the setting and the props; they were part of the drama; they gave me a sense of myself as a metropolitan man just for a minute or so.

Angela gave me a certain amount of encouragement. She told me she liked me; she told me my color was like the color of some people in her country. But there was a man in her life, an Englishman she had met in Italy during the war. He was a rough, common man, liable to become violent. I never saw him; it was Angela herself who described her lover in that way—half asking you to condemn the man, half asking for sympathy for herself, speaking of the relationship as though it was something unavoidable.

She said that one night, during a quarrel, he had become so violent that she had run out of the room or flat naked except for a coat which she had grabbed as she ran. She had decided after that to live by herself. That was when she had moved to the Earl's Court house. Her lover was absent; at least I never saw him. Was he in a foreign country? I gathered from things that other people said that he might have been in jail. But I didn't raise the question with Angela, and she didn't say. I should have asked her, but because of my feelings for her I didn't want to. She was loyal to this man nonetheless. And the encouragement she gave me was oddly chaste. Her room was open to me; but it was only when she had other visitors that she encouraged me to be playful—as though witnesses made my playfulness all right. She was more distant and careful when there were no other visitors.

It was because of Angela—in fact, as Angela's friend—that I went to the Sunday lunch given by the manager, Mr. Harding, and his wife. Mr. Harding I had hardly seen. And even after this lunch—which became part of my "metropolitan" material, something I obsessively wrote about for many months, not only in London in the summer, but also later in Oxford in the autumn, altering the reality to make it fit my idea of what was good material, suitable for someone like myself to write about—even after all that writing I have no impression of what the man and his wife looked like.

The lunch was in a large room on the ground floor at the back of the house. The room at the front, choked with brown furniture and seldom used, was the "lounge." The room at the back was not so full of furniture; but the walls were as stripped as the walls of the other rooms in the house, as though the war itself had visited some disaster, some looting, on the house. I gathered that this back room was part of the quarters or rooms that the Hardings enjoyed as managers of the boardinghouse.

The tall windows looked out onto the garden—or, more properly, untended ground—that ran to the high brick wall of the underground railway station. There was a tree; there was a view of trees in neighboring plots. The ground was bare in the shadow of the brick wall of the underground station. It was not unpleasant to me; I liked the colors; I liked the feel of a space enclosed and shaded but cool.

There were other friends of the Hardings'. Mr. Harding was the star of the lunch. I believe he was drunk. He wasn't incapacitated; but he had been drinking. Mrs. Harding—again, I have no picture of her—and Angela looked after the serving of the lunch. Mr. Harding talked. He was not only the star, but also the comic turn; he had a strong idea of who he was, and he talked with the confidence of a man among people whom he knew, people who would laugh at his jokes and be impressed by his manner.

Had he been drinking at home, in a room somewhere, or had he gone to the pub? I didn't have the social knowledge of London drinking to ask or to guess. I knew nothing about pubs. I didn't like the idea of pubs; I didn't like the idea of a place where people went only to drink. I associated it with the rumshop drunkenness I had seen at home, and was amazed that to ordinary people on the London streets a drunk man was comic, and not hateful. Just as I was slightly amazed now that Mr. Harding, drunk at the lunch table, should not be treated with contempt by his guests but with tolerance and even respect. He was listened to. I cannot tell what sort of accent he had. It sounded good to me, like something from a film.

The most memorable moment of the lunch came during the telling of a story by Mr. Harding. I have a memory of Angela chuckling while Mr. Harding spoke; and a memory of Mrs. Harding doing a kind of straight-woman act.

What Mr. Harding's story was about I do not remember. But there came a moment when he said, slowly, his deliberate drunken accents filling the room, "One of my wives—Audrey, yes Audrey." And then he spoke directly to Mrs. Harding: "Do you remember Audrey?" And Mrs. Harding, not laughing, not smiling, not looking directly at Mr. Harding, doing her straight-woman act, Mrs. Harding said, "I loved Audrey. She was such a sweet kid."

I was dazzled by that passage of dialogue. It seemed to me sophisticated, big-city, like something in a film or play or a book—just the kind of thing I had traveled to London to find, just the kind of material that would help to define me as a writer. And in many of the pieces of writing I attempted, in London at the boardinghouse, and later in Oxford during the terms and then the holidays, I brought that passage in. Though I had no social knowledge to set it off; though— to put it at its simplest—I had no idea what Mr. Harding had been doing that morning, where he had come from, and where he would be going that afternoon; though I could hardly see the man or judge his speech; though I never even thought to ask whether he had fought in the war or had spent his time in Earl's Court drinking.

Writing about Mr. Harding and that passage of dialogue, I had a setting. Sunday lunch in a big London house. In some of the writing I attempted I improved the condition of everybody. I improved my own condition as well (without overt boasting), because to have heard and recorded that passage made me as "knowing" as I thought a writer should be when he moved among people. So to me, as a writer, that passage gave as much pleasure as it had given to both Mr. Harding and Mrs. Harding.

But what of Mr. Harding? What other clue do I have to a more complete person? Has he really vanished from my memory? Can I not recall more than an impression of middle-aged, baldish whiteness, and a lazy, deliberate way of speaking? Did he know that the eighteen-year-old among the guests at his lunch was a writer who would cherish those words of his and go up to his room and write them down? He couldn't have known. The sophistication, then, the play, was for the people at the table; it was a thing Mr. Harding could waste. And that little deduction, in retrospect, makes him more interesting than what I noted down about him at the time. My passion to gather metropolitan experience and material, to give myself stature as a writer, this overreadiness to find material that I half-knew from other writers already, my very dedication, got in the way of my noting the truth, which would have been a little clearer to me if my mind had been less cluttered, if I had been a little less well educated.

As I wrote that passage of dialogue between the Hardings, I often improved everybody's circumstances, as I have said. But now, with my experience of Mr. and Mrs. Phillips at the manor house, and my knowledge of Bray, the car-hire man, I see that lunch in the Earl's Court boardinghouse as slightly less than it seemed to me even at the time. I see the participants as servants, in a degraded setting, the gentlefolk whom the servants were meant to serve being gone, with the war, and leaving a looted house, full of foreigners now. So possibly the deliberation of Mr. Harding's speech was not only the deliberation of the habitual drinker after drinking, but also the genteel precision of the servant, whose vowels might have betrayed him to people in the know. But at that lunch Mr. Harding was safe. To his English friends his sophistication and wit would have been part of a familiar and loved act; and his Englishness worked—wonderfully—for the foreigners present, for both Angela and me.

If Mr. Harding was less than I made him in my writing at the time, then he was also more. To make him grand in my writing, equivalent to his wit, I suppressed the boardinghouse background. But in suppressing aspects of the truth, I did more: I managed to suppress memory. And it was only when I began to concentrate on the lunch that Sunday for this chapter that I remembered that the lunch was special. For this reason, which I never mentioned in my writing: it was the Hardings' last lunch in the house; they had been sacked. They were to be replaced by—Angela. So about the drinking and the wit and the byplay about "one of my wives," and Mrs. Harding's "I loved Audrey," there was an element of great and admirable bravado. But that was not the material I was looking for; it was not the material I noted.

About Angela, I concentrated, in my writing, on her running away at night from the flat or room of her violent lover, wearing only a fur coat over her nakedness. I knew the fur coat. Its quality I couldn't (and still can't) assess; but it developed for me an alluring sexual quality (as no doubt it had for Angela herself, telling the story of her near-naked night flight). The sexual detail suggested a sexual knowingness; it concealed the innocence of the writer. But I could do little with the material. Unwilling as a writer ever to fabricate, to invent where I had no starting point of knowledge, thinking of it as a kind of trespass, I came to the end of my Angela material very quickly.

As with Mr. Harding, I didn't know where Angela had come from. Her past in London, her life away from the Earl's Court boarding-house, was mysterious to me. New to London, I couldn't even begin to imagine the furnishings of her lover's room or flat, his family background, his geographical background, far less his conversation. And as mysterious was Angela's time in Italy. There was a story there—if it had occurred to me that there was. And there was a means of finding the story out. I could have asked her. But I never thought of asking her. I hadn't arrived at that stage.

How had she met her lover? What had life been like in Italy during the war? What had happened to other people in her family? And the various Italians and Maltese and Spaniards and Moroccans of Euro-pean origin who came to her room and were her friends—what were their stories? How had these people found themselves in England and in that Earl's Court area?

The flotsam of Europe not long after the end of the terrible war, in a London house that was now too big for the people it sheltered—that was the true material of the boardinghouse. But I didn't see it. Perhaps I felt that as a writer I should not ask questions; perhaps I felt that as a writer, a sensitive and knowing person, it was enough or should have been enough for me to observe. But there was a subject there that could have been my own; something that would have ex-ercised my indelible pencil to good purpose.

Because in 1950 in London I was at the beginning of that great movement of peoples that was to take place in the second half of the twentieth century—a movement and a cultural mixing greater than the peopling of the United States, which was essentially a movement of Europeans to the New World. This was a movement between all the continents. Within ten years Earl's Court was to lose its prewar or early-war *Hangover Square* associations. It was to become an Aus-tralian and South African, a white-colonial, enclave in London, pres-aging a greater mingling of peoples. Cities like London were to change.

They were to cease being more or less national cities; they were to become cities of the world, modern-day Romes, establishing the pattern of what great cities should be, in the eyes of islanders like myself and people even more remote in language and culture. They were to be cities visited for learning and elegant goods and manners and freedom by all the barbarian peoples of the globe, people of forest and desert, Arabs, Africans, Malays.

Two weeks away from home, when I had thought there was little for me to record as a writer, and just eighteen, I had found, if only I had had the eyes to see, a great subject. Great subjects are illuminated best by small dramas; and in the Earl's Court boardinghouse, as fellow guests or as friends of Angela's, there were at least ten or twelve drifters from many countries of Europe and North Africa, who were offering themselves for my inspection, men and women, some of whom had seen terrible things during the war and were now becalmed and quiet in London, solitary, foreign, sometimes idle, sometimes half-criminal. These people's principal possessions were their stories, and their stories spilled easily out of them. But I noted nothing down. I asked no questions. I took them all for granted, looked beyond them; and their faces, clothes, names, accents have vanished and cannot now be recalled.

If I had had a more direct, less unprejudiced way of looking; if I had noted down simply what I had seen; if in those days I had had the security which later came to me (from the practice of writing), and out of which I was able to take a great interest always in the men and women who were immediately before me and was to learn how to talk to them; if with a fraction of that security I had written down what passed before me, frankly or simply, what material would I not have had! For soon the time would come when I would look, professionally, for material for a London book about the time of my arrival, and then I would find very little.

What remained in my memory was what I had written about obsessively in those early days, and much of that was about Angela's sexuality: the feel of her breasts when, sitting or reclining on the bed beside me in her room, our backs against the wall, and the room full of her strange friends, she had allowed me to press my hand against her breast; the shape of her mouth; the brilliant wartime red of her lips; and the feel of her fur coat; and the sight, thrilling and unexpected, of her apron in the restaurant.

Of Angela's past and time in Italy I noted down nothing, never thinking to ask. I noted down only her railing against the Italian priests of the south, who became fat during the war, she said, when everybody else went hungry. I noted that down, I remember it now, because it was "anticlerical." "Anticlericalism"—that was one of the abstract issues of European history that I had got to know about, from teachers' notes and recommended textbooks, at Queen's Royal College in Trinidad. History as abstract a study for me as the French or Russian cinema, about which I could write essays, just as I could write essays on French history without understanding, without having any idea about, kings and courtiers and religious sects, any idea of the government or social organization of an old and great country.

And how could my knowledge of the world not be abstract, when all the world I knew at the age of eighteen was the small colonial world of my little island in the mouth of the Orinoco, and within that island the world of my family, within our little Asian-Indian community: small world within small world. I hardly knew our own community; of other communities I knew even less. I had no idea of history—it was hard to attach something as grand as history to our island. I had no idea of government. I knew only about a colonial governor and a legislative council and an executive council and a police force. So that almost everything I read about history and other societies had an abstract quality. I could relate it only to what I knew: every kind of reading committed me to fantasy.

I was, in 1950, like the earliest Spanish travelers to the New World, medieval men with high faith: traveling to see wonders, parts of God's world, but then very quickly taking the wonders for granted, saving inquiry (and true vision) only for what they knew they would find even before they had left Spain: gold. True curiosity comes at a later stage of development. In England I was at that earlier, medieval-Spanish stage—my education and literary ambition and my academic struggles the equivalent of the Spanish adventurer's faith and travel-er's endurance. And, like the Spaniard, having arrived after so much effort, I saw very little. And like the Spaniard who had made a long, perilous journey down the Orinoco or Amazon, I had very little to record.

So, out of all the things I might have noted down about Angela's Italian past, I noted down only her anticlericalism. It was a confir-mation of what had up till then been abstract; it thrilled me because I had expected to find it.

The flotsam of Europe after the war—that was one theme I missed. There was another, linked to that.

Shortly after she had taken over from the Hardings, Angela took me up to a room one Saturday afternoon to show me "something," as she said. She behaved as though this "something" was something she had just discovered, something the deposed Hardings might have been responsible for. Though this couldn't have been true: Angela had been connected with the house for some time.

She took me to a room on the second or third floor. It was a big and dark room, much bigger than mine. The curtains were closed. The room smelled of old dirt and urine, old unwashed clothes, old un-washed bodies. It was as though the smell hung on the darkness of the room; as though the darkness was an expression of the smell. There was an old man on the bed; he was the source of the smell. A stick was leaning on the bed. Angela said to the figure on the bed, "I've brought someone to see you."

He paid no attention. Playfully, and greatly to Angela's amuse-ment, he took the stick that was leaning on the bed and tried to raise her skirt with it. She was showing me the old man and his sexual play-fulness as an oddity; that was how I accepted it. She told me nothing else about him and I didn't ask. The questions come only now. Had he come to the house before the war, when the lounge might still have been a lounge and the dining room perhaps a true dining room? Had he stayed there throughout the war, and was he too old now to move? Had the Hardings taken up his meals to him, and did Angela do so now? Was he utterly dependent on the people who ran the boarding-house?

If, as I thought (though at the age of eighteen I had no means of assessing the age of old people), he was now about eighty, it meant that he had been born in 1870. Born in the year Dickens died; the year Lord Alfred Douglas was born; the year the Prussians defeated the French. Or, considering it from another angle, the year after Mahatma Gandhi was born. As a young man he would have known people whose memories went back to the early decades of the nineteenth century; he would have lived among people to whom the Indian Mutiny was a recent affair. Now, after two wasting wars, after Gandhi and Nehru, he was ending his days in one of the big houses of Victorian London, a part of London developed in the Victorian time. And now the houses there, which had survived so much, were too big for the people; and the old man in the big dark room was like a stranger among the people who lived in the house. Against these houses there beat a new tide of people—like myself, and the other Asiatics in the house, and Angela and the other Mediterraneans—who still hardly knew where they were.

I saw the old man once later. He was shuffling about one of the staircase landings. There was an odd, humorous-seeming restlessness about his old face. It might have been that that was the way the flesh and muscles on his face were now set; it was as though his face was, very slightly, twitching with age. He didn't look at me with any kind of recognition; he just had his fixed seeming smile. He was concentrating on his steps and what for him would have been the long walk down to the hall and the street. It was summer, late August, but he was wearing an overcoat. It was dark blue and looked heavy; it might have been made to measure some time before. He was tall; and the overcoat, though he needed it for warmth, seemed too heavy for his shoulders. He had his stick. His smell preceded him and lingered after him. I suppose he was going out for a little walk; it would have taken him a long time to prepare.

Did he have visitors? Where did he get money? I never asked. And when I came back to the boardinghouse for the second and last time, for the Christmas holidays after my first term at Oxford, I never asked after the old man; and Angela never told me anything about him. I never saw him then; and I suppose that he had died in the twelve weeks or so since I had seen him on the landing in his heavy blue overcoat. Such a link with the past, so precious to me, with my feeling for the past. Yet I didn't ask about the old man.

*I*T WASN'T only that I was unformed at the age of eighteen or had no idea what I was going to write about. It was that the idea given me by my education—and by the more "cultural," the nicest, part of that education—was that the writer was a person possessed of sensibility; that the writer was someone who recorded or displayed an inward development. So, in an unlikely way, the ideas of the aesthetic movement of the end of the nineteenth century and the ideas of Bloomsbury, ideas bred essentially out of empire, wealth and imperial security, had been transmitted to me in Trinidad. To be that kind of writer (as I interpreted it) I had to be false; I had to pretend to be other than I was, other than what a man of my background could be. Concealing this colonial-Hindu self below the writing personality, I did both my material and myself much damage.

To wish to ask questions, to keep true creative curiosity alive (creative rather than the mindless curiosity of gossip, forgotten about almost as soon as it is received), it was necessary for me to make a pattern of the knowledge I already possessed. That kind of pattern was beyond me in 1950. Because of my ideas about the writer, I took everything I saw for granted. I thought I knew it all already, like a bright student. I thought that as a writer I had only to find out what I had read about and already knew. And very soon—after "Gala Night" and all my many writings about the Hardings and Angela—I had nothing to record and had to stop.

Things, objects, endure. The little pad I had taken aboard the Pan American World Airways plane at Trinidad—cheap stuff, five-cents-store stuff, cheap ruled paper set in a folder or binder with envelopes in a pouch on the inside cover—the little pad was still with me, like the indelible pencil. But after that very first day no true excitement had been transmitted to its pages. It recorded smaller things, false things; it recorded nothing; it was put aside. The pencil survived, continued to be used. Writing implements, whether pen or pencil, were not thrown away in those days. And that indelible pencil, which brightened only when water fell on it, grew shorter and stumpier, lasting on long beyond its purely literary duties. It wrote letters; it wrote my name on the front page of the books I bought, books which were many of them like *South Wind*, books of England associated with "culture," which I had read about or which the more cultural of my teachers had recommended to a boy who was going to England to be a writer.

The separation of man from writer which had begun on the long airplane flight from Trinidad to New York became complete. Man and writer both dwindled—the preparations of years seeming to end in futility in a few weeks. And then, but only very slowly, man and writer came together again. It was nearly five years—a year after Oxford was over for me, and long after Angela and Earl's Court had passed out of my ken—before I could shed the fantasies given me by my abstract education. Nearly five years before, quite suddenly one day, when I was desperate for such an illumination, vision was granted me of what my material as a writer might be.

I wrote very simply and fast of the simplest things in my memory. I wrote about the street in Port of Spain where I had spent part of my childhood, the street I had intently studied, during those childhood months, from the security and distance of my own family life and house. Knowledge came to me rapidly during the writing. And with that knowledge, that acknowledgment of myself (so hard before it was done, so very easy and obvious afterwards), my curiosity grew fast. I did other work; and in this concrete way, out of work that came easily to me because it was so close to me, I defined myself, and saw that my subject was not my sensibility, my inward development, but the worlds I contained within myself, the worlds I lived in: my subject turning out to be a version of the one that, unknown to me, I had stumbled upon two weeks after I had left home and in the Earl's Court boardinghouse had found myself in the too big house, among the flotsam of Europe after the war.

Until that illumination, I didn't know what kind of person I was, as man and writer—and both were really the same. Put it at its simplest: was I funny, or was I serious? So many tones of voice were possible or assumable, so many attitudes to the same material. Out of a great mental fog there had come to me the idea of the street. And all at once, within a matter of days, material and tone of voice and writing skill had locked together and begun to develop together.

I came in time to the end of that first inspiration. And in 1956, six years after leaving home, I could go back. Six years! That was the time-scale ship travel imposed on people. To go abroad was indeed to say good-bye. That large family farewell at the Trinidad airport, though conventional in many respects, did hint at the nature of the journey I had been about to make. Six years in England!

Travel was now to become more frequent for me, journeys more matter-of-fact. Yet every journey home and every journey back to England was to qualify the one that had gone before, one response overlaying the other.

I went back in 1956 by steamship, traveling directly from England, experiencing the slow change in weather, noting with pleasant surprise the day when the wind began to blow and it was not necessary to brace oneself, because the wind was mild and warm; experiencing the ritual of shipboard life, the extravagant printed menus, the officers changing from temperate black uniforms to warm-weather white uniforms. After thirteen days on the Atlantic I awakened one morning to silence; after thirteen days and nights of the steamer's engines, the silence was something that filled the ears.

We were at Barbados; and every porthole of my cabin framed a bright, shocking, beautiful picture: blue sky, white clouds, green vegetation. So that, at this first landfall on my first journey back home, I was momentarily like a tourist, seeing the publicized, expected thing. This was the way that as a child I had been taught to draw and color my island, the local scene; it was the way the mulatto curio makers of Frederick Street and Marine Square in Port of Spain, the people with

stalls on the pavements below the overhanging upper floors of the old
buildings, it was the way they painted the local scene for the visitors
who got off the tourist ships of the Moore-McCormack line and walked
about the town for an hour or so.

I hadn't believed in that way of seeing. I had thought it was a convention, something for the posters, the advertisements in the American magazines. And, indeed, the island that revealed itself to me when
a party of us went ashore had no relation to those beautiful porthole
pictures. The island of Barbados was flat; it looked worn out, by
sugarcane fields and people; the roads were narrow; the wooden houses
were small, very small, and seemed to sit lightly on the flat land, to be
insubstantial, though this island had been cultivated and peopled for
centuries; and there were little children everywhere.

The children were black. There was not in Barbados that mixture
of races we had in Trinidad; and especially there was not in Barbados
an Indian or Asiatic population. But after my six years in England, to
come upon Barbados like this, suddenly, after thirteen days at sea, was
less like coming upon a landscape than like seeing very clearly an aspect of myself and a past I thought I had outlived. The smallness of
that past, the shame of that smallness: they had not been things I could
easily acknowledge as a writer. They were things that the writer of
"Gala Night" and "Angela" and "Life in London" thought he had left
behind for good. I was glad when the morning tour (in a shared taxi)
was over, and I could get back to the ship.

As though there was safety in the ship; as though the next morning the ship wasn't to set me down at my own island. And I found,
when I landed there, that everything had shrunk to Barbados size. But
much more than in Barbados, I was looking less at a landscape than
at old, personal pain. Six years before—and at that age six adult years
was half a life—everything in Port of Spain was tinged with the glory
of my good-bye to it: the cambered streets, the wooden houses, the
big-leaved trees, the low shops, the constant view of the hills of the
Northern Range in morning light and afternoon light. Everything was
tinged with the excitement of departure and the long journey to famous places, New York, Southampton, London, Oxford; everything

was tinged with the promise and the fantasies of the writing career and the metropolitan life. Now six years later the world I thought I had left behind was waiting for me. It had shrunk, and I felt I had shrunk with it.

I had made a start as a writer. But neither of the two books I had written had as yet been published; and I couldn't see my way ahead, couldn't see other books. Six years before, I had been only a boy, following a fantasy, answerable to no one. Now my father had died; there were debts; there were family responsibilities. But I had no means of helping anyone; I could barely help myself. I had only a newly discovered talent; and the only thing I could do, the only way I could look after myself, was to be in England—no longer now a country of fantasy, but simply a place where as a writer I might make a living in a small way, from radio scripts and bits of journalism while I waited for the books to come.

I left after six weeks. The scholarship that had taken me out to England in 1950 had given me the return fare back; this second trip to England was paid for by me, precious money from my very small store. I left on another banana boat, which went by way of Jamaica. I left the ship at Kingston and joined it again three days later at Port Antonio, where it was loading up with bananas—a memory of a green coastline, of dark-green vegetation as in a lagoon overhanging a dark-green sea, and an ache in my heart at my own insecurity and my consequent inability to enjoy the landscape. And then the ship took me north, to the shortening days of England in winter.

The winter itself, the gray tossing seas, I didn't mind, on that nearly empty ship. Winter, in fact, I still liked, for the drama, for the contrast with the tropics of my childhood. It was the uncertainty at the other end that bothered me; and the knowledge now that at either end of my own "run" there was uncertainty. No scholarship money; no vague, warm idea of Oxford and writing at the end of the journey; no note taking. No Angela and the Earl's Court boardinghouse; no sense of the big-city center, with the noise of the underground trains. Instead of Earl's Court and its old Victorian grandeur there was a working-class Kilburn house of gray, almost black, brick in which I had a two-room flat sharing lavatory and bathroom with everybody else.

There was an English brewer on the ship, a tall, heavy, elderly man. I knew he was a brewer because I heard him say it to someone. I also heard him give his name and his title to the purser when he took a book from the small banana-boat library. Giving his title, although there were so few of us on the ship. He, the brewer, three or four English ladies, a Jamaican mulatto, and I. The ladies played cards together.

Six years before, the brewer and these ladies would have been very closely studied by me. Not now. It wasn't that they were alien, and too far from my experience; it was that, having arrived at some intimation of my subjects as a writer, I was no longer interested in English people purely as English people, looking for confirmation of what I had read in books and what in 1950 I would have considered metropolitan material. One of the ladies ran a boardinghouse on the south coast of England. She had given herself a *Caribbean cruise*! I heard the words in her conversation, saw them in her eyes, could hear them in reports she would make to her friends when she got back: the experience itself seemed to matter less than the report she would make of it. What different values the words had for her and for me! Though we might have traveled on the same Fyffes banana boats, the *Cavina*, the *Golfito*, the *Camito*, what different journeys we had made!

Four years later it had all changed for me: the world, my mood, my vision, that very Atlantic. In those four years, out of the panic of that winter return to England, I had pulled much work out of myself, had written a book which I felt to be important. And it was with a security that was entirely new, the security of a man who had at last made himself what he had wanted to be, that I went back to the island, ten years after I had left it for the first time.

And everything I saw and felt and experienced then was tinged with celebration: the hills, the spreading shacks, the heat, the radio programs, the radio commercials, the noise, the route taxis. That landscape—with all its colonial or holiday motifs: beaches, market women, coconut trees, banana trees, sun, big-leaved trees—had always, since I had known it, been the landscape of anxiety, even panic, and sacrifice. The education that had made me had always been like a competition, a race, in which the fear of failure was like the fear of extinction. I had never, as a child, felt free. On afternoons like these, where now in 1960 I could go for drives or dawdle over lunch, I had had to stay with the books; on nights like these, when now I could go visiting or could simply talk, I had had as a scholarship boy to study or memorize things to a late hour. My abstract learning had been dearly bought!

If there was a place, at this stage of my career, where I could fittingly celebrate my freedom, the fact that I had made myself a writer and could now live as a writer, it was here, on this island which had fed my panic and my ambition, and nurtured my earliest fantasies. And just as, in 1956, at that first return, I had moved from place to place, to see it shrink from the place I had known in my childhood and adolescence, so now I moved from place to place to touch it with my mood of celebration, to remove from it the terror I had felt in these places for various reasons at different times. Far away, in England, I had recreated this landscape in my books. The landscape of the books was not as accurate or full as I had pretended it was; but now I cherished the original, because of that act of creation.

And it was as if, then, having won through to a particular kind of achievement, and having come to the end of a particular kind of fear, my relationship with my island had come to an end. Because after this I never found in myself any particular wish to go back. When for one reason or another I did go back, I found that, having neither fear now nor a wish to celebrate, my interest in the island was satisfied, even sated, in a day. I might, on the way from the airport on the morning of an arrival, be struck by the colors, and think I would like to stay for many days or weeks. But after the first day and first night and the first jet-lagged predawn rising, and the first sight of the hummingbirds in the garden, I became restless, anxious to move on.

People had no news; they revealed themselves quickly. Their racial obsessions, which once could tug at my heart, made them simple people. Part of the fear of extinction which I had developed as a child had to do with this: the fear of being swallowed up or extinguished by the simplicity of one side or the other, my side or the side that wasn't mine.

It was odd: the place itself, the little island and its people, could no longer hold me. But the island—with the curiosity it had awakened in me for the larger world, the idea of civilization, and the idea of antiquity; and all the anxieties it had quickened in me—the island had given me the world as a writer; had given me the themes that in the second half of the twentieth century had become important; had made me metropolitan, but in a way quite different from my first understanding of the word, when I had written "Gala Night" and "Life in London" and "Angela."

When, in 1960, with that mood of writer's celebration on me (as I have described), I began my first travel book, it was from my little colonial island that I started, psychologically and physically. The book was in the nature of a commission: I was to travel through colonies, fragments of still surviving empires, in the Caribbean and the Guianas of South America. I knew and was glamoured by the idea of the metropolitan traveler, the man starting from Europe. It was the only kind of model I had; but—as a colonial among colonials who were very close to me—I could not be that kind of traveler, even though I might share that traveler's education and culture and have his feeling for adventure. Especially I was aware of not having a metropolitan audience to "report back" to. The fight between my idea of the glamour of the traveler-writer and the rawness of my nerves as a colonial traveling among colonials made for difficult writing. When, the traveling done, I went back to London with my notes and diaries, to do the writing, the problems were not resolved. I took refuge in humor—comedy, funniness, the satirical reflex, in writing as in life so often a covering up for confusion.

In order to do more of this kind of writing, it was necessary for me to acknowledge more of myself. I soon had the opportunity. Not long after finishing that first travel book, I went to India, to do another. This time I left from England. India was special to England; for two hundred years there had been any number of English travelers' accounts and, latterly, novels. I could not be that kind of traveler. In traveling to India I was traveling to an un-English fantasy, and a fantasy unknown to Indians of India: I was traveling to the peasant India that my Indian grandfathers had sought to recreate in Trinidad, the "India" I had partly grown up in, the India that was like a loose end in my mind, where our past suddenly stopped. There was no model for me here, in this exploration; neither Forster nor Ackerley nor Kipling could help. To get anywhere in the writing, I had first of all to define myself very clearly to myself.

So, from the starting point of Trinidad, my knowledge and self-knowledge grew. The street in Port of Spain where I had spent part of my childhood; a reconstruction of my "Indian" family life in Trinidad; a journey to Caribbean and South American colonies; a later journey to the special ancestral land of India. My curiosity spread in all directions. Every exploration, every book, added to my knowledge, qualified my earlier idea of myself and the world.

But Trinidad itself, the starting point, the center—it could no longer hold me. It was no longer connected in my mind with an Atlantic crossing, a journey by ship over a fortnight, with the ship ritual, the change of the weather, the putting back of the clocks every other morning, the colors of the sea and the sky, the waves and swells, the rainbow-shot spray, the dolphins, the flying fish that, once one entered Caribbean waters, flew at night at the ship's lights and could sometimes in the morning be found expiring, slippery and flapping, on the decks. Passenger ships no longer went to Trinidad or anywhere else; Trinidad was an airline halt, its airport the scene of matter-of-fact departures and arrivals. And it was easy for me to quell whatever longing I occasionally felt for the landscape of my childhood by recreating in my mind the tedium that I knew would come to me on the second day, after the glory of arrival and the glory of the first dawn.

Then I accepted a commission from an American publisher to write a book for a series on cities. I chose my own city, Port of Spain, to write about, because I thought it would be easy for me and also because I thought there was little to write about: Trinidad, after its discovery and dispeopling, had not been peopled again or settled until the end of the eighteenth century. I thought of the project as the labor of a few months, journalism in hard covers. Then I discovered that the source books didn't really exist. The idea that historical truth is preserved somewhere in libraries, in semi-divine volumes, with semi-divine guardians, is something that many of us have, I suppose. But books are physical objects, created or manufactured to meet a demand; and there were no such semi-divine source volumes about Trinidad. I had to go to the documents themselves. Such an irritation; but then the documents began to draw me in; and the longer I stayed with them the harder it was to give up the project.

The idea behind the book, the narrative line, was to attach the island, the little place in the mouth of the Orinoco River, to great names and great events: Columbus; the search for El Dorado; Sir Walter Raleigh. Two hundred years after that, the growth of the slave plantations. And then the revolutions: the American Revolution; the French Revolution and its Caribbean byproduct, the black Haitian revolution; the South American revolution, and the great names of that revolution, Francisco Miranda, Bolívar. From the undiscovered continent to the fraudulence and chaos of revolution; from the discovery and Columbus and those lush aboriginal Indian "gardens" he had seen in 1498 in the south of the island (along beaches I knew, wide beaches down which freshwater streams flowing from woodland cut little channels to the sea, where yellow Orinoco floods mingled with the Atlantic), from the discovery by Columbus, a man of medieval Europe, to the disappearance of the Spanish Empire in the nineteenth century—this was the historical span of my story. At the end of the period of my story, Trinidad, detached from South America and Venezuela and the Spanish Empire, was a full British West Indian colony, an island of sugar and slaves (the aboriginal population extinct, forgotten). And then, within years, slavery was to be abolished; sugar was to cease to be of value; and this little corner of the New World, all ideas of its promise now abandoned, was to sink into its long nineteenth-century colonial torpor. While revolutionary Venezuela, no longer part of the Spanish Empire, was beginning its century of chaos.

I could see, in the documents of this later period, the lineaments of the world I had grown up in. Asian-Indian immigrants had come in the period of nineteenth-century torpor. As a schoolboy I had assumed that torpor to be a constant, something connected with the geographical location of the island, the climate, the quality of the light. It had never occurred to me that the drabness I knew had been manmade, that it had causes, that there had been other visions and indeed other landscapes there.

Reading the transcript (miraculously preserved) of the trial of a Negro slave for the murder of another slave in Port of Spain in the Spanish time, and picking up inconsequential details about the houses, the street life, the backyard or slave-yard love affairs and jealousies, I found I could easily think myself back into that Port of Spain street of two hundred years before. I could see the people, hear the speech and accents. In that street I could see the origin of the Port of Spain street I had spent part of my childhood in—the street whose life and people had been the subject of my first book.

That my Port of Spain street, which as a child I had studied with such intentness, could be material had come to me as an illumination in 1955, fully five years after I had come to England, five years after "Gala Night" and "Life in London" and "Angela" and other attempts at "metropolitan" writing. That illumination was still to some extent with me. I was still working out, in my writing, all the implications of that discovery. But it was astonishing to me to discover that the street life I had written about had such a past, that the street life I had witnessed as a child, or something like it, had existed in Port of Spain in 1790. While Trinidad was still part of the great and old Spanish Empire; while slavery still existed, and was forty-four years away from being abolished; when the French Revolution was still new, and the black Haitian revolution was still a year away.

These references—to the Spanish Empire and the Haitian revolution—would not have occurred to me when I had lived on the street. Even when at school I had got to know (as part of school learning) the historical facts about the region, they did not have any imaginative force for me. The squalor and pettiness and dinginess—the fowl coops and backyards and servant rooms and the many little houses on one small plot and the cesspits—seemed too new; everything in Port of Spain seemed to have been recently put together; nothing suggested antiquity, a past. To this there had to be added the child's ignorance; and the special incompleteness of the Indian child, grandson of immigrants, whose past suddenly broke off, suddenly fell away into the chasm between the Antilles and India.

So, just as at the moment of takeoff in 1950 in the Pan American World Airways plane, I had been amazed by the brown-and-green pattern of fields which gave my island the appearance of other places photographed from the air, so now I was amazed, reading the documents of my island in London, by the antiquity of the place to which I belonged. Such simple things! Seeing the island as part of the globe, seeing it sharing in the antiquity of the earth! Yet these simple things came to me as revelations, so used had I been, in Trinidad, to roadside views, to seeing the agricultural colony at ground level, as it were, at the end of the great depression and the century-long colonial torpor. The landscape in my mind's eye during the writing of this book became quite different in its feel and associations from the landscape of the earlier books.

The labor which at the beginning I had thought of as the labor of six months stretched to two years. Ever since I had begun to identify my subjects I had hoped to arrive, in a book, at a synthesis of the worlds and cultures that had made me. The other way of writing, the separation of one world from the other, was easier, but I felt it false to the nature of my experience. I felt in this history I had made such a synthesis. But it tired me.

And many months before finishing this book I thought I would put an end to my time in England; shed weariness, not only the weariness of the writing, but also the weariness of being in England, the rawness of my nerves as a foreigner, the weariness of my insecurity, social, racial, financial; put an end to the distortion of my personality that had begun on the very day I had left home; put an end to that journey which—in spite of the returns and other journeys in the interim—had remained the fracturing one that had begun that day when the Pan American plane, taking me up a few thousand feet above the island where I had lived all my life, had shown me a pattern of fields and colors I had never seen before.

I sold my house. A few weeks' writing remained; and in the house to which I moved I began to feel very tired. I used to have two baths a day. The first bath was after breakfast, to wash away the effects of the sleeping pill that had kept my mind quiet during the night, had stopped me dealing in words, solving the problems of various parts of my book, had stopped me seeing all these problems come together into one unsolvable and alarming threat (in daylight I knew that writing problems were solved one by one). The second bath I had at the end of the day's work. So morning and evening for ten or fifteen minutes at a time I soaked in warm water. One morning the idea came to me that I was like a corpse at the bottom of a river or stream, tossing in the current. I gave up the morning soak. But the idea of the corpse was hard to get rid of. It came back to me every time I had a bath.

At last the book was handed in, and I could leave England. I had no long-term plans. I could think ahead only to the freedom, the freedom of not having a book to write any more, the freedom to spend each day as I chose, the freedom to move from place to place, to say good-bye. I intended to be a roamer for a while, to live the hotel life. I intended also—at last—to spend a little time in the United States. Before that, there was some journalism to do: pieces on the Caribbean islands of St. Kitts and Anguilla, then in the news; and a piece on Belize, British Honduras, my first piece on Central America.

I went first of all to my own island, Trinidad. I wanted to see the island where I had been living in a new way in my imagination for the last two years, the island I had restored, as it were, to the globe and for which now I felt a deep romance.

I found an island full of racial tensions and close to revolution. So, as soon as I had arrived at a new idea about the place, it had ceased to be mine.

Through writing—knowledge and curiosity feeding off one another—I had arrived at a new idea of myself and my world. But the world had not stood still. In 1950 in London, in the boardinghouse, I had found myself at the beginning of a great movement of peoples after the war, a great shaking up of the world, a great shaking up of old cultures and old ideas. And just as my own journey had brought about a change in me and set me looking for new ideas and a resolution beyond anything I had imagined as a bright schoolboy at Queen's Royal College in Port of Spain, so restlessness and the need for a new idea of the self had driven many other people, including the people I thought I had, in every sense of the word, left behind.

The muscular, weight-lifting Trinidad Negro in the tight, buttoned-up sports jacket in Puerto Rico, on the way to Harlem; the other black man on the S.S. *Columbia*, handling himself carefully, returning to the life in Germany he preferred to his life in the United States—these men in whom (unwillingly, since I was Indian and Hindu, full of the tragedy and glory of India) I saw aspects of myself, echoes of my own journey and the yearning at the back of that journey, these men had been isolated in 1950, vulnerable, their nerves raw.

There had since been many more like them. They hadn't all traveled to find fulfillment—or to be abraded. In Trinidad on my return now that rawness of nerves among black people had become like a communal festering. It couldn't be ignored. And so to return to my island in the Orinoco, after the twenty years of writing that had taken me to a romantic vision of the place, was to return to a place that was no longer mine in the way that it had been mine when I was a child, when I never thought whether it was mine or not.

That romance was now a private possession. The island meant other things to other people. There were other ways of responding to a knowledge of the world or an idea of the past, other ways of asserting the self. The Negro in the Puerto Rico hangar and the man on the *Columbia* had asserted propriety, their wish to live within an old order, their wish to be treated as others. Twenty years later the Negroes of Trinidad, following those of the United States, were asserting their separateness. They simplified and sentimentalized the past; they did not, like me, wish to possess it for its romance. They wore their hair in a new way. The hair that had with them been a source of embarrassment and shame, a servile badge, they now wore as a symbol of aggression. To keep my idea of romance, I had—as before in Trinidad, but now in a new way—to look selectively.

(That had been necessary in London as well. Part of my story, in the history I had just written, concerned the first British governor of the island, who had been accused of illegally ordering the torture of an under-age mulatto girl. All the witnesses in the case had been brought to London in 1803 and lodged for years at the expense of the government. One man had been lodged in Gerrard Street, Soho. The number of the house was given; the house still existed. But Gerrard Street, at the time I wrote, was full of Chinese from Hong Kong: restaurants, food shops, packing cases on the pavements. Could I see the past there? I could, when I looked above the Chinatown at ground level, the imperial backwash of the late-twentieth century. Above, in the flat facades, I could see a remnant of the late-eighteenth century, could imagine the rooms. My knowledge of London architecture had grown beyond the Dickens-inspired fantasies.)

Now in Trinidad—leaving aside the people and the anger that was like madness—to see the landscape I had created in my imagination for the last two years, to look for the aboriginal, pre-Columbus island, I had to ignore almost everything that leapt out at the eye, and almost everything in the vegetation I had been trained to see as tropical and local, part of our travel-poster beauty—coconut, sugarcane, bamboo, mango, bougainvillea, poinsettia—since all those plants and trees had been imported later with the settlement and the plantations. The landscape of the past existed only in fragments. To see one such fragment I looked at the drying-up mangrove swamp—green thick leaves, black roots, black mud—outside Port of Spain, ignoring the rubbish-strewn highway and the bent and battered median rail and the burning rubbish dump and the dust-blown shack settlement beyond the highway and the shacks on the hills of the Northern Range. From the top of Laventille Hill, among the shacks, I could imagine myself at the beginning of things if I looked selectively down at the Gulf of Paria— gray, leaden, never blue—and the islets in the gulf.

Private that view I forced on myself, private the romance. My vision of the history was not the vision that set the young black people marching in the streets and threatening another false revolution. The story had not stopped where my book had stopped; the story was going on. Two hundred years on, another Haiti was preparing, I thought: a wish to destroy a world judged corrupt and too full of pain, to turn one's back on it, rather than to improve it. After the book I had written, after my two years' exaltation, I saw this anger from two sides: from the side of the Negroes, the people with the hair, and also from the side of the Asian-Indian community, the people mainly threatened, not black, not white.

I went on after a fortnight to St. Kitts and Anguilla, to do my articles. St. Kitts was very small, thirty thousand people. It had no Asian-Indian population and therefore, for me, no personal complication. To the Negroes there I was just a stranger, someone not black, and with straight hair. Judgments could be as simple as that here. This absence of personal complication, the smallness, and the simplicity of the geography made the past extraordinarily graphic.

St. Kitts was the earliest British colony in the Caribbean, established in a region from which Spain had withdrawn. In shape it was —apart from a tail—round. It had a central mountain, forested at the top; and the slopes, covered with even sugarcane, ran all the way down to the sea. The island was edged with a narrow asphalt road, and there were the little houses of the workers, descendants of slaves, along this road. Sugar and slavery had created that simplicity, that unnaturalness in the vegetation and landscape.

In a shallow, dry ford not far from this littoral road there were boulders in the sugarcane. These boulders were incised with very rough figures: aboriginal Indian work: the earlier past, a reminder of the horror before slavery. No aboriginal Indians now existed in St. Kitts; they had been killed off three hundred years before by English and French; the rough carvings on those boulders were the only memorials the Indians had left. The accessible past was the English church and churchyard—in a tropical setting. No yews; instead, the palms known as royal palms, with straight and stout gray trunks, with grainy ridges all the way up like healed wounds, each ridge marking the place where a frond had grown. (And how different, in this colonial setting, were the associations of an English churchyard from the associations of a churchyard in England!) The past was also accessible in the eighteenth-century main square, called Pall Mall, of the little town, where newly arrived slaves from Africa were put up for sale after being rested in the barracoons. For one hundred and fifty years in St. Kitts the memory of this past had lain dormant. Now, in mimicry of Trinidad and the United States and other places, the memory revived, when the memory had really ceased to humiliate, serving instead as a political stimulus, a communal rhetoric of sentimentality and anger.

And in the island of Anguilla, even smaller than St. Kitts, not green, less productive, there was another aspect of that three-hundred-year-old slave simplicity. The people of Anguilla were not pure black; they had their own past; they were separated by that past from the people of St. Kitts. The population of Anguilla—there were about six thousand people in all—was made up of a few mulatto clans with British names. They had the vaguest idea of their history, of how they had got to that flat barrenness in the Caribbean Sea so far from the big continents, so far even from the other islands; some people spoke of a shipwreck.

I saw all this under the spell of the book I had written, the past I had discovered far away in England from the documents and felt I had almost created, as much as my novels had been created. And still under that spell, I went on later to Belize. To do that, I had to go to Jamaica first; from Jamaica there was one airplane a week.

It stopped at Guatemala City. In the dark airport building—beyond the jagged, mud-colored volcano craters that the airplane, landing, had shown: like giant anthills or like the extravagant towers of a fairy tale, on the level surfaces of which houses clung in clusters—in the lounge of the airport building, when I saw the faces of the short, plump girls behind the counter and saw the fresh-vegetable or fresh-pepper relishes in the glass case, I remembered that this was absolutely my first time in Central America, my first time in the land laid waste by Cortés and his successors. The girls were Chinese-looking, but they were not Chinese. That half familiarity made them very strange, remote. And those chopped-up vegetable relishes in the glass case— they suggested a matching strangeness. Foods distinguish cultures and even historical epochs. (What would the food of ancient Rome have been like?) And I remembered reading somewhere that the chocolate drink consumed by the jar in Montezuma's court was drunk cold and bitter and spiced.

In the glimpse of the strange food; in the strange, Chinese but not Chinese faces of the girls behind the counter; in the Spanish but not Spanish of the menu boards; in the fairy-tale volcanic spires of the land outside; in the vegetables and flowers that grew unnaturally large and bright in the high, clear, temperate air, I had an intimation of the wonder of the New World and the tragedy and pathos of the Spanish usurpation.

It was a short flight on to Belize City—Belize, British Honduras, the British intrusion on the coast of the Spanish Empire, the British mahogany colony, the origin of the Guatemalan claim to Belize (the subject of my article), and the source of much of the Georgian furniture in the London salerooms (but there was no mahogany in Belize now; it had all been cut down). On the coast there would have been among the Negroes descendants of the slave mahogany log cutters. Inland, there was a Mayan population and there were mighty Mayan ruins. In the shadow of one such ruin a Mayan boy (whatever his private emotions) giggled when I tried to talk to him about the monument. He giggled and covered his mouth; he seemed to be embarrassed. He was like a person asking to be forgiven for the absurdities of long ago; though there was no British colonial architecture worth the name in the mahogany colony, and all the monuments were Mayan. To the north, near the Mexican border, and still barely excavated, there was a whole Mayan town, abandoned centuries before the coming of the Spaniards, and now covered by forest, every tall, steep-stepped temple making a green hill.

From London to Trinidad to St. Kitts and Anguilla, Guatemala City and Belize: the journey might have been planned by a man wishing to move backwards in time, to see his history take concrete expression. So that for many weeks after finishing my book I continued to exist in its aura and exaltation, finding confirmation of the world I had dreamed about and created from the documents.

I had given myself a past, and a romance of the past. One of the loose ends in my mind had vanished; a little chasm filled. And though something like Haitian anarchy seemed to threaten my little island, and though physically I no longer belonged to the place, yet the romance by which I had attached it to the rest of the world continued to be possessed by me as much as the imaginative worlds of my other, fictional books.

Still, there was no word about the book I had written from publisher or agent in the United States. The time came when I had to move on. I stuck to my original plan, which was to go to the United States, to travel for a while, using the advance I had hoped to get from the book.

I left from Jamaica. It was February. The weather was bad in the north. The plane, just after it crossed Jamaica, landed again at Montego Bay. We stayed there for many hours. A hotel lunch was served by sulky, aggressive Negro waiters who had got too used to waiting on tourists and despised them. (Once, more than twelve years before, in a time of anxiety and almost grief, I had left for England from Port Antonio on a banana ship, at the other end of the island.) In the late afternoon we took off again, and the airplane flew and flew into the night and then it flew around in the night. We flew for hours. We flew until our fuel was exhausted and then we landed at Baltimore, to take on more fuel. Passengers were not allowed to get off; Baltimore was not an official port of entry. We took off again and flew some more. Like hijacked passengers. It was like the slow, slow flight of nineteen years before in the little plane of Pan American World Airways (a flight which had set me making notes in my cheap pad every hour). Now we were flying around and unable to land because of the weather, the snow. So we flew until we could land. We landed finally some hours after midnight.

No coins; no knowledge of the different sounds made by American telephones. And landing in that great cold, I found the next day or that day that my book had been judged unsuitable by the publisher who had commissioned it, that the decision had been made weeks before, while on my journalistic travels I had been uplifted by my own vision of romance, the product of the writing, coming at the end of a vocation that had lasted twenty years.

I had been briefly in New York twice since 1950, the year of my overnight stay. But the city I had seen on those later occasions had remained quite separate from the first city, the city of Raimu and *Marius* and *South Wind* and the gray, seemingly canopied sky. It was only now, in a time of anxiety that was like the anxiety of my first arrival, that I thought to look for that city. It was only now that I could begin to acknowledge the humiliation the taxi driver had caused me when he had cheated me; the humiliation I had felt at not being able to tip the Negro in the hotel.

I remembered the name of the hotel: the Wellington. I remembered its writing paper, on which for the sake of the drama I had written my diary on the night of my arrival. On this writing paper the letters that spelt out the name of the hotel sloped backwards, next to a drawing of what I suppose was the hotel building. Did the hotel still exist? My friend Robert Silvers, who had run my articles on St. Kitts and Anguilla in his paper, the *New York Review of Books*, said, "It's a hotel where musicians stay."

And yet it was astonishing to me to come upon it one day, a working hotel in a busy street. It should have been an archaeological site, to match its mythical nature in my mind. So modest at pavement level, in spite of the drawing of the skyscraper on the writing paper. Door, lobby, none of these things I had remembered: the hotel had lived in my imagination rather than memory like something from earliest childhood. An impression of darkness all around—I had arrived early in the morning, and was very tired, and nervous. And within that darkness, sensations rather than pictures: eating the chicken over the wastepaper basket, avoiding the scalding water in the bath cubicle. Like dreams rather than memories, and yet suited to the occasion, for me: for on that day space and time had become one. Both space and time separated me from my past at the end of that day; and the writer's journey that had begun that day had not ended.

I had planned to spend the advance for the book in the United States. There was no advance; but I stuck to my plan. I spent my own money. It was like watching myself bleed. Eventually I moved away, west. And in Victoria, British Columbia, in a brand-new rented flat with rented furniture I started work again. The writer's life: whatever one's mood, it was always necessary to pick oneself up and start again.

I started on a sequence about freedom and loss. The idea had come to me more than three years before, in East Africa. It had come suddenly, during the afternoon of a day-long drive between Nairobi in Kenya and Kampala in Uganda. It had come as a mischievous, comic idea, matching the landscape and exhilaration of the long drives I had been used to making in that part of Africa. Now the idea was all that I had at the moment in the way of writer's capital; and it was touched with the mood of the historical book I had written; my disappointment; and the homelessness, the drifting about, I had imposed on myself. I had as it were—and as had happened often before—become one of my own characters.

After some weeks I came to the end of my original impulse, and could go no further with the writing. I lost faith in what I was doing. The days in Victoria, which had passed easily when I was writing, began to drag. And then I faced the simple fact that as a man who made his living by writing in English and had no American audience, I had only England to go back to; that my wish to be free of the English heaviness had failed; that my departure from my island in 1950 —with all that it implied in homelessness and drift and longing—was final.

From Victoria to Vancouver. The very tall stewardesses in the very short skirts: a dreadful frivolity. Toronto; London. The grind and grind of the airplane engines, hour after hour; stages in a return I didn't want. So that twenty years on I was making a journey that mimicked my first. If twenty years before I could have been granted a glimpse of myself as a writer, someone with a talent that had been developed, and with books to his name, I would have considered myself blessed. The blessing I felt as a blessing still; but—as with the pain that attends love—the disappointment that had come with the blessing I felt as a terrible solitude.

I had no house. In London I rented a serviced flat in Dolphin Square. It consumed my money in steady installments, every week so much. The bills came up in a woman's handwriting: round, easy, the lower line of the writing creating a regular, almost scalloped pattern. The handwriting spoke of a woman absolutely at peace, sexually fulfilled, without anxiety. I envied her this calm, this absence of ambition. And when I went down to the office to settle the bill, I tried to work out which of the women it was—among the clerks who might have passed as wage slaves—which woman it was who, perhaps without knowing how blessed she was, had written out the figures of my fierce, debilitating demand.

The summer was over. For the first time in England, after nineteen years, I felt cold, imperfectly clad. Until this time I had had the same kind of clothes summer and winter and had not felt the need for a pullover or for warm underclothes or even an overcoat. I had longed for frosty weather, short days, electric lights in the early afternoon. Now, with this need for warm clothes, a need that seemed to grow and grow, I felt the winter as winter, darkness.

One day there were workmen somewhere below my window. They began to talk to one another. It was like listening to a play: different voices, careful dialogue, characters, sentences, ideas, showing off, acting, style. In all my time in England I had never heard workmen talk like that, among themselves, so loudly, in the open air, for so long. It was a little frightening, this eavesdropping on what was like an unknown country. I knew another side of England: Oxford, people in broadcasting, writers. I had never been brought into contact like this with the country I had been living in for so long. I hadn't read about working men like the ones I was now listening to; I hadn't seen films about them.

I went eventually to stay in a private house in the town of Gloucester. It was a wet day. The railway station was cold, damp, indicating the nearness of the River Severn. Gloucester, away from its grand cathedral, was a small, mean, common town. It was not a place I would have gone to out of choice. But now it offered a house, shelter, hospitality.

The house was at the edge of the town: mean houses making mean the fields they had been set down among: the pollarded willows, the narrow tainted brooks in which industrial litter floated, willows and brooks like features of city slum. It was not a house I would have chosen. But it was a home for someone and had been furnished like that and had the atmosphere. It was welcoming.

At lunchtime on this first day the house also offered a coal fire. The French windows looked out onto a long narrow garden, scrupulously stripped and forked over for the winter. Far off were the sounds of a railway marshaling yard—oddly comforting at this distance. Everything about this house was welcoming and good. And in this unambitious setting I felt protected, isolated, far from every wounding thing I had known. For the first time in many weeks I felt at ease.

That afternoon, in the front room of the house, where the furniture was old but cared for, I looked for the first time for weeks at the typescript of the book I had tried to get started on in Victoria, the sequence about freedom and loss. I found it better than I had during the writing. I even saw the sentence where it had come alive—a sentence written out of concentration, from within the mood created by the words. That critical creative moment had been missed by me in Victoria, perhaps because of my anxiety about what was to follow in the writing; and perhaps as well because of my anxiety about what was to follow Victoria.

Now, recognizing the validity of that good sentence, I surrendered to the pictures the words created, the other pictures they trailed. I summoned up again, and sank back into, the mood of Africa, the mood out of which the sentence had been written. I heard—or created—snatches of dialogue from different stages of my story; this particular story in the sequence was full of dialogue. I made brief notes. And it was only when I came back from the mood or came out of the concentration that I understood how far away I had been.

In my early days as a writer, when my talent was declaring itself,

I had developed (or discovered) this ability to concentrate and to compose in the midst of harassment, which was an ability (given a clear run of an hour or two—shorter periods didn't work) suddenly to withdraw, to shed even acute anxiety, like an engine cutting out when too much was asked of it, to push the world to one side and to enter my writing as I might enter a walled garden or enclosure (the image that often came to my mind). Writing strengthened me; it quelled anxiety. And now writing restored me again. My book was given back to me. I began to write slowly, day by day.

The book of the summer was given back to me in the winter. Without the book and the daily act of creation I do not know how I would have gone through that difficult time. With me, everything started from writing. Writing had brought me to England, had sent me away from England; had given me a vision of romance; had nearly broken me with disappointment. Now it was writing, the book, that gave savor, possibility, to each day, and took me on night after night.

I had intended to stay for a week or so in Gloucester. I stayed nearly three months, unwilling, apart from everything else, to cut myself off from the good magic of the place.

Several weeks of original composition lay ahead of me when I left Gloucester and went to Wiltshire, to the valley. For the first four days it rained and was misty; I could hardly see where I was. It was a good way of making the transition from the front room of the Gloucester house, which had been kind to me, kind to my African creation. It was good for the book, which was still in the delicate, suggestible state of its first draft. When a book was in that state, things around me could get written into it, could become part of the emotional charge of the narrative and, once written into a book, hard to take out. So I tried, during the composing of a book, to avoid disturbance. And that Wiltshire valley fog was right.

In my imagination, at that stage of my story, I was living in a made-up Africa, a fairy-tale landscape that mixed (according to my need) the high, rainy plateau of Rwanda with the wet, terraced, cultivated hills of Kigezi in western Uganda.

As a child in Trinidad I had projected everything I read onto the

Trinidad landscape, the Trinidad countryside, the Port of Spain streets. (Even Dickens and London I incorporated into the streets of Port of Spain. Were the characters English, white people, or were they transformed into people I knew? A question like that is a little like asking whether one dreams in color or in black and white. But I think I transferred the Dickens characters to people I knew. Though with a half or a quarter of my mind I knew that Dickens was all English, yet my Dickens cast, the cast in my head, was multiracial.) That ability to project what I read onto Trinidad, the colonial, tropical, multiracial world which was the only world I knew, that ability diminished as I grew older. It was partly as a result of my increasing knowledge, self-awareness, and my embarrassment at the workings of my fantasy. It was also partly because of the writers. Very few had the universal child's eye of Dickens. And that gift of fantasy became inoperable as soon as I came to England in 1950. When I was surrounded by the reality, English literature ceased to be universal, since it ceased to be the subject of fantasy.

Now, in Wiltshire in winter, a writer now rather than a reader, I worked the child's fantasy the other way. I projected the solitude and emptiness and menace of my Africa onto the land around me. And when four days later the fog lifted and I went walking, something of the Africa of my story adhered to the land I saw.

I walked out between the stripped beeches and between the old, untrimmed yews, solid and dark green; and along the public road, past the cottages of flint and brick and thatch (but not yet seen clearly), and up the hill beside the windbreak to the barn at the top. I saw Stonehenge from a gap in the windbreak: a very wide view, the downs pimpled with tumuli and barrows. I walked down the hill to the farm buildings at the bottom. I asked a man the way to Stonehenge. He told me to go on past the farm buildings and then turn to the right, along the wide grassed way. Around the farm the ground was muddy, churned up by tractor tires. Water, puddles, reflected the gray sky. The grass on the grassed way, up the slope to the barrows from which a closer view of Stonehenge was to be had, the grass was tall and wet and entangling.

Another day I walked along the public road in another direction, towards Salisbury. I came to a marked footpath. It was muddy, the mud deep. I turned back after about two or three hundred yards. (As once, four years before, in Kigezi in Uganda, getting out of the car one rainy afternoon to be in a village with separate little terraced hills and huts and afternoon smoke, wishing to be in the middle of that enchanting view, I had found myself mired in animal excrement, tormented by the stares and constant approaches of Africans, who were puzzled by my intrusion, and I had had to turn away, get back into the car, drive on.)

I didn't explore too much on the public road after that. I left all the marked public footpaths untrodden. I stuck to the downs, the grassed droveway, the walks around the farm at the bottom of the valley. And I continued easily in that rhythm of creation and walk, Africa in the writing in the morning, Wiltshire in the hour-and-a-half or so after lunch. I projected Africa onto Wiltshire. Wiltshire—the Wiltshire I walked in—began to radiate or return Africa to me. So man and writer became one; the circle became complete.

The Africa of my imagination was not only the source countries —Kenya, Uganda, the Congo, Rwanda; it was also Trinidad, to which I had gone back with a vision of romance and had seen black men with threatening hair. It also now became Wiltshire. It was also the land created by my pain and exhaustion, expressed in the dream of the exploding head. A little over a year before, towards the end of the book about the New World, I had had the waking fantasy of myself as a corpse tossing lightly among the reeds at the bottom of a river (a river like the one in the Pre-Raphaelite painting of the drowned Ophelia, reproduced in the *Nelson's West Indian Reader* I had used in my elementary school in Trinidad, a river that turned out to be like the river in Wiltshire at the back of my cottage). Now every night at some stage an explosion in my head, occurring in a swift dream, giving me the conviction that this time I had to die, that this time I could not survive the great, continuing noise, awakened me.

Such violence in my Africa, in the security of my stone cottage, where I had a coal fire every night! So much had gone into that Africa of my fantasy. As a point of rest, as a refreshment, a promise of release, I allowed myself to play, lightly, with the ancient Mediterranean idea that had come to me from the Chirico painting, *The Enigma of Arrival.*

The empty wharf; the glimpse of the mast of the ancient ship; the doorways; the wicked, hypnotizing city towards which the two cloaked figures walk.

For two days they had sailed, staying close to the shore. On the third day the captain wakened his deck passenger and pointed to the city on the shore. "There. You are there. Your journey's over." But the passenger, looking at the city in the morning haze, seeing the unremarkable city debris floating out on the sea, unremarkable though the city was so famous—rotten fruit, fresh branches, bits of timber, driftwood—the passenger had a spasm of fear. He sipped the bitter honey drink the captain had given him; he pretended to get his things together; but he didn't want to leave the ship.

But he would have to land. Such adventures were to come to him within the cutout, sunlit walls of that city. So classical that city, seen from the ship; so alien within, so strange its gods and cults. My hero would end as a man on the run, a man passionate to get away to a clearer air. In desperation he was to go through a doorway, and he was to find himself on the wharf again. But there was no mast above the walls of the wharf. No ship. His journey—his life's journey—had been made.

It did not occur to me that the story that had come to me as a pleasant fantasy had already occurred, and was an aspect of my own.

I had no means of knowing that the landscape by which I was surrounded was in fact benign, the first landscape to have that quality for me. That I was to heal here; and, more, that I was to have something like a second life here; that those first four days of fog—before I went out walking on the downs—were like a rebirth for me. That after twenty years in England, I was to learn about the seasons here at last; that at last (as for a time as a child in Trinidad) I would learn to link certain natural events, leaves on trees, flowers, the clarity of the river, to certain months. That in the most unlikely way, at an advanced age, in a foreign country, I was to find myself in tune with a landscape in a way that I had never been in Trinidad or India (both sources of different kinds of pain). That all the resolutions and franknesses I was going to arrive at through my writing were to be paralleled by the physical peace of my setting; that I was to be cleansed in heart and mind; and that for ten years I was to turn this landscape of down and barrow, so far from my own, into the setting for concentrated work.

The man who went walking past Jack's cottage saw things as if for the first time. Literary allusions came naturally to him, but he had grown to see with his own eyes. He could not have seen like that, so clearly, twenty years before. And having seen, he might not have found the words or the tone. The simplicity and directness had taken a long time to get to him; it was necessary for him to have gone through a lot.

A long time later, seeking as always a synthesis of my material, my worlds, my own developing way of seeing, I thought of the present book and returned to live in the past. And it was actually during the writing of the first chapter or section that I remembered something from the first week of my time in London, when I was staying in Angela's boardinghouse. My writer's ambition, my social inexperience and anxiety, had suppressed so much of that empty time, had expunged so much from my memory.

I used to go out doing the sights. It was what tourists did. And one day, somewhere in central London, perhaps along the Embankment, I saw someone from the S.S. *Columbia* sitting on a bench below a statue. He was like part of the monument. He was in a dark suit; a small man hot in the month of August (the month and the weather were fitted together later by the writer). He was tired. He had been doing the sights and possibly having as little idea of what he was doing as I had: travel was a pleasure so much in the mind, so much something for later narrative.

He was a butler, I thought, the man from the *Columbia*. Perhaps he had told me that on the ship; or perhaps I had made it up, finding in him a resemblance to a butler in some film. He was slightly offhand with me. It was as the night watchman had said during the gala night on the *Columbia*, when he had lectured those of us who were outside the dance lounge on the quirks of human behavior. After three days on a ship everyone was faithless, he had said; on shore, though, people became themselves again and forgot shipboard romances and even acquaintances.

The butler was going on to France. A week there—no doubt in Paris: more sights—and then another ship would take him from Le Havre or Cherbourg back to New York, and the wandering holiday life would be over. He would be back home, free of hotels and the daily tramping and the fatigue and the strange food. And I passionately wanted to go with him. I didn't want to be his companion or talk to him or be in his house or apartment. I wanted to be as he was at that moment, a man on the move. I passionately wanted, though hardly arrived in London, to be free of London. I didn't want to go back home, though; I knew there was nothing there. I just wanted that day, trying to engage the offhand butler in conversation, trying to claim acquaintance with him in the strangeness of London, I wanted that day to feel that England was temporary for me too.

Like the character in the story that came to me twenty years after, when I first came to the valley, I wanted to stay with the ship.

*M*ORE THAN ten years after I had moved to the valley, when I was almost at the end of my time there, my time in the manor cottage, my second life, I was strongly reminded of my first week in England. I had a letter from Angela.

I hadn't heard from her or about her for thirty years. Even her name had ceased to be familiar; it was something I had to fumble for when I thought back to those early days. And this letter from Angela was more than a word or a note. It was many pages long, written over many days and, as the handwriting showed, written in many moods.

It was a round, fluent, thin-nibbed hand, now erect, now leaning to the right. Now the lines were straight, now crooked; now the letters were carefully shaped, now they moved up and down and were left unfinished. But the writing had an essential mode: it was the feminine English hand, round and fluent, the round shapes of the letters occasionally flattened, becoming wider than they were tall, egg shapes, speaking of a passive sensuality. The Englishness of the handwriting was a surprise; it was as though, purely by living in England, Angela had acquired that hand. The envelope carried the postmark of a town in Buckinghamshire: middle-class, commuter country.

The surname Angela gave (in brackets) at the end of her letter was English. I had forgotten her Italian surname, having seldom used it; but this English name seemed odd, seemed not to go with the person I knew. Yet she had given me an English name the first day we met. She called me Victor. She said that my Hindi or Sanskrit name was too hard for her and she didn't intend to try to use it. Thirty years later she remembered the name. *Dear Victor.* I was surprised. But perhaps no one (except very famous actors and dancers and sportsmen and people in the entertainment world who live by the physical admiration they receive from other people) perhaps no one forgets an admirer; and this may be truer of women, who as they get older must check over and over and count lovers and adventures.

Dear Victor. And it worked for me, too: through all the intervening sensualities, all the uses to which I had put my body, the name Angela had given me called up the enigma and false promise of that early time in London, and Angela's waitress clothes and red lips; it even called up the feel of her fur coat (in which, according to her story, she had run away from her lover's room or flat one night when he had turned too violent); it called up the feel of her breasts, the liberty she permitted in her room when other people—her friends, displaced people from Europe and North Africa—were there. It called up—what I had very nearly forgotten, because there had been so much real writing since—my attempts in those days, out of my great ignorance, to turn Angela into suitable material. How often I had written about her, her breasts, her fur coat; how often I had introduced myself; how often I had improved or sought to improve everybody's circumstances!

She had heard me on the radio, she wrote; she had heard me many times and even seen me on television, but hadn't thought of troubling me until now. She reintroduced herself. And she rewrote her past as once I had done. She said she "managed" the "hotel" in "Kensington" where I had stayed before going up to Oxford. Nothing about the Italian restaurant in the Earl's Court Road. "I don't think you know but I had a daughter in Italy my sister was looking after her until I could send for her. Well Victor this daughter is now a grown woman of thirty-five with children and a lovely baby girl of her own and speaking English you wouldn't know she was Italian." That was the end of the first part of the letter, all of it written in one kind of handwriting, regular, swift, strong, faltering only towards the end.

After this the lines began to slope, the letters leaning more sharply, the spacing irregular: much time, perhaps days, had passed since she had written the first part of the letter. "I used to walk out with someone you didn't like at all. And to tell you the truth Victor I didn't care for him all that much. But it was the war, things looked different then, you get mixed up with strange people. You hate the priests you don't care what they say and you know that youth is ignorant."

"Walk out"—extraordinary language. I had never heard the phrase used by anybody. So dainty, quaint, so old-fashioned sounding and coy for Angela's association with a violent man who was a criminal and was probably in jail when I got to know her. They had met during the war in Italy. She had been glad to follow him from the mess of Italy after the war to the peace and order of London—though of London she would have known as little as I.

"It got bad after you went to Oxford and stopped coming to the hotel I was getting like one of these battered wives you read about in the papers these days only I wasn't a wife. And he started coming to the hotel and carrying on many a time I thought I was for the sack. But then one day somebody came to the hotel. A tall man in a tweed jacket and the second time he talked to me with his level steady gaze I felt he had been sent by God himself Victor you know I am no great believer but I saw the hand of God there I must say. I went to the Catholic church and lighted a candle which I hadn't done since I was a child. When your good friend heard what was happening he came over hotfoot to the hotel ready for blood I don't know what he expected. But as soon as he saw the man he had to deal with he went crazy it was pathetic it made me ashamed he was like a man ready to cry. Class is class, I saw it then, the English Gentleman Victor you cannot beat it, you cannot say you know England until you know the English Gentleman. Our good friend went away with his tail between his legs but then up to his old tricks as per usual he began to telephone me effing and dashing every other word going on and on about the tweed coat."

The man in the tweed coat married Angela—though again she knew as little of his background or the life to which he was taking her as she had done of the man she had first followed to England. She brought her daughter over from Italy; and they all lived in Buckinghamshire until her husband died. In Angela's letter those many happy years were passed over quickly; the man who had given her those happy years was hardly a presence.

Most of Angela's letter was about matters that had happened since the death of her husband, her savior. Most of Angela's letter was about her daughter, the daughter whom Angela had left behind as a child in Italy for some years, to follow—for very good reasons—her rough lover to London. The daughter had been brought over to live in Angela's Buckinghamshire house, had been sent to the local school. But suddenly, growing up, the daughter had declared herself Angela's enemy. The daughter's boyfriends had been wrong, according to Angela; and then the daughter's husband had been very wrong, had even been to jail. Daughter and husband tormented Angela, and this had become especially bad since Angela's husband had died. They had turned their children against Angela; they had forbidden Angela to come to their house.

This was the burden of the largest part of Angela's letter. It was of this, rather than of the past, that she had settled down to write. This was the letter she had written at different times, in different moods, with different degrees of stability, in different versions of the handwriting she would no doubt have picked up from both her daughter, educated at the local school, and her husband. And this part of the letter was hard to read. It was very much like the letters I received sometimes from obsessed people: addressed to me, but not really meant for me. I couldn't read it in a connected way. I read it in snatches, jumping from page to page.

"But this I know Victor the little girl will grow up and learn to use the phone though her mother doesn't think so and the little girl will want to telephone her gran who loves her. You have my address and telephone number Victor I don't have yours, please telephone and let us meet and talk over the good old days always the best I say."

I read this letter in my cottage. I felt my surroundings very acutely, felt their foreignness, felt the unrelatedness of my presence there. Beyond the garden wall, and where the water meadows began, were the great aspens. There had been three; they had made a giant fan; I had watched them grow. In the gales of one winter I had actually been watching when two of the giant aspens had snapped, twice, leaving jagged, raw stumps. The stumps had grown to look less raw; there were powerful shoots from the stumps. I had trained myself not to feel grief for things like that; I had trained myself in the belief that change was constant. On the other side of the cottage, the view in one direction was of the water meadows, seen beyond the fast-growing wild sycamores and the tall, unpruned box hedge. In the other direction there were the old beeches, the yews, the dark, overshadowed lane to the road. Though I had never noted it down, I had had an intimation of a world in flux, a disturbed world, when I had first seen Angela and her friends in Earl's Court. We had both, it seemed, continued to travel versions of our old route; we had both made circular journeys, returning from time to time to something like our starting point.

I didn't go to see her. I didn't telephone her. It would have been physically hard for me to go to where she was. And her disturbance, her instability—which perhaps had always existed and which perhaps as an ardent young man I couldn't see, preferring to see the shape and color of her mouth—her instability, created no doubt by the terrible war and then her time in a London which she could hardly have understood, that was too unsettling to me. I preserved my own balance with difficulty.

I was also deep in a book. My thoughts were of a whole new generation of young people in remote countries, made restless and uncertain in the late-twentieth century not by travel but by the undoing of their old certainties, and looking for false consolation in the mind-quelling practices of a simple revealed religion. Angela took me back to the past. I wasn't living there, intellectually and imaginatively, any longer. My world and my themes had come to me long after I had ceased to write of Angela.

Her letter was soon covered over by the paper that accumulated in various piles in various places in my cottage. After some months it would not have been possible for me to get at it easily. She never wrote again.

IVY

I NEVER spoke to my landlord. And in all my years as his tenant I saw him—or had a glimpse of him—only once. (There was another glimpse; but that was even briefer, was from a distance, and was of his back.) The true glimpse came on the public road one afternoon, at the end of my walk; and I was so little prepared for it, and it was so brief, that I couldn't say afterwards what my landlord looked like.

That day I hadn't done the walk up the lark hills to the barrows and the closer view of Stonehenge. I had done the other, shorter walk, on flatter ground. At the farmyard at the bottom of the hill I had turned down the wide straight stretch of the droveway, bisected for some time now by the barbed-wire fence.

It was there, down the free part of the wide way, that I had seen Jack driving back early one Sunday afternoon after his midday drinking at the pub, bumping and banging along in his old car, plowing through the tussocky grass like a launch in choppy water. And it was along that way that on the Christmas Saturday before he died he had driven his car twice, once out, once back, to have his last evening with his friends in the pub.

On the barbed-wire fence there were still the shredded remains of one or two of the plastic-sack paddings Jack's father-in-law had rolled at his crossing places. And at intervals down that way there were the older relics Jack would have known. On one side, the empty, abandoned gray beehives set down in the grass in two crooked rows; on the other side, in the shade of bush and silver birch, the abandoned gypsy caravan with its cambered roof and variegated colors, the caravan itself still appearing in working order. Further on, on that same side, past the young wood, there was the old hayrick shaped like a cottage and covered with the black plastic sheeting that had over the years grown ragged at the edges, had lost its shine and its ability to crackle, and had thinned and weathered to a texture like that of a faded rose petal or the skin of a very old person. Beyond that, the mysterious house ruin, all walls, with a boundary line of sycamores that had grown tall, those regularly spaced sycamores now like part of the mystery of the place. When they were planted, and for many years afterwards, the seedlings or saplings would have seemed far apart and would have made no impression in the wide way. Now the crowns of foliage on the sturdy trunks met and cast a solid cold shade in which even in the hottest summer no grass could grow; the earth, though flinty, was always damp and black around that ruin, like ground trodden on by sheep.

The straight stretch of the droveway ended in an abrupt bare slope marked with lines and welts and indentations that suggested old agriculture or old fortifications. The way itself curved, to run beside this slope, which, though not high, shut out a further view and led the eye up to the sky. Nothing now on that striated, antique hillside; hardly pasture. Only a water trough, no grass around it, the flinty soil trampled into black mud. From time to time steers (on the upper slope outlined against the old sky) were penned there, blank, healthy, heavy-bellied, responsive to every human approach, waiting now only for the covered trailer and the trip along the winding valley road to the slaughterhouse in the town.

On the other side of the way there was a wide tilled field that led gently up to a wood. The tilling of such flinty soil (and the flints could be big and heavy) was new. I had been told that it had started only during the war, when the discovery was made that (in addition, of course, to fertilizer) ground like that needed to be merely scratched rather than deeply plowed. In the wood at the top were reared pheasants for shooting, pheasants which, when grown, wandered all over the valley. It was in that wood that I had gone walking during my very first week in the valley and, in a muddy lane overhung with trees I had later learned to be blackthorn, I had met Jack's father-in-law.

The droveway here was deeply rutted, tall grass growing in tufts on the ridges, the ruts themselves narrow and bare and flinty, with loose gravel. Hard to walk on; ankle-turning.

On this path one day—during my first or second year, when hares still delighted me, and I looked for them during every walk—I had seen the dusty, ragged, half-rotted-away carcass of a hare. The area was famous for its hares; a traveler in the previous century, William Cobbett, had once seen, not far away from here, a field full of hares. And there were still hare shoots—curiously feudal occasions in one way, with hired beaters driving the animals over the downs towards the shooters, hidden behind bales of hay on the droveway; and at the same time occasions on which landowners and laborers and men from the small towns round about were at one, united by old country instincts. Perhaps the hare had been shot during one of those shoots; perhaps the wounded animal had been mangled and dragged out to the droveway by a dog. Dead and soon useless, soon less than carrion, it had perhaps been turned over inquisitively by a farm worker or a walker, kicked or pushed along a deep rut and left finally to dry and molder away.

What mighty hind legs! Folded in death. (Such a skeleton, or something that reminded me of it, I saw again more than ten years later on a high rocky islet midway in the narrow channel between southwestern Trinidad and Venezuela. This was an islet of pelicans and frigate birds, but pelicans above all. Here pelicans lived and also died. In the central dips of the islet the ground was springy with guano; and on the rock ledges there were whole pelican skeletons, as though, knowing themselves to be in their sanctuary, the big birds had folded their powerful wings and settled down to die. The pelican bones on that islet—called by the Spaniards Soldado, "the soldier," and after-wards by the English Soldier's Rock—looked like the strong hind legs, bones within dusty fur, of that hare.)

The antique, bare slope at one side of the droveway receded and became high and steep, so that there was something like a field or paddock on that side of the droveway. There was a pond in this field; and at various points down the high, steep slope trees had been planted. The inexplicable little pond, the abruptness and height of the slope, the scattered trees—the land here had a feeling of oddity, ancientness, even sanctity.

The elms in the paddock or field at the foot of the steep slope had all been cut down—like the elms all over the valley—and showed now only as level stumps sawn off about a foot or so above the ground. There were one or two horses in the paddock. Unbridled, broad-backed, with muzzles perhaps a little too sloping, they looked heavy, primitive animals, and as emblematic as everything else in that setting: the pond, the paddock, the elm stumps, the steep green slope with the scattered trees, each tree casting a perfect shadow. As though, as in a primitive painting, every element here had to be perfectly realized, separately realized. In the very simplicity and clarity of the view there was a kind of mystery: it linked neither to the bare downs to which it led in one direction, nor to the lush river vegetation, the water meadows, to which it led in the other direction.

The rutted droveway, running past little houses and gardens (one of them the old farm manager's house, with its full, many-colored suburban-English garden), became paved and then, very quickly losing mystery, met the public road. This road ran on a ledge or cutting in the down just above the river. It was the road Jack, after his drinking that Sunday lunchtime, had decided not to take. There was a steep drop down to the river. To the right there was a weir. And, beyond, water meadows that were like the water meadows Constable had painted one hundred and fifty years before.

After antiquity, Constable and also the more recent past. It was of Augustus John that I had first thought, very vaguely, when I had seen the gypsy caravan across the droveway from Jack's cottage and the old farm buildings. Then (after I had got to know the book) the caravan brought to mind, at the same time as it gave a reality to, the drawings and colored illustrations by E. H. Shepard for *The Wind in the Willows*. That book itself, about a river like the one I now saw, still seemed new, contemporary. And the paint on the caravan—which appeared to be in such good order and seemed to have been temporarily parked—was still so bright that it was easy to imagine that the caravan might be on the road again one day, and that just around the corner on the droveway (by the silver birches, say) one might come upon the old world—in which that caravan once had a real place—going on.

Just in this way now the water meadows had the effect (in one corner of the mind) of abolishing the distance between Constable and the present: the painter, the man with his colors and brushes and boards, seemed as near and contemporary as what he made us now see: the water channels and pollarded willows he had settled down one day to paint. This idea of the painter, this glimpse of the painter's view, made the past ordinary. The past was like something one could stretch out and reach; it was like something physically before one, like something one could walk in.

Shepard and Constable—they had imposed their vision on an old landscape. But on their vision was imposed something else now, a modern picturesque. Beeches as old as the century lined the narrow road. Hundreds, thousands, of young beeches grew on the leaf-strewn slope between the main row of beeches at the edge of the down and the asphalted road; and thousands more on the steeper slope from the road down to the river. All the shades of delicate light-shot green, of overlapping, transparent green leaves, hung over the road. This was the scenic drive the taxi drivers of the town took visitors along.

The beeches had been planted at the turn of the century by the father of my landlord and were now like a natural—wasting—monument of the father's grandeur. This grandeur had come from the consolidation and extension in imperial times of a family fortune established

earlier, during the beginnings of the industrial revolution. The family
had its roots elsewhere; many branches of the family now flourished
elsewhere. But my landlord lived on here—where once his family had
owned nearly all the land and many of the houses—in a few acres
beside the river.

And it was here, on this road, at the end of my walk, below the
trees planted by his father before he, the son, had been born, that I
had my first and only true glimpse of my landlord.

It was a confused glimpse. The road was narrow, curving. I was
nervous of the car, as I was nervous of all cars or vehicles on this
stretch of road with its blind curves. Then—rather late—I saw that
it was the manor car; then I thought to look for Mr. Phillips, and to
acknowledge him. Mr. Phillips was smiling. It was a friendly, happy
smile, and it was odd in a man whose manner and instincts were au-
thoritarian and protective, and whose usual expression in public was
one of sternness and irritability. The smile, then, the conviviality and
relaxedness of it, told me that the occasion was special and his passenger was special.

And I knew at once, I had an immediate idea, that the person sitting beside Mr. Phillips was my landlord, the man in the manor, the
man I had got used to not seeing. And before—forgetting Mr. Phillips's smile and the dangers of the road—I could properly focus on
the stranger, the car had gone. This was my only glimpse of my landlord, his face; and I wasn't sure what I had seen.

I had an impression of a round face, a bald head, a suit (or the
jacket of a brown suit), a benign expression. What I most clearly
remembered—it was the detail I was sure of: not the kind of detail
that imagination could supply—was a low, slow wave of a hand. A
wave just above the dashboard, so that from the road I saw the tips
of his fingers making an arc at the bottom of the windshield.

We had never met. Mr. Phillips must have told him who I was;
and—in spite of the bad sight he was said to have, one of his many
afflictions—he must have seen me before I had seen him. And secure
in the car, with Mr. Phillips at his side, he must have seen me more
clearly than I had seen him. My glimpse had been so hurried, so shot

through with the confusion of the moment—coming at the end of a swift sequence of little alarms and recognitions—that I wasn't sure whether my imagination, as instantaneously as in a dream, hadn't suggested certain of the details I thought I had seen, to supply me with a picture of the man I had more or less created in my head already.

I had an impression of benignity above the wave. But I had cause to question that impression when I spoke to Mr. Phillips on the telephone in the evening. With a laugh that was like a carry-over from the smiling good humor I had seen in him in the car that afternoon, he said yes, the man I had seen in the car was my landlord. And then, as though explaining my doubt, Mr. Phillips said, "He always wears dark glasses in the car. Otherwise his stomach gets upset, and then he gets a migraine." How then, if he had been wearing dark glasses, had I seen a benign expression in his eyes?

So this glimpse of my landlord—this glimpse of someone unexpectedly ordinary—made him, after all, more mysterious. And more than the man, it was the occasion that was memorable: the manor car with the descendant of the manor builder and the planter of the trees, driving below the beeches on the ledge at the rim of the down, just above the river and the water meadows. So that more than ever for me the personality of the man continued to be expressed by his setting, by these beeches on the public road, by the permanently closed front gate of the manor and the overgrown garden at the back.

My imagination had given me a glimpse of a benign elderly man in a brown jacket making a shy wave from his car. This picture—created in a flash as the car had gone by—answered my own need. It was how I wished to think of the man in whose grounds I had so unexpectedly, for the first time in my adult life, found myself at peace.

I soon learned that the picture wasn't true. Neither was the other picture which I carried, a contrary, slightly sinister picture I had allowed my fantasy to work up from details given then and at other times by Mr. Phillips: of a fat, round-faced man buttoned up in a suit, with dark glasses and a hat, being taken out for a spin through countryside he would never otherwise see; being taken out for thrilling but safe glimpses (safe, as for a child standing behind a rail at the top of

a tower and looking down) of the world from which he had withdrawn; yet never too thrilling, not London, for instance; just the countryside, and the houses of a few people he knew very well, and some
hotels on the south coast, where he went in fine weather to have lunch
or to get his hair cut. (This last detail, given me quite innocently by
Mr. Phillips one day, added long, lank hair to the dark-glassed and
otherwise formally suited recluse of my fantasy: I saw my landlord
being at once pushed and supported into the lobby of some Victorian
hotel by Mr. Phillips, Mr. Phillips holding on with both hands to the
left arm of his charge, while the free right hand of my landlord blindly
groped.)

Neither picture, neither the man I thought I had seen, nor the man
I had invented, answered to what I was told about my landlord by
people in London who knew him and sometimes came to visit him.
That other man, coming to me in fragments as it were, remained far
away.

A pampered childhood here, in the grounds where I now walked
about. In the cold shade of the overgrown orchard there was a round,
two-story children's house, solidly built, thatched, and still more or
less whole, though the surrounding vegetation was partly strangled
and decayed, as in true forest. In the room downstairs there was a real
fireplace, with inset stone or concrete shelves in the wall on either
side, and with ladder steps to the upper room, which had dormer windows in the conical thatched roof. More than a doll's house on a grand
scale, and yet less than a child's play house: an adult's idea, rather, of
a children's house, with nothing left to the imagination.

After that pampered, protected childhood, a young manhood of
artistic talent and promise and of social frivolity. I was shown photographs of those days both by Mr. Phillips and by Bray, the car-hire
man, whose father had worked all his life at the manor. Bray lived in
the flint and brick cottage his father had bought long ago from the estate; but though Bray was now independent of the manor and proud
of it, refusing even to serve people in the manor, he had all kinds of
manor souvenirs to show and he liked showing them. Blurred black

and white photographs of parties in the grounds, the gardens not yet grown, undergrown; photographs of young people sitting in uncertain light (dusk or dawn?) on the rails of new timber bridges over the creeks in the water meadows. (Photographs—snapshots—melancholy in their effect: each snapshot, capturing a moment of time, with all its unconsidered details, forcing one to think of the tract of time that had followed, and being a kind of memento mori in the way a good painting of the same occasion—charged with the spirit and labor of the painter—would never have been.)

Then in early middle age, after the parties, after the second war, a disturbance of some sort, a morbid, lasting depression, almost an illness, resulting in withdrawal, hiding, a retreat to the manor, complicated after a while by physical disorders and—finally—age.

I was his opposite in every way, social, artistic, sexual. And considering that his family's fortune had grown, but enormously, with the spread of the empire in the nineteenth century, it might be said that an empire lay between us. This empire at the same time linked us. This empire explained my birth in the New World, the language I used, the vocation and ambition I had; this empire in the end explained my presence there in the valley, in the cottage, in the grounds of the manor. But we were—or had started—at opposite ends of wealth, privilege, and in the hearts of different cultures.

Twenty years before, when I was trying to write at the Earl's Court boardinghouse, residence in the grounds of the manor would have seemed suitable "material." But the imperial link would then have been burdensome. It would have tormented me as a man (or boy) to be a racial oddity in the valley. And I would have been able as a writer (at that time) to deal with the material only by suppressing certain aspects of myself—the very kind of suppression and concealment that narrative of a certain sort encouraged and which had led me, even as an observer, eager for knowledge and experience, to miss much.

But the world had changed; time had moved on. I had found my talent and my subject, ever unfolding and developing. My career had changed; my ideas had changed. And coming to the manor at a time of disappointment and wounding, I felt an immense sympathy for my landlord, who, starting at the other end of the world, now wished to hide, like me. I felt a kinship with him; was deeply grateful for the protection of the manor, for the style of things there. I never thought his seclusion strange. It was what I wanted for myself at that time.

I wanted, when I came to the manor, after the pride of ambition, to strip my life down. I wanted to live as far as possible with what I found in the cottage in the manor grounds, to alter as little as possible. I wanted to avoid vanity; and for me then vanity could lie in very small things—like wishing to buy an ashtray. Why a special ashtray, when the empty tobacco tin could serve? So I felt in tune with what I saw or thought I saw at the manor; I felt in myself the same spirit of withdrawal. And though I knew that men might arrive at similar states or attitudes for dissimilar reasons and by different routes, and as men might even be incompatible, I felt at one with my landlord.

Privilege lay between us. But I had an intimation that it worked against him. Whatever my spiritual state at the moment of arrival, I knew I would have to save myself and look for health; I knew I would have to act at some time. His privilege—his house, his staff, his income, the acres he could look out at every day and knew to be his—this privilege could press him down into himself, into non-doing and nullity.

So though we had started at opposite ends of empire and privilege, and in different cultures, it was easy for me, as his tenant now, to feel goodwill in my heart for him.

I never thought it odd or "creepy," to use the word given me by Alan, a literary visitor, that I never saw my landlord. His wish to be unseen by me was matched by my wish not to be seen by him. A remnant of my old colonial-racial "nerves"; but I was also nervous of undoing the magic of the place. If I had seen my landlord, heard his voice, heard his conversation, seen his face and expression, been constrained to make conversation back, to be polite, the impression would have been uneffaceable. He would have been endowed with a "character," with vanities, irritations, absurdities; and this would have led me to make judgments—the judgments that, undoing acceptance, can also undo a relationship. As it was, the personality of my landlord was expressed for me by the mystery of the manor and the grounds.

*T*HE MANOR grounds grew on me. Unused to the seasons (in the way I have described) and, so far as architecture went, still perhaps tending to take things too much for granted, seeing "ordinary" buildings too much as natural expressions of a particular place, it took me time to understand what I was seeing. It took me time to see that my cottage, in spite of its name, was not a simple building.

It was a long low building on two levels (there was a slight, graded slope from the road to the water meadows and the river). It was at the far side of the lawn or manor "green." Whatever my mood, and however long or short my separation from the cottage, whether I had gone on an overseas assignment of many months or had simply gone to Salisbury or had gone for my afternoon walk, the first sight of the cottage on my return, breaking in upon me at the end of the short, dark lane from the public road, never failed to delight and surprise me.

The lane from the public road was overhung with yew; and summer added the layer-upon-layer shade of beech and copper beech; so that even while I was in that gloom, the openness of the lawn and the soft warm colors of the cottage were visible. I felt delight at the long, low shape of the building set right against the beeches. The roots of one or two beeches began just beyond the cottage wall—and yet, for some reason, there was never any shifting or subsidence of the cottage foundations. I felt delight at the setting, the naturalness, the rightness. And surprise that this was where I lived.

It took me time to understand that this was no country "naturalness," that the cottage had been designed to create just that effect. The walls were thick, perhaps rubble-filled; but on the surface they were a considered mixture of flint and brickbats and warm yellow stone. And once I saw the design and the intention, I also saw that the masonry was craftsman's work. One day, on a block of stone set high up on a side wall, I saw the carved initials of the builder or designer—the last initial proclaimed him a member of my landlord's family—with the year, 1911.

Play, from someone of the family, in that secure, far-off year, the coronation year of the king-emperor, George the Fifth. With my instinct to accept what I found, it took me time to recognize the element of play, and the extent of it, in the ordering of the manor grounds.

A short yew hedge separated my cottage from a small, single-roomed wooden building, unpainted, and now weathered gray-black. This building, square in plan and taller than my cottage, was extravagantly rustic in style. The walls were of thick, rough-sawn planks. The lower edge of the planks kept the shape and the bark of the trunk from which they had been sawn. The whole structure rested on mushroom-shaped stones.

I thought that this fanciful house or shed was intended by the builder—whether it was the same member of the family who had built my cottage I didn't know—to be the forester's hut in the play settlement or village around the lawn or manor green. Until one summer afternoon, in my third or fourth year, Pitton, the gardener, coming back after lunch in a relaxed mood, opened the weathered door to show me. And how easily and sturdily that door swung open, though the building had not been used for years!

What I had thought of as the forester's hut was no such thing. It had been a stable. It even had a hay loft. There was still hay in the loft; and there were still ropes and harness hanging on nails, and leather and trappings connected with horses; and still a smell of horse; and a timber floor quite clean below the cobwebs. Everything was weathered outside. Inside—and the wooden house or box was much taller and bigger than it seemed from the outside—everything was protected, in spite of the starlings that besieged it at certain times and especially for two or three weeks in the spring.

A stable like a forester's hut (I allowed my fantasy to persist); and across the lawn a squash court built to look like a farmhouse, its apparently rough walls as carefully thought out as the walls of my own cottage. Next to that were the rough-timbered garages or wagon sheds. And then the antique, ivy-covered, flint-walled storehouse or granary whose back formed part of the churchyard wall. So that after the spaciousness of the downs and the water meadows, the country openness, there was suddenly here a remnant and a reminder of medieval huddle and constriction. And just as, along the droveway, the modernity of the old farm manager's bungalow was set next to the antiquity of the worn, striated slopes, so here the modern fantasy of my cottage and the forester's hut and the farmhouse was set next to, ran into, the Middle Ages.

And yet it made a whole. It worked. You could take it all for granted, as I had done at the beginning, and see it as something that went with an Edwardian big house in this part of the country. Or you could enter the fantasy, a child's vision made concrete, child's play by an adult or adults: extraordinary, this gratuitous expression of great security and wealth in this corner of an estate that once was so much bigger (and far from places like Trinidad, where the word "estate," when I first got to know it, especially if it was a sugar estate, didn't hold any idea of grandeur or style, carrying connotations instead only of size and sameness, and many small lives and small houses at the edges). And yet it was this element of play—the child's play of the toy settlement around the manor green or lawn—which, when I recognized it, I yielded to.

Across the "lane" from the forester's hut, and visible from the side window of my cottage, was what looked like a little country cottage on its own. It was really a shed, built against the wall of the manor's vegetable garden; but it had been designed like a half cottage, a cottage sliced down through the middle from the ridge of the roof, to suggest, from certain angles, a cottage with a door and a window.

The lane that ran around this settlement and its green was lined with mushroom-shaped stones. These stones, I was told, were a local feature. Barns used to be built on them to keep the rats out. They had kept the rats out of the stable, the forester's hut. But it was their decorative, fairy-tale quality that was exploited here. Every mushroom stone had been made to look different from every other. The tops were chipped differently and sometimes the supports were carved into a curve. Over the years many of these mushrooms had been damaged.

They were too delicate a fantasy. Many of the mushroom tops had in fact disappeared, been got out of the way; and even some of the supporting stones had been knocked flat. But by a miracle, outside my cottage door, on the lane side, in front of the wall of the vegetable garden, there had been preserved five or six of these mushrooms as they had been originally designed: the tops chipped into different degrees of thickness, chipped rough, each mushroom top supporting a little moss forest in winter.

This was the fantasy to which I returned—the many-featured fantasy of manor, manor village around its green, manor garden—and always felt welcomed by, in that first winter, while I was working on my book. It was the fantasy of the original builder or builders, the family fantasy which my landlord had inherited and which now, I felt, as I entered more and more into it, best expressed his character.

The rest of the grounds—the orchard, the garden at the back of the main house, the water meadows, the walk along the river—all of that came later, in the late spring or early summer, when I was ill and couldn't do the long walks along the droveway. This was the time I learned to fix that particular season, to give it certain associations of flowers, trees, river.

After I had finished my book (the one with the African center-piece) I had gone abroad to do some journalism, for the money, the travel out of England, and the spiritual refreshment. The assignments had been exhausting, the second in a place not served by many airlines. I had fallen ill on the slow journey back, through many climates; and in one place had spent four days and nights in a hotel room, in a stupor of ache and sleep.

I was light-headed when I returned to the valley and the cottage. I felt its welcoming quality, its protectiveness, and was moved by the unearthly beauty (as it seemed to me) of every growing thing around my cottage. The peonies below the sitting-room windows made an especial impression. My fantasies, both waking and sleeping, constantly played with the shapes of these developing, tight, round, dark-red buds.

The doctor found nothing seriously wrong with me, no infection of lung or blood. He said I was tired. He said (and we were in a military area): "Battle fatigue."

And as the weeks passed that indeed was what my illness seemed to resolve itself into: a great tiredness, not unpleasant, a tiredness with the little delirium that—alas, too rarely—had come to me as a child with a tropical "fever," this fever associated with the chill of the rainy season, the season of extravagant, dramatic weather, of interruptions in routine, of days off from school because of rain and floods, and the coughs and fevers to which they gave rise. How often, as a child, having had my fever, I had longed to have it all over again, to experience all the distortions of perceptions it brought about: the extraordinary sense of smoothness (not only to one's touch, but also in one's mouth and stomach), and, with that, voices and noises becoming oddly remote and exciting. I had never had fever as often as I would have liked. Instead, very soon, as I had grown up, fever had been replaced by the real misery of bronchitis and asthma, exhausting afflictions without a good side.

Now, in my welcoming cottage, deliciously, for the first time since my childhood, I felt I was having "fever." Exhaustion—work, travel—had brought it on: the doctor's diagnosis felt true.

In my welcoming cottage, hidden by layer upon layer of beech and yew from the public road, I began to feel oppressed by the labors and strains of the last twenty years; the strains connected with writing, that passion; the personal strains as well that had begun that day when the Pan American World Airways plane had taken me up and shown me that pattern of the fields I had been surrounded by as a child in Trinidad but had never seen till that moment.

All the work, all the strain, all the disappointments and recoveries, now seemed to sit in a solid mass in my head. But I had no vision now of being a corpse at the bottom of a river; no dream of an exploding head that left me shaken up, exhausted, after a struggle to wake. All the stress had turned to fever. So that in my welcoming cottage I was like a child again. As though I had at last, after twenty years, traveled to the equivalent of the fantasy I had had in mind when I left home.

And it was in this mood that when I recovered sufficiently to go outside, I began—with the encouragement of Mr. and Mrs. Phillips, who asked me to dismiss the idea that I might be trespassing on my landlord's privacy—to explore the spring of the overgrown garden. The spring that had begun for me, and had been fixed for me, by the peony pushing up tight, swelling buds on rhubarblike stalks below the sitting-room window of my cottage.

In my twenty years off and on in England I must have seen many thousands of peonies. They were a common flower, as I was to see when I was fit enough to take bus rides into Salisbury. Right through the valley, in open, sun-struck gardens, small and large, country-cottage or suburban-style gardens, I saw them blooming away too fast in bright light, losing their tightness and deep color, rapidly losing their virtue. None of the many thousands I had seen before this spring had made an impression on me; I had never been able to put the name "peony" to any of them; I had never been able to attach them to a season or a time of year or to the appearance of other flowers or to other natural events. These peonies of my convalescence, these peonies around my cottage, were my first; and they stood for my new life.

The clump outside the sitting-room window was on the north of the cottage; there was another clump, in the shade of the yew hedge between my cottage and the forester's hut. They came out slowly, preserving their shape, developing an especially deep color. From the lane below the yews and the beeches, the peonies of my cottage made two deep points of color in an otherwise green expanse, edged with wilderness.

ONCE THERE were sixteen gardeners. Now there was only Pitton. He grew vegetables in the walled garden; there he also grew certain flowers for the manor and my landlord; he looked after a private lawn of my landlord's somewhere else in the grounds. He was like Jack, marking out and maintaining areas of cultivation in the midst of wasteland. But much of what Pitton did was hidden from me. What I saw was mainly wilderness, through which once or twice in the season Pitton would cut—for him and me—the narrowest of paths, quite literally. One swath up; one swath down.

This two-swathed path of Pitton's began at the end of the lawn, almost opposite the shaded lane that led from the public road. The path ran through an enclosure hedged with old box, unpruned, grown out now almost into trees, meeting above the entrance to make an arch, almost as if that had been intended. The enclosure was empty, without any sign of old planting or old flower beds. In one corner a sycamore had been planted or had seeded itself (there were a number of sycamores about, growing apparently at random); and on this syc-amore, a tree now rather than a sapling, someone had trailed a wisteria vine—itself now an old thing, speaking of the old days and the many gardeners and of people having the time and means and wish to em-bellish a hidden corner.

In the winter the enclosure had been full of the dried-up stalks of weeds, sometimes as tall as dried maize plants, and clumps of thin, long-bladed grass. Now the weeds, on succulent, thick, green stalks were growing tall again. But in spite of those weeds and the wild grass, the path Pitton had cut, one swath up, one swath down, showed grass as tight and fine and level as the grass of a lawn—as though the wil-derness was only on the surface and awaited only this cut to reveal the old order and beauty and many seasons' tending that lay beneath.

This enclosure seemed to be part of the garden of the manor. But I was told by Bray, the car-hire man, that it was older; and the over-grown box hedge suggested a greater age. The enclosure belonged to the house that was here before the manor, Bray said; and he said that before that, there had been a monastery or nunnery on the site. The idea was not a fantastic one. In medieval times everything would have lain along the little river; just a few miles away, at Amesbury, where the river went wide and shallow and clear, there was an abbey and perhaps also the remnant of the nunnery to which Guinevere came from Winchester-Camelot when the Round Table of King Arthur broke up.

An enclosure, then, as stripped of human presence as that damp stone ruin on the droveway, the stone ruin surrounded by sycamores that, ignoring the decay and death of the house they were intended to shelter, continued to grow, casting a cold shade on the black, grassless earth—as stripped as that far-off ruin, this emptiness within the tall box hedge, just a few steps from my cottage, where (if Bray was right) religious men or women of another age, renouncers of the world perhaps, pampered people, possibly also half prisoners, had taken the air or told their beads, secluded in the medieval huddle of a village, between the village center of church and churchyard and the busy river and wet fields, water meadows, busy with peasant labor turning over the heavy, rich black earth.

At the end of this enclosure was the orchard. Old, even decayed, it stood among older forest trees; and the box hedge here was straggly; at the exit the top branches did not meet to form an arch. From here, until the summer green hid it, the river and the willows could be seen across the water meadows—not cropped now, the meadows, no hay taken off them, never busy, and closed even to cattle. No question of taking a shortcut across the water meadows to the river. The land was permanently "drowned," cut up by choked channels, and with the remnants (like minor Roman engineering ruins) of abandoned control hatches.

It was said that the secrets of drowning and draining the meadows were now lost—labors once as matter-of-fact and seasonal as, say, the water bailiffs' cleaning of the river and cutting of the over-long river weeds, floating entanglingly up. Once the wealth of the valleys lay in the wet meadows. Now it lay more in the wide, unencumbered uplands. All that grew now in the manor meadows beyond the orchard —and were never cropped—were the wild yellow irises.

One side of the orchard, as you came into it from the enclosure, was like a wood. There were many tall old forest trees and the ground was choked with weeds and tree debris. Suitably, this wood was where the two-story thatched children's house was. I couldn't get to it in the spring. There was no path. Pitton cut a path here much later, and then it was a four-swathed path, first for the hand barrow with garden refuse, and then for the big caged barrow or trolley Pitton used to ferry dead leaves to the grass-and-leaf-and-flower graveyard he had established, out of everybody's sight, at the back of the children's house.

This vegetable graveyard or rubbish dump Pitton described as a "garden refuge," and a certain amount of ingenuity went into finding or creating these hidden but accessible "refuges." That was how Pitton used the word: I believe he had two or three such refuges at different places. Refuse, refuge: two separate, unrelated words. But "refuge," which Pitton used for "refuse," did in the most remarkable way contain both words. Pitton's "refuge" not only stood for "refuse," but had the additional idea or association, not at all inappropriate, of asylum, sanctuary, hiding, almost of hide-and-seek, of things kept decently out of sight and mind. He might say, of a fallen beech branch on the lawn, or a heap of grass clippings: "That'll be going to the refuge." Or: "I'll take it down to the refuge presently."

I thought at first that it was only Pitton's way with the word. But then I discovered that it was more or less common usage in the valley. I heard it from Bray, the car-hire man, Pitton's neighbor. I heard it from him at the time the council workers went on strike for a week or so, or—as little printed notices pinned to trees and bus stops up and down the valley said—the council workers had decided to take "industrial action." "No refuge this week," Bray said, meaning that there was to be no refuse collection. "You don't have to tell me who's behind this. It's the commonest among them. Commonest in name and in deed."

I also heard the word from Mr. Phillips's father. After the death of his wife the old man sometimes came on a Saturday afternoon to visit, and also (Saturday being Pitton's day off) to walk through the grounds. He stopped sometimes in front of my cottage to talk. He had started life as a carrier's boy, and he was full of information about the old days. He told me why laborers' cottages beside the public road could be so very narrow. The old coach and cart roads had to be wide; when they were paved they became narrower, and there were strips of ground on either side which for a time were nobody's property. Laborers squatted on these strips and built their cottages. He told me why so many had elder hedges, and why the hedges could be so mounded up and high. Elder grew fast, and a hedge was a squatter's way of staking out his claim. The hedges were high, not with the vegetable growth of centuries, as I had imagined, but with the imperishable household rubbish of the last century. Many of the hedge mounds had been built up with bottles and metal junk and old shoes, rubbish that couldn't be got rid off. And the old man explained: "There was no refuge in those days, you see."

And I heard the word again from the neat, well-dressed, and anxious man who came to deal with a plague of mice that scuttled about the ceiling of my bedroom, sounding at times as though they were pushing or rolling little pebbles back and forth. This man told me all he knew about rats and mice. Rats were terrors, but they were creatures of habit; they had their runs and could be caught. Mice, on the other hand, could live in small cracks or cavities in a wall; they never pined for light or a freer life; they could live on a gram of food a day, a crumb of biscuit. But the man's heart wasn't in the mouse hell or purgatory or mouse nullity he was describing. Once he might have spoken the words with relish and enjoyed the response of his listener. Now he, the mouse expert, spoke by rote. He was worried about his health; he had had a heart attack quite suddenly one day when he was laying down some poison for some mice. He was worried, above all, about his job, worried that the government or the local authority might close down his little department altogether and put the mice and vermin business out to contract with a private firm. Suddenly, with an accusing stab of the finger, he said, with a use of the word that was as two-edged and apt for him as Pitton's "refuge" was for Pitton: "Do you know the next thing to go? The next thing to go will be refuge. Soon there'll be no public refuge in this place."

To one side, then, as you came out into the orchard, were the children's house and Pitton's refuge, as yet unreachable by a path, since that had not been cut. To the other side lay the great manor gardens, filling first the space between the water meadows and the vegetable garden and then the space between the water meadows and the manor.

Nestlings cheeped in the knotholes in the old orchard trees. Last year's nut shells—the work of gray squirrels—were crunchy on the nut walk that linked the orchard and the big manor lawn. The nut walk ran beside the vegetable garden; the slender boughs of the nut trees had been bent with old skill—or at least before Pitton's time—to meet above. Still visible among the fast-growing nettles and wild rose growth was the stone path around the old rose beds. Then came the lawn proper. And here, fearful of intruding (in spite of what the Phillipses said), I walked at the very edge, beside the water meadow.

The water meadow or marsh had already clearly claimed part of what had once been cultivated garden. Certain decorative trees, pink hawthorns especially, now grew in the marsh and were surrounded by marsh debris and vegetation. Many of the marsh plants, and especially the reeds, which might have been planted at one time for the beauty (like Chinese or Japanese calligraphy) of their spearlike leaves, many of these plants had jumped the path Pitton had tried to keep clear at the edge of the wet meadow, and seeded themselves in the lawn—like the trash from a sugarcane fire jumping a firebreak and sending arrows of flame into the adjoining green field.

The lawn sloped gently up all the way to the house. In the middle there was a big evergreen tree that must have been older than the house. The quarters and little terrace of Mr. and Mrs. Phillips—with washing on the terrace—were at one side, behind some statuary. The house was not old. It had been built early in the century, but built to look old. Like the reconstructed church across the lawn from my cottage, it was part of the taste of the time for a special idea of the past, the assertion—with the wealth and power of an unbelievably extensive empire—of racial and historical and cultural virtue. The back of the house made a gray impression: gray stone mottled and mildewed.

I never looked very hard at the back facade. There was my wish not to intrude. And there was another reason. I didn't know the internal arrangements, and didn't know from which window my landlord—with his limitless time, his long, empty days—might be looking out.

He would have looked out on something like perfection: the lawn with the great tree in the foreground, the forest or wood to one side, the beaten-down water meadow beyond this lawn, with all the growth of willow and reeds and bamboo clumps and dogwood and the shrubs that loved water; the river with its river growths, the water meadows beyond, the willows, the channels, the drowned fields catching the morning light and, at a sufficient distance, the evening light; and then the bare downs again. (And what effects of moonlight on these water meadows, with the moon rising above the bare downs! What effect, on a moonlight night, of river and mist!)

There were only a few acres, relatively speaking, attached to the manor now. The land just beyond the river belonged to another land-owner. But by a series of accidents—the water meadows no longer needed for pasture, the shrinking of the small valley villages with the mechanization of agriculture at the end of the last century, the dis-appearance of many agricultural cottages, the taking over by the mil-itary of the distant bare downs—by these and other accidents, the view from the back of the manor, the view through which I walked, was of a nature almost unchanged since Constable's day: a view without a house, without the peasant or river activity of the Middle Ages or the age before the plowing of the downs, a view almost of a nature park. And all this just a few miles from the famous old towns of Salisbury and Wilton, the modern urban clusters of Southampton and Andover, the red brick, old and new, of the Victorian railway town of Basing-stoke, and the Victorian Gothic black-brick ring around the cathedral heart of ancient Winchester.

The toy village of which my cottage formed part was only an aspect—together with the children's thatched house in the pathless forest—of the greater design of the manor grounds. But perfection such as my landlord looked out on contained its own corruption. Per-fection like that could too easily be taken for granted. There was noth-ing in that view (of ivy and forest debris and choked water meadow) which would irritate or encourage doubt; there was nothing in that view which would encourage action in a man already spiritually weakened by personal flaws, disappointments and, above all, his knowledge of his own great security. The view—so complete, so simple—seemed to say or could appear to say: "This is the world. Why worry? Why interfere?"

At the far end of the lawn, where a new wood began, offering little glimpses of hedges and overgrown paths and covered walks and stone urns, a wood which I was never to explore, at that end of the lawn there was a very large greenhouse. Its timber frame was solid, so solid that from a distance it all looked whole, a greenhouse in use. But the green behind the glass was the green of weeds growing unusually tall in the protected conditions of the greenhouse—a wilderness of weeds; and many of the glass panels had fallen. To me (with what I knew of old Trinidad estate houses, estate houses in the French Caribbean style) there was about this greenhouse something—over and above the fact of its size—that suggested wealth. It had been "overspecified": its timbers, the depth of the concrete floor (on two levels on the sloping site), its door, its hinges, its metalwork—everything was much sturdier than was strictly necessary. It was the way—perhaps without being asked—builders built for the rich; just as shopkeepers sent up their best to the big house. There was something very satisfying about this style of building; everything seemed so much itself; everything seemed built for long use; there was no fragility, no anxiety.

Over the hill, Jack also had a greenhouse, at the back (or perhaps the front) of his cottage, facing the old farmyard. That greenhouse would have been bought from a catalog, like those advertised in the magazines with the television or radio programs. And how frail Jack's greenhouse had always looked, how slender its timber frame, how fragile its thin glass, even its floor of concrete! And indeed, when its time had come, how quickly it had all gone, all but the concrete floor (and even that had later disappeared)! How quickly it had been cleansed of its greenhouse spirits! But this manor greenhouse, after two decades of neglect, still stood and from fifty yards still looked solid and whole, its timbers still painted, its thick concrete floor still uncracked, its door swinging easily on its hinges. It would have been the work of a day to clean it inside, and the work of less than a week to recommission it again, to replace its wilderness with order.

Bush inside the great greenhouse, bush outside. Pitton's lawn mower didn't come here until late in the season; and then, as everywhere else after the lawn mower had been, the grass showed level and flat and lawnlike and tended. But, before that cut of Pitton's, it was necessary to hack through the nettles and the bush that grew thick and fast in the dampness to get to the first of the bridges that led across the water channels and creeks of the water meadow to the riverbank.

At the other end of the lawn, where the water meadow met the orchard, there was a barbed-wire fence in a ditch, in the midst of the water bush, to deter intruders. At this end there was only bush and something like forest debris. But here, in the days of the old life of the manor, there had been a series of railed timber bridges over the channels—channels which, overgrown with willows that had then been blown down by equinoctial gales, had become like forest creeks: water appearing to be black over old leaves and mud, until you noticed the clear clean colors of the leaves and the sky that the water reflected. In these hidden black creeks (so unlike the open meadows with yellow irises at the other end) there were often mallards. They took fright at one's approach, so used were they to their untroubled possession of these waters, or a particular willow-blocked arm of a creek.

The bridges over the creeks of the water meadows had been built to high specifications; but over the years they had rotted in the water and had been further broken up by the growth of vegetable matter, even sturdy, tall-stalked nettles, and especially by the growth of the roots and trunks of willows. There still remained, that first spring of my walks and discoveries, a heavy gate at the end of the first bridge. This gate dragged; but its posts, though black and green with damp and disagreeable to the touch, still stood, and the gate could still be pulled shut and latched with a rusting catch. As a gate, a barrier, it was meaningless. The levels of ground and water had changed; the gate no longer guarded a dry walk across the water meadow. One could simply walk around the gate. There was a merest dip in the ground now, and the only inconvenience came from the nettles. But the nettles were everywhere.

At one stage of this cross-meadow walk the weeds and reeds and willows and other wild growths were so tall it was hard to see the river. Then, quite suddenly, from the very last bridge—with many broken planks, big rusted nails alone remaining whole, the planks they had fixed having rotted away altogether—suddenly from the last bridge the end of the bush was clear, and the trimmed path along the river-bank, beside the collapsed boathouse.

This boathouse was a spectacular ruin. The mooring for the boat or boats was in a creek, one of the old channels of the water meadow. The thick timber posts or pillars of the corrugated iron–roofed shelter stood on either side of the creek. But tame though the river looked— a few feet deep, a few feet wide—the water it channeled was a force of nature, not wholly predictable; and the banks of that river and its inlets were constantly changing. The boathouse creek, widening or simply shifting, had caused the boathouse to collapse on one side. The angle of collapse, the rotting timber, the black-looking water, the rust-ing corrugated iron suggested a tropical river ruin, somewhere on the Orinoco or Amazon or the Congo. And yet, passing this ruin, and as though belonging to another order of nature, another order of society almost, was the trimmed path along the riverbank.

It was to that easy path, a path for fishermen, that the water-meadow bridges were meant to lead. And the river itself flowed tidily and gently; and neat planks bridged the channels from the wet meadows to the main river. It was the hand of man, the hand of the water bailiffs and people like them, that suggested an orderly nature. Left to itself, the river, like the water meadow at the back of the manor, would have become a forest ruin. It took only one collapsed willow—blown down during a gale, say—to create a mess in the river: the banks wrecked, easy passage gone, tangled islands of river weeds and river dross with rippled skins of milky-brown scum building up in a few days between the branches.

The color of the river depended on what grew on the banks. And small though the scale was, the bank was varied. Where there were tall reeds or grasses on the water's edge, and the bank was overhung with trees, and if there were little indentations—miniature coves—in the bank, then the water was dark green, deep-seeming, and mysterious. Where the bank was clear the water was clear, showing the white sand or chalk of the bed or the rippling green river weeds.

There came a stage on my walk along the riverbank when I stood directly in front of the water meadow where the yellow irises grew. Beyond that was the old orchard, with the box enclosure that lay to one side of my cottage. Above the orchard and the vegetable-garden wall I saw the roof and chimneys of my own cottage below the beeches, and was surprised all over again, every time, that that was where I lived.

Not far beyond this point the walk that was permitted to me came to an end. Beyond that was another river "beat," belonging to another landowner, and though it would have been easy to climb over the makeshift fence, I preferred not to do so.

The river curved here. On the opposite bank the down ended abruptly in a wooded cliff, giving a great depth and a hint of surrounding forest to the river color. There was also a new channel here from the bare down, a spring breaking out of the chalk and quickly turning into a noisy cascade. So that again, in this neat, tame, smooth landscape, with a bare green-white down and with a river a few feet deep divided neatly into numbered beats, there was a reminder of the unpredictable force of water. Old corrugated-iron sheets served as hatches in the new channel: an unexpected touch, in a landscape without people, of the urban slum.

The water bailiffs had released young trout near here, and they hadn't wandered far. They were unexpectedly unattractive, as nervous as rats, of that color as well, and as swift and devious and silent as rats as they made for the camouflage of the dark river weeds.

This was the river walk, barely ten minutes, hardly a walk to someone used to walking most days for about an hour and a half. But the walk was always new; the river and what I saw always changed. There was the blue iris I saw in my first spring. Solitary among the weeds and nettles at the edge of the water meadow. I was transported at the sight, and instantly had the wish, if I ever were to plant a garden of my own, to try to achieve that effect. And then, in the light-headedness of my convalescence, I began (until I sobered up again) to walk through the nettles to the iris, as though the beauty of what I saw lay not in the setting, but in that particular iris.

There were the scented old roses in the wild rose bed. And the roses I saw that first summer were the last: I was in at that particular death. Because in the autumn Mrs. Phillips pruned them, "cut them right back," as she said; and those old rose bushes, cut down to the quick, all turned to brier again.

There was a time of the spring or summer—every year—when a pale blue lawn weed floated like a blue mist above the daisy-spotted lawn. And always there was the river. It was the river, with its overwhelming beauty of reeds and weeds and moving water and changing reflections, that made me say, long before I felt myself in tune with other plants and truly in tune with the seasons: "At least I've had a year of this." And then: "At least I've had two years of this."

And just as, on the walk over the downs past Jack's cottage, I always in the beginning looked for the warm brown fur of the hares, so on this shorter river walk I looked for the miniature volcano of the salmon's nest in the white chalk of the riverbed; and the still, dark pike waiting in a deep pool where the water was dark in the shadow of reeds. And I looked for the vole or water rat. I knew the little tree on whose lower branch he liked to sun himself, after shaking his fur. I often saw him swimming across the river; and once I saw him so soundly asleep that—thinking he was dead—I went and stood over him. I often heard the surprised plop of his fellows as they dived into their river holes, sending up silent muddy clouds.

Every winter and spring created fresh havoc in the manor gardens and water meadows. The bridges over the channels decayed and decayed. The gate at the very last (or the first) bridge was eventually left open one year and collapsed finally of its own rot. The river changed its course by a few feet, washing over the path that the water bailiffs had kept clear; and the planks that spanned the channels were lost below water. New two-plank bridges were built, one plank plain, one covered with wire netting, for the grip it gave both to shoes and to the wheels of the bailiffs' barrows.

On this walk, as on the longer walk on the downs past Jack's cottage, I lived not with the idea of decay—that idea I quickly shed—so much as with the idea of change. I lived with the idea of change, of flux, and learned, profoundly, not to grieve for it. I learned to dismiss this easy cause of so much human grief. Decay implied an ideal, a perfection in the past. But would I have cared to be in my cottage while the sixteen gardeners worked? When every growing plant aroused anxiety, every failure pain or criticism? Wasn't the place now, for me, at its peak? Finding myself where I was, I thought—after the journey that had begun so long before—that I was blessed.

And then one day, quite unexpectedly, walking with freedom at the back of the manor, walking at the edge of both the ruined water meadow and the wild manor lawn, I saw my landlord.

*T*HIS WAS my second glimpse of my landlord; there never was to be another. And it was as confusing as my first, when I had seen him sitting beside Mr. Phillips in the motorcar, driving along the narrow road below the beeches planted by his father. I had barely seen him that time in the motorcar, had barely had time to focus on him, and the car had moved on, leaving me with a more precise, and surprising, picture of Mr. Phillips—happy, not at all irritable in the company of his master, more like an impresario, like a man who was fully himself, had a proper idea of his duties and worth.

And just as after that first sighting my imagination had played with a half-impression of my landlord, now making him benign, now making him buttoned up, with dark glasses and the long hair of a Howard Hughes recluse, so now, because (being as nervous myself of being seen as he was) I turned away as soon as I saw him and never looked back, my memories were as much of the shock of the moment as of the man I had glimpsed.

I saw him from a great distance, almost as soon as I had walked past the old rose bed (without roses now, a brier wilderness, long after that first summer of thorny, densely petaled, scented, lilac-pink roses) and had stepped onto the lawn proper, full of daisies.

He was sitting in the pool of sunlight between the great evergreen that shaded much of the lawn, the big, partly broken greenhouse, and the wood at the side of the house, through which I had seen little paths, which I had never explored, for fear of intruding, for fear of disturbing my landlord, for fear of something very like this moment.

He was sitting (as I thought or felt afterwards) in a canvas-backed easy chair in the sunlight, facing south, with his back to me. He was wearing a wide-brimmed hat. That hat obscured the shape or the baldness or otherwise of his head, just as the canvas back of his chair obscured the bulk or otherwise of his back or torso.

From the first sighting I had had of him I had retained one clear physical detail: the little low wave he had given against the dashboard of his car. I had invested that wave with his shyness, the shyness of his illness, the shyness that went at the same time (as I thought) with a great vanity, the shyness that wasn't so much a wish not to be seen as a wish to be applauded on sight, to be recognized on sight as someone stupendous and of interest; and I had also invested that wave with his benevolence.

From this second glimpse I again retained just one clear physical detail: it was of his crossed leg and his bare bent knee—shining in the sun. He was wearing shorts; they were tight around the plump thigh I saw. This wish of my landlord for nakedness and physical self-cherishing—stories had come my way, from the Phillipses and from Bray, the car-hire man, whose father had worked in the manor long ago, of the great beauty of my landlord as a young man—this idea of beauty and the flesh now went with an opposite reality: the fatness of self-indulgence and inactivity.

It is that detail—the pool of sunlight in the wilderness, the sun on the fat shining leg—that fixes the season for me. I knew of course that he kept to his room in the cold weather, and went out of doors only in fine weather. He had been granted at birth a great house and a wide view in the dampest part of the county, on the riverbank, in a valley (which often, looking down from the viewing point on my other walk, I had seen covered entirely with mist). But his instincts were Mediterranean, tropical; he loved the sun. Inertia, habit, friendships, a wish to be where his worth was known—perhaps these things had kept him in his inherited house. Perhaps if he could have taken friends and social connections, the knowledge in others of his social worth, everything that protected him, he might have moved. But he stayed in his house, which was his setting, and dreamed of being elsewhere, dreamed in his own way.

He had sent me poems—in my first year as his tenant—about Krishna and Shiva. Mrs. Phillips had typed the poems out and then she had brought them over in person to the cottage. It was my landlord's gesture of welcome to me; and so Mrs. Phillips treated it, adding to the gesture her own surprising reverence for the act of poetry making. Mrs. Phillips typed out and brought over more poems. She became as it were the living link between my landlord and me. I don't think he intended the courtesy to be quite like that; but that was how it fell out, and it made my settling into the cottage very much easier.

Krishna and Shiva! There, beside that river (Constable and Shepard), in those grounds! There was nothing of contemporary cult or fashion in my landlord's use of these divinities. His Indian romance was in fact older, even antiquated, something he had inherited, like his house, something from the days of imperial glory, when—out of material satiety and the expectation of the world's continuing to be ordered as it had been ordered for a whole century and more—power and glory had begun to undo themselves from within. Ruskinism, a turning away from the coarseness of industrialism, upper-class or cultivated sensibilities, sensibilities almost drugged by money, the Yellow Book, philosophy melting away into sensuousness, sensation—my landlord's Indian romance partook of all of those impulses and was rooted in England, wealth, empire, the idea of glory, material satiety, a very great security.

His Indian romance—which had very little to do with me, my past, my life or my ambitions—suited his setting. His Krishna and Shiva were names and in his poems they were like Greek divinities, given the color of antique sculpture, literally touched with night-blue, the color of wantonness, the promise of a pleasure (and beauty and Keatsian truth) that made the senses reel.

The conceit about the painted statues was pleasing (I felt it was an old poem). And there was knowledge of a sort of the blue, aboriginal gods of the Hindu pantheon, the lascivious Krishna, the drug-taking Shiva (blue standing, in fact, for the black of the aboriginal inhabitants of India). But in later poems—some typed by Mrs. Phillips, some printed (single sheets, with drawings)—a similar heady sensuousness was attributed to Italian youths of apparently the previous century or young Conradian sailors (again of apparently the previous century) in Peruvian or Malayan or Brazilian ports.

His fantasies (sensual rather than explicitly sexual, to judge by the poems) were unconfined but also unfocused: a warm blur, something that was owed him but which perhaps might disappear with definition: something out there, outside himself, and eventually an aspect of his acedia, the curious death of the soul that had befallen him so early in his life. His anchor was his house, his knowledge of his social worth. Through all the ups and downs of his illness or his acedia, the knowledge of who he was remained with him. All the poems he had sent by Mrs. Phillips had been signed, extravagantly. There was about his signature—in addition to its size—something of the experimental nature of a boy's signature; it spoke of someone still savoring his personality.

And now he sat before me, in a pool of sunlight in the grounds of his house, the house he had known all his life, next to the broken-paned weed-filled greenhouse, in the ruin of his garden. Seminude, his legs crossed, the fat right thigh (the thigh that was raised, and which I saw) tightly encased in his shorts.

It was the Phillipses who had encouraged me to walk through the back garden and along the riverbank, pooh-poohing as an unnecessary delicacy my wish to walk at the very limit of the lawn, beside the water meadow. (Their own visitors were less circumspect.) My landlord had his own patch, they told me; it was somewhere at the end of those overgrown walks through the wood at the far side of the house; I could walk with freedom. And I had done so for some years. I had certainly been observed by my landlord from one of the manor windows. And I believe that in his appearing where he was, there might have been an element of willfulness. His movements out of the house were major affairs. Someone would have had to take the chair out for him, for instance. And perhaps it was out of a wish to "show" him— for his pettishness, his petulance—that neither Mr. Phillips nor his wife had told me that my landlord was sitting out in the back garden that day.

His house, his garden, his view, his name. What did he see? Whatever he saw would have been different from what I saw. And so, after learning and possessing that view and the river for so many seasons, I was suddenly shocked, suddenly felt an intruder, as much as I did when one day Bray, the car-hire man, in a special nostalgic mood (he had been quarreling with his wife and with Pitton, the manor gardener, who was his next-door neighbor) showed me a social magazine of the 1920s, and I had seen a handsome, self-aware group of young people of the period, sitting on the rails of one of the bridges over the creeks between the back lawn and the river. Another view, another place!

What did he see, sitting there in his canvas-backed chair? Did he see the tall weeds in the solid greenhouse, the tops of some of the weeds flattened against the glass? Was he agitated by the wish to put things right or by the idea of decay and lack of care? Did he see the ivy that was killing so many of the trees that had been planted with the garden? He must have seen the ivy. Mrs. Phillips told me one day that he liked ivy and had given instructions that the ivy was never to be cut.

What were his feelings, then, when a tree collapsed? So many trees had collapsed. Such a wilderness now ruled in the water meadows, such a forest litter, with so many fallen willows, and the exposed Norfolk reeds then laid flat by the floods of a winter that for a week or so had cut an extra channel through the meadows on the opposite bank.

He liked flowers. Pitton grew flowers for him in a corner of the walled vegetable garden. And from what I heard, he became passionate for flowers as soon as the weather brightened. He could not always wait for the flowers Pitton grew. He insisted then, after his winter seclusion, on going out to flower shops in Salisbury and other towns, sometimes making long journeys to certain favored garden centers to buy flowers and plants in pots.

It was Pitton who reported to me that, on the way back from one of the flower expeditions, my landlord had seen the peonies below my window and in the shade of the yew hedge and had felt as I did about the depth of color of the overshadowed peonies.

Pitton, reporting this (to please me), found himself in a quandary. The difficulty lay in my landlord's pronunciation of the word "peony." Pitton didn't want to be disloyal to his employer.

"He doesn't say 'peony' like you and me," Pitton said. "He says pe-*ony.*" The word in this pronunciation rhymed with "pony."

Somewhere—was it at Oxford, or was it in the pages of Somerset Maugham—I had read or heard of this Edwardian affectation, an affectation known to be an affectation. Bal-*cony* rhyming with "pony"; and pe-*ony* rhyming with "pony." And the affectation that Pitton reported was strange. Like my landlord's knowledge of the value of his name, this affectation, the badge of a particular group, this class lesson from another age, had survived his desperate illness, his acedia.

And—forgetting this affectation—how did his taste for flowers go with the ruin of his own garden—the ruin through which, from his windows, he would have often seen me walking? Did he in fact see decay? Or did he—since vegetable growth never stopped—simply see lushness? Or did he cherish the decay, seeing in it a comforting reflection of his own acedia?

That wouldn't have been too fanciful. It would have been like my own wish, coming to the cottage in his grounds, not to interfere, to take things as I found them; and then my later wish, out of my own delight in the place, not to see decay, not to be saddened by that too ready idea of decay, to see instead flux, constant change; and the feeling which I grew to cherish, that in the very dereliction of the grounds I had come upon them at their peak, that the order created by sixteen gardeners would have been too much, would have made for strain and anxiety, that the true beauty of the place lay in accidental, unintended things: the peonies coming out very slowly below the thick dark green of the yews; the single blue iris among the tall nettles; the young deer that for many months lived among the reeds beside the rotting bridges over the water channels, having learned that the place was not frequented by men.

I had come to the manor in a mood of withdrawal myself, and I understood how in that mood one would have felt mocked, it would have debilitated one, to make gestures that were too affirmative. As part of that wish to be unaffirmative, to take things as I found them, not to interfere, I had painted my room in the cottage a deep mauve. It was the least assertive color I could think of, and it came from something in my childhood.

My elementary school in Port of Spain was in a street, Victoria Avenue, that ended in a cemetery. Nearly every afternoon after school I saw the horse-drawn hearses and the mourning procession on foot passing the high, rubble-filled wall of the cemetery, named Lapeyrouse after the French explorer La Pérouse by our late-eighteenth-century French settlers (fleeing the effects of the French Revolution in Haiti and the other French islands). The horses that pulled the hearses to Lapeyrouse were covered with a reticulated pall, black or mauve. As a result, mauve—purple—was never for me the color of power and pomp; it was the color of death. In the mood I was in when I came to the cottage, any more affirmative, life-encouraging color would have been only mocking. (Later that color became associated with the beauty and benignity and welcome of the place.) And since one seeks to understand people by looking for aspects of oneself in them, I was willing to attribute something of the attitudes of my own withdrawal to my landlord.

But perhaps there was as little pattern in his emotions, his sensual responses, as in his poems. He liked summer, the sun, flowers, ivy. Perhaps he was incapable of any effort to put things right. Or perhaps he was merely spoilt, and thought that however much the ivy and the gales destroyed in his garden, there would still be something for him to see; there would still be some sunshine in the summer and some clearing in the ruined garden for him to sit out in.

Ivy so covered and smothered some trees it was hard—especially for me, who knew so little—to tell what kinds of trees they were. A tree that collapsed one year turned out to be a cherry tree. I had known it only for its fitful blossom breaking through the ivy matting. Pitton and Mr. Phillips between them cut up the cherry trunk into discs; they used a chain saw, and the discs were perfect little things, like toys, when freed of the ivy matting. I was offered some of the discs for my fire. I put the discs I had been given in my outbuilding (the half-cottage against the vegetable-garden wall) and left them there to dry. When they did dry out, I couldn't bring myself to burn them all.

One disc I kept, as a souvenir of the garden, and I had it smoothed down and varnished. It had dried with its sheeny bark on; there were only a few spaces between the bark and the wood; and drying as slowly as it had done, the wood had hardly cracked. Just showing sawmarks, and nondescript as wood, without a definite color, growing dusty in my outbuilding, the cherry-wood disc came up beautifully when it was smoothed down. I counted the rings. There were forty-seven.

For its first two or three years the cherry tree might have grown in a nursery. So it might have been planted in the autumn of 1930. For the first twenty-six years the sapwood had grown at a healthy pace; and the color of the wood at the center was blond. But then, for its last twenty-one years, the growth of the sapwood had slowed down; the lines of the heartwood had grown close together; and the outer wood of the disc was dark.

Here in the secret vegetable life of the cherry tree of the garden was something like confirmation of what I had heard about the life of my landlord. In 1949 or 1950—1950 being the year I had left my own home island, had made my roundabout journey to England, looking for material to write about, and being as a writer (in the pieces I attempted) much more knowledgeable than I was as a person, hiding myself from my true experience, hiding my experience from myself —in 1949 or 1950 my landlord had withdrawn from the world, out of an excess of knowledge of that world. That probably was when he had given orders that the ivy was not to be touched. Up to that time the garden laid out by his parents had been more or less tended, in spite of everything, in spite of the war. Four or five years later, going by the evidence of the rings on my disc of cherry wood, the ivy had taken; and twenty-one years after that the choked, strangled tree had collapsed and become part of the debris of the garden, the debris of a life.

It occurred to me one day that at the time the ivy had taken or become established on the cherry tree, at the time my landlord's acedia had become permanent, while he was still a youngish man, I would have left Oxford. And since I had to do something, and since I had left home to be a writer, and no other talent or vocation had declared itself in me, I had set myself up as a writer—as deliberately as that. There was no joy in that decision. That was the blankest and most frightening year of my life. And one day in the valley, for no reason, perhaps only for the sake of the thrill, as I was walking up the hill beside the windbreak of pine and beech and hawthorn and field roses to the viewing point, walking in that setting which had given me joy of place like no other place in the world, I found myself thinking myself back into my personality of twenty-five years before, and felt again a panic I had all but forgotten, and the wish it had given rise to, to run and hide: having no money, no job, having developed no talent, having no place to return to that evening except a dark and very damp basement flat rented by a cousin; having nothing to offer my family who, since the death of my father the previous year, were psychologically dependent on me.

Somehow I had done the writing. Somehow—and twenty years later, it was to seem such a piece of luck—I had engaged myself in the world. And twenty years of a life which had been the opposite of my landlord's had brought me to the solace of the debris of his garden, the debris of his own life. Debris which nonetheless never ceased to have an element of grandeur.

A man with a simpler idea of himself, a simpler idea of his name, would have seen the great value of his property, might have realized its value, and lived elegantly elsewhere on the proceeds. But my landlord preferred to be with what he knew. Other people might contemplate a move for him. He himself could not think of a life away from his house and garden, which perhaps he continued to see in his own way, perhaps even saw as whole and perfect, the way we fail to see the tarnishing that has gradually come to flats or houses where we have lived a long time.

*T*HE MANOR seemed so much itself, the style of things there so established, that the recentness of the decay was a surprise. And having learned to see that, I saw it in other places as well. I saw it in the cold frames just outside my cottage.

These frames, intended as little nurseries, had low walls of brick, with the northern wall a foot or two higher than the southern; and they were roofed with great timber-framed glass covers, hinged to the higher, northern wall, so that the glass covers sloped south. These covers could not have been easy to lift. Like many other things in the manor grounds, they had been overspecified: heavy glass, oversolid timber frames. At some stage the cold frames had been abandoned; and the heavy covers, taken off their hinges, had been set against the high vegetable-garden wall. That was where I found them.

They looked very old, with the weeds and grass growing around them. But when in the summer, going beyond what was strictly my own territory, and cutting the grass between my back door and the garden wall (with the manor's mower, filled by Pitton with the manor's fuel), when in the summer I first cut that grass and took the mower right up to the garden wall and the glass covers, what a transformation! What had looked like bush in a long-neglected corner of the grounds came up, after its cut, looking level and neat. And it was as if the glass covers had been set against the wall just a few months before.

The earth there, against the wall, had been made up partly of wood ash and reddish coal ash, perhaps even from the fireplaces of my own cottage (and perhaps before the days of "refuge"). Between this made-up earth and the side wall of my outbuilding there was a depression with a bulky metal grille: a soakaway, one of many set about the grounds, to drain the water that ran off the downs, the road, the paved lane, the lawn, the drive. Nothing was natural here; everything was considered. Grass and trees concealed as much engineering as a Roman forum. Just one cut with the mower did away with the idea of wilderness outside the back door of my cottage, showed up the considered lines of wall and earth and outbuilding, and the solidity of the timber-framed glass covers against the wall.

Still firm, the timber of those covers, still showing white paint. Few of the glass panes had broken; four or five had merely slipped from their cracked putties. And although the soil was poor, and was on the north side of the garden wall, and for much of the day was in the shade of the beech trees, yet the grass and weeds that grew between the glass covers had grown unnaturally tall and rich. And though in the brick-walled frames themselves (still edged with timber to receive the glass covers) there were drifts of beech leaves and beech mast, and out of the oddly yellow sand there grew nettles and ground elder and weeds whose names I didn't know and many thorny blackberry bushes, yet that one cut with the mower around the cold frame did away with the idea of old decay—as, five or six years later, the rings in the disc of the collapsed cherry tree were also to do.

It was oddly unsettling to see the ground at the back of my cottage "come up" again; unsettling to deal with the idea that the dereliction of the place was new, the dereliction which to me had made it perfect as a place of refuge, and in which I had taken such comfort; that the place had been let go just a year or two before I had arrived; that the process of contraction, though begun twenty or twenty-five years before, had recently accelerated; and that my own presence there was part of that accelerating process.

And the Phillipses too: when I had first met them, they had seemed to belong, to be part of their setting, to have been molded by the neglect by which they were surrounded. I had sat in their sitting room and looked out onto the mottled stone terrace, with its views of the untended gardens, the big trees, the overgrown water meadows obscuring everything beyond; the branches of shrubs in the foreground now hung with seed bells for the birds; and to one side, empty washing lines with a supporting pronged pole.

All that had seemed of a piece with the manor. And because I knew nothing of big-house interiors and life, and brought to that interior and view only an imagination fed more by cartoons and films than by literature (I could think of no particular book with the setting); and because, in an unfamiliar setting in England, I fell into my old way of accepting or categorizing what I found as another example of English life, I thought that the Phillipses were examples of staff or servants living in the staff quarters of a biggish house. I attributed to them the manners of such people.

It was disappointing to me to learn, as I did after a few months, that the Phillipses had come to the manor less than a year before me; that their manners were not the manners of servants or household staff but simply their own manners, the manners of people looking for peace and relishing the peace they had found at the manor.

Though they looked settled in the quiet of the manor, and though they were of the region, they were not "country" people, but people of the town, with country-town tastes. Though they seemed to be absolutely part of the manor—at ease in their quarters and indifferent to the dereliction around them, as though that had come so slowly they had not noticed—they were in fact rootless people; less rooted than Jack, over the hill.

They had no house of their own, were planning for none. They lived in houses that went with the jobs they took; and though they were people nearing fifty, as I thought, they seemed unconcerned about the time when they would be too old to work. Like their employer, my landlord, Mr. and Mrs. Phillips appeared to think that there would always be shelter for them.

The car, the outings, the shopping in any one of the three or four towns that were near to us, the visits two or three times a week to a pub they knew well in any one of those towns—these were their pleasures: town pleasures, not country pleasures. And that appearance of being long settled and comfortable in their quarters (where the furniture, most of it, would have belonged to the manor), that appearance which so reassured and comforted me that first day, was part of their talent as rootless people. It was a talent not unlike Jack's, though it was not so immediately apparent.

In the middle of farmyard dereliction and his own insecurity in his job and cottage, Jack kept his elaborate gardens and did his digging for vegetables and flowers and kept his plots in good heart. So, in the middle of an equal insecurity—since at any time their employer might die, and they would have to move on with their possessions to another job and another set of rooms—the Phillipses made their cozy home. Jack was anchored by the seasons and the corresponding labors of his gardens. The Phillipses had a different kind of stability. It was events outside their home, festivities outside, that gave rhythm and pattern and savor to their townish life: the outings, the visit two or three times a week to their pub, their annual holiday in the same hotel in the south.

Probably this aspect of their life would have given the Phillipses away. They were not by social habits people of the village; they were not by instinct or character servants of a big house; they were people of the town, the outer world. And—if I had been told nothing at all —Mrs. Phillips's pruning of the old rose bed in the garden would have made me wonder about them. Such roses in the summer in that rose-bush wilderness! And then in the autumn the bushes had been cut down to thick knotted stumps a few inches high, and Mrs. Phillips had often spoken of what she had done. "I've cut them right back." Asserting so many things at once: boasting of her attempt to tame the wilderness at the back of the house; liking, at the same time, the severe business of cutting "right back"; and intending some slight rebuke to Pitton, the solitary gardener, who might so easily—had he been interested, had he really cared—have done the pruning she had had to do herself.

There were no more roses. In the next summer there was only brier, a rampant, flowerless thicket. Brier swallowed the evidence of Mrs. Phillips's pruning; and she never mentioned it again, did nothing further in the manor gardens while Pitton was there. (And perhaps when the cycle of the manor has truly ended, when everybody who knew the place then has disappeared, and new people with new plans walk about the grounds, that wild brier patch will be noted as proof of what can happen to untended, unpruned roses.)

Where, as a new arrival, accepting everything, I had seen people exemplifying their roles, soon it was the ambiguity of the Phillipses that made an impression, caught in my mind. They were people of the outer world acting out their role as house servants. And the ambiguity was real. Mr. Phillips had been a male nurse in a mental hospital; then he had worked in a hotel. In one of those places—a hospital or a hotel—Mrs. Phillips had begun to suffer from her nerves; and it was because of those nerves that they had come to the manor, to be a little withdrawn, to look after my landlord.

So far from being a servant, Mr. Phillips had been in the business of restraining and disciplining people. And as often happens, people attracting people they need, Mr. Phillips, the strong man, attracted people—like his wife, with her nerves—whom he had to look after. And perhaps there was an extra happiness of this sort as well in his job in the house, with his employer. Which would have explained his oddly happy, fulfilled look that day when I saw him driving his employer below the beeches on the ledge above the river.

He was a man of medium height; perhaps even a small man. The cold-weather clothes he wore—a heavy zip-up pullover, for the most part—concealed his physique. It was only in my second summer—perhaps because of what I had been told about him, and what he had told me about himself—I noticed his well-developed back, his great shoulders and powerful forearms, as of a man used to lifting weights.

Every afternoon at about three I heard him shout from somewhere beyond the vegetable garden. After some time I knew what he was shouting. He was shouting: "Fred!" It was his call to Pitton to tea. Whether this was a gesture of friendship; whether it was something he was required to do; whether they all had tea together in the Phillipses' sitting room or in the kitchen, or whether Pitton just went and took away his tea, I don't know. There was an irritation and authority in that shout that made me think of the other "Manor" (as it was known locally) where Mr. Phillips—and Mrs. Phillips as well, before her nerves—had worked.

❋ ❋ ❋

ONCE THERE were sixteen gardeners. Now there was only Pitton. It was some time, a fortnight perhaps, before I got to know him, got to know that he wasn't just a visitor to the grounds; and it was some time again before I understood that he was the gardener, the last of the legendary sixteen. He didn't quite fit the role. There was nothing antique or forlorn or elegiac about Pitton's appearance. He was in his mid-fifties, middle-aged rather than old; he certainly wasn't one of the original sixteen. He was a sturdy man, with a firm paunch, and of the utmost respectability in his dress. He wore—it was winter when I first saw him—a felt hat, a three-piece tweed suit, and a tie. (Always a tie on Pitton, winter and summer.)

Not only did he not look like one of the sixteen, he didn't even look like a gardener. At least, he wasn't my idea of a gardener. And that is a better way of putting it, because this business of gardens and gardeners called up special Trinidad pictures and memories, called up the history of my own small Asiatic-Indian community, late-nineteenth-century peasant emigrants, and touched a nerve.

As a child in Trinidad I knew or saw few gardeners. In the country areas, where the Indian people mainly lived, there were nothing like gardens. Sugarcane covered the land. Sugarcane, the old slave crop, was what the people still grew and lived by; it explained the presence, on that island, after the abolition of slavery, of an imported Asiatic peasantry. Sugarcane explained the poor Indian-style houses and roughly thatched huts beside the narrow asphalt roads. In the smooth dirt yards of those little houses and huts there were nothing like gardens. There might be hedges, mainly of hibiscus, lining the foul-water ditches. There might be flower areas—periwinkle, ixora, zinnia, marigold, lady's slipper, with an occasional flowering small tree like the one we called the Queen of Flowers. There was seldom more.

There were gardens in Port of Spain, but only in the richer areas, where the building plots were bigger. It was in those gardens that as a child, on my way home from school in the afternoons, I might see a barefoot gardener. And he would be less a gardener, really, less a man with knowledge about soils and plants and fertilizers than a man who was, more simply, a worker in a garden, a weeder and a waterer, a barefoot man, trousers rolled up to mid-shin, playing a hose on a flower bed.

This barefoot gardener would be Indian—Indians were thought to have a special way with plants and the land. And this man might have been born in India and brought out to Trinidad on a five-year indenture, with a promise of a free passage back to India at the end of that time or a grant of land in Trinidad. This kind of Indian contract labor had ended only in 1917—antiquity to me in 1940, say; but to the barefoot waterer in the garden (still perhaps knowing only a language of India) a time within easy recall. This kind of gardening was a town occupation, barely above, perhaps even merging into, that of "yard boy," which was an occupation for black people, and something so unskilled and debased that the very words were used as a form of abuse.

After the war a new kind of agriculture began to develop. Port of Spain had grown, and the lands of the Aranguez Estate, not far from Port of Spain, were taken out of sugarcane cultivation (Aranguez, named in the late eighteenth century by the Spaniards after the town of Aranjuez in Spain, with the famous royal gardens). There was a certain amount of house building at Aranguez; but to the south, on the edge of what was swampland, liable to flooding from the Gulf of Paria when the Orinoco River in Venezuela rose, on this land, on either side of the highway embankment the Americans had built during the war, former estate workers had leased plots from the estate, a few acres each, and had begun to develop vegetable gardens, slowly redeeming the land from swamp, building it up.

The vegetables they grew—aubergines, beans, okras—had a shorter cycle than sugarcane and they were correspondingly more demanding. They required finer attentions; and every day during a vegetable cycle the vegetable growers could be seen weeding or digging or watering or spraying, even when there was horse racing or an international cricket match in Port of Spain or some big festive event, working the way men work only when they work for themselves.

Cocoa created the effect of a forest or wood; sugarcane was a tall grass. The straight lines of these vegetable plots, the human scale, the many different shades and textures of green, gave us a new idea of agriculture and almost a new idea of landscape and natural beauty. The vegetable growers were Indian, but these vegetable plots were like nothing in peasant India. The skills, the practices, came from the experimental plots of the Imperial College of Tropical Agriculture—famous throughout the British Empire—which was just a mile or two away. Many of the Indian vegetable growers had worked there as garden laborers. And it was only some years after I had been in England that I saw that the landscape the Indian vegetable growers had created on either side of the highway in south Aranguez—a landscape which had no pattern in Trinidad or India—was like the allotments I saw in England, at the edge of towns, from the railway train. English allotments in a tropical and colonial setting! Created by accident, and not by design; created at the end of the period of empire, out of the decay of the old sugar plantations.

Thirty years later the Aranguez vegetable plots were to cover many square miles, land built up from swamp, season by season, creating a flat, wide, Dutch effect, extending all the way to swamp mangrove in one direction, and in the other appearing to go to the foot of the Trinidad Northern Range, now no longer green and empty, but covered on its lower slopes with the shacks of illegal black immigrants from the other islands. The landscape which, when I was a child, still retained some of its aboriginal, prediscovery features, was to be irrevocably altered, and the people with it.

Thirty years later, at the time of the oil boom, many of those vegetable growers (or their descendants) were to become people of wealth, with children at schools or universities in Canada and the United States. But at the beginning, just after the war, when there were still damp, palm-thatched huts in the aboriginal reeds and sedge of the swamp beside the American-built highway, the labor of those vegetable plots, scientific though it was, still looked brutish and underpaid, an extension of plantation life, of mud and sun and bare feet, damp huts, and oily or sweated felt hats folded at the back to fit the head like a visored cap.

Flowers were beautiful; everyone loved them. In Port of Spain there were the many acres of the Royal Botanical Gardens, established after the British conquest of the island; and the lily ponds and rockeries of the Rock Gardens. Both places were recognized beauty spots. But the idea of "gardeners" was not contained in the idea of the garden; in fact, it ran contrary to the idea of the garden. The garden spoke of Port of Spain and comfort and a good office job and Sunday drives around the Queen's Park Savannah. The gardener belonged to the plantation or estate past. That past lay outside Port of Spain, in the Indian countryside, in the fields, the roads, the huts.

Literature or the cinema (though I cannot think of any particular film) would have given the word different associations. But that knowledge—of swamp and estate and vegetable plot—was the knowledge I took to England. That was the knowledge that lay below my idea of the P. G. Wodehouse gardener and my idea of the gardener in *Richard II*, poetically conversing with a weeping queen. And inevitably I acquired new knowledge. There were the gardeners of the great parks of London. There was the gardener of my Oxford college, a mild, humorous, pipe-smoking man with (as I thought) the manner of one of the dons. And just as in the allotments beside the railway I had grown to see the original of the Aranguez plots; so, coming to the manor (with its echoes of the estate big house and servants), and seeing around me the remnants of agricultural life (the remote, distorted original of the Trinidad estates), that earlier knowledge revived in me.

But Pitton, the last of the legendary sixteen, was quite original. He appeared at nine every morning at the wide, white-painted gate at the end of the lawn. And in his three-piece tweed suit he looked so unlike a gardener or any sort of manual worker; he so studiously avoided looking at my cottage, so carefully kept his distance, kept to the far path; that I thought he was going on through the back of the manor grounds to some quite different duties, and in opening the white gate was simply exercising some old public right of way.

There was a certain amount of movement in and out of the manor grounds. And until his punctuality and regularity gave him away, I thought that Pitton might be one of those visitors, someone perhaps approaching the farmyard or the churchyard from a back way; and someone also with a right to use the water tap near the garden shed at the side of the squash court built like a farmhouse.

We also had animal visitors. There was a black and white cat that came down the way Pitton came and, in the tall grass and weeds near the box hedge, became a great hunter. There was a Labrador dog that made an opposite circuit. He belonged to a house further up the valley; his master was away in London during the week, and on weekday mornings this dog did its own circuit of the water meadows. On sunny mornings from my sitting room I saw his tail bouncing up and down far away, saw no more; until eventually, having pushed through water meadow and overgrown orchard, the animal fetched up in front of my cottage, underbelly black and wet, paws black and wet. Like Pitton, he stuck close to the buildings on the other side of the lawn; and there was in his hunched shoulders, his looking straight ahead (a little like Pitton trying to give the assurance that he was minding his own business), some hint that he knew he was in territory not his own. The elegant fawn-colored creature was not liked by everybody. His morning circuit was not of the water meadows alone. He was also a haunter of dustbins. The Phillipses at the manor complained; even Pitton complained. A disappointment there, about the dog. A little like the disappointment I felt in Pitton himself when he, the carefully dressed, paunchy, staid figure, became known to me and turned out to be only the gardener.

The wilderness that the black and white cat and the fawn-colored Labrador explored was the wilderness that claimed Pitton (or so it seemed), the wilderness which he entered every day as gardener. But he never came out as dirty or as wet as the Labrador; he came out as clean as the cat.

The main reason was his steadiness, his refusal to hurry himself. Pitton knew how to pace himself. There was nothing in Pitton's labor of the attack or boisterousness of Jack when I saw him in his allotment or garden. On some summer afternoons Jack worked bare-backed. Pitton

would never have done that. Pitton cared too much for the idea of
clothes. If Jack's varied labors and varied dress (as I saw them in his
after-hours garden) were like successive illuminations in a book of
hours, exaggerated and emblematic, Pitton was a more modern man,
a man of fashion.

Yet in Pitton's fashionableness, his careful but regular buying of
clothes that matched the seasons and were meant for that season's wear,
in this very steadiness, this absence of waste, there was something
like ritual. Clothes and the seasons ritualized Pitton's year. There was
a time for the felt hat and the three-piece suit, thornproof. There was
a time for the straw hat; there was a time when the three-piece suit
became a two-piece. There was a time for pullovers, one pullover, two
pullovers. There was a time for "country" shirts, a time for lighter
shirts; a time for a quilted jacket; a time for a dark, thin, plastic raincoat. His dress was absolutely suited to the work he was doing and
the time of year. In that fine judgment about clothes and the weather,
as well as in his steadiness, his physical pacing of himself, lay Pitton's
extraordinary neatness.

And in his clothes, his appearance, his refusal to look like a gardener or farm worker, a laborer, lay much of his pride. I thought that
at least some of the vanity would have been given Pitton by his wife.
She was a woman of a great, delicate beauty, which was extraordinary
in someone of her station; her complexion and features and her car-
riage suggested the nearness of some fine strain.

Both Pitton and his wife were people without the gift of words.
They had trouble finding words for what they had to say, so it seemed
that they had very little to say. But the beauty of Pitton's wife was of
such a sort that it overcame her intellectual, which was also her social,
disability. It was always good to see her; her near-dumbness was always a surprise. Beauty is beauty, though; and beauty is rare; no one
who possesses it can be indifferent to it. And I thought that Pitton's
clothes were meant—either by Pitton himself or by his wife—to match,
to set off, Mrs. Pitton's looks.

Then another idea was given me by a middle-aged English writer, a friend for many years, who was visiting one day. As a writer he was socially scrupulous, knowing how in England to look through both the caricature and the self-caricature.

The writer saw Pitton—it was summer now, and Pitton was in his summer clothes, with his straw hat—picking his way back slowly to the white gate. Pitton's morning work was done; he was going home for lunch. He timed his lunchtime exit so that he would reach the white gate more or less at one o'clock. Pitton was on the far side of the lawn, not looking at my windows, staring ahead like the fawn-colored Labrador.

Tony said, "Is that your landlord?"

"He's the gardener."

Tony said, "It proves something I've long held. People get to look like their employees."

I hadn't truly seen my landlord and didn't know what he looked like. Tony had perhaps seen him years before, in London, in the days when my landlord was socially active, a man about town, before he had withdrawn.

But Pitton's resemblance to my landlord—if such a resemblance did exist—couldn't have been induced in the way Tony was suggesting: the employee imitating the employer, and the employer then, out of laziness, out of being flattered, imitating the imitation of his employee. Pitton's resemblance to my landlord would have been an accident, a coincidence; because Pitton had come to the manor at about the time my landlord had withdrawn, at the beginning of my landlord's great depression. Even now, as I heard from the Phillipses, my landlord came out of his room only on the finest days; and Pitton hardly saw him. It was the Phillipses who mediated between my landlord and the gardener—or, more properly, the garden.

My landlord couldn't have been Pitton's model. But I felt at once that there was something in what Tony had said or implied about Pitton; that the style was modeled on that of a superior. Pitton, as I heard, had been in the army in some capacity before coming to the manor —we were in a military area. And turning over this question of Pitton's model after Tony's visit—in fact, never losing the idea as long as I saw Pitton—it came to me that Pitton's model (with the encouragement of Mrs. Pitton) would have been an army officer of twenty or twenty-five years before whom Pitton had served or served under (someone still alive in Pitton's memory: Pitton's imitation this officer's chief memorial, perhaps).

The army was still important to Pitton. His son was in the army. The progress—or the postings—of this boy was the only topic which could make Mrs. Pitton, blinking fast, speak a sentence or two; normally she only smiled and looked pretty. We met occasionally at the bus stop, in the shade of the dark yews and beeches. There were not many buses; the road was fairly quiet; and voices at the bus stop sounded and echoed almost as in a room. We spoke about her son as though he were no more than a boy at school, as though, say, he was doing reasonably well with the books, but doing a little better in the swimming and the sports.

The word "school" did in fact come up in Mrs. Pitton's talk of her son's army life. She told me at the bus stop one day, "They've sent him to the artillery school." This would have been at Larkhill. Apt name once: these downs around Stonehenge rang at the appropriate season with lark song. But now—untouched though the green downs looked—Larkhill was the name of the army artillery school, booming away during the day and sometimes during the night and sometimes, if there was a big exercise, night and day.

Because Pitton's son was there, and because Pitton told me of the great event, I went in my first summer to the artillery school's "open day." It was like one of the summer rowing occasions at Oxford, when the families of undergraduates occupied the college barges. It was like the sports day at my school, Queen's Royal College, in colonial Trinidad. I recognized the occasion at once. Instead of masters and boys, there were officers and soldiers; instead of sports, displays with guns, displays of great skill. But there was the same atmosphere of the fair, of food and women's clothes, of unusual colors, of normally hidden family relationships now publicly exposed; the same half-humorous loudspeaker announcements, the same atmosphere of dressing up and showing off, the same atmosphere of a society especially mixed for that day—boys and masters showing off at the school sports, men and officers showing off here, whole families showing off, women and girls displaying themselves, the poorer very concerned not to be outfaced.

I could see the attraction of the occasion for the Pittons. I could see that it might well have been their most important social occasion for the year. And the open day did provide a little extra conversation for a while with Mrs. Pitton at the bus stop.

Then she told me one day that her son had finished his training at the artillery school. It had gone well. "His friends gave him a little momento." And believing perhaps that "momento" might be an army word, another special army word, as new and puzzling to me as it had been to her, she repeated it and explained it. "A little momento of his time with them. An old-fashioned brass cannon set in clear plastic, like a diamond."

A cheap souvenir; the smiling, empty-faced woman speaking of her son as of a child still. The "momento," the bad art: the reality—the army, the soldier son—should have matched. But the reality was different. The reality was serious. The Pitton boy was being trained as a killer soldier, the new-style British soldier. And he was suited to the part. He was a giant, with very big feet. The fineness of the strain that had produced Mrs. Pitton's features had ended with her or had skipped her son.

It was astonishing that now—after its ineptitude in the nineteenth century, which was yet the century of the great glory of the empire; and after its great but wasting achievements in the Second World War, at the end of that imperial glory—it was astonishing that now, when there were no more big wars for the country to fight, the British army should be concentrating on producing this kind of elite soldier. There were occasional incidents in the little towns around Salisbury Plain; the taxi drivers sometimes had trouble at night. But in our valley we seldom saw a soldier or an army vehicle. Army vehicles seemed not to be allowed there; in our valley we lived protected from what surrounded us, just as in the nineteenth century the big industrialists lived in country estates outside the industrial towns where they made their fortunes.

Pitton's boy came home one weekend with his "girl." On Sunday afternoon he took her up to the viewing point. That was when I saw them. I was coming down the hill at the end of my own walk. The small girl clung to the giant, seeming to wrap herself around him, in a demonstrative way I had never seen in the valley. Or it might have been that I was at the age when I was able to observe these things with detachment, the detachment and knowingness I was aiming at when I was eighteen, and doing my drafts of "Gala Night." The boy, the girl; the parents' house; the walk before tea—the tribal ritual, setting the observer at a distance.

But how disquieting that boy's face was! In spite of his size, one could see the child his mother still saw: the unformed features still, the conflation of the two gentle faces, Pitton's and Mrs. Pitton's, the two simple, inarticulate people I knew, inarticulate but with their own vanities, the two faces meeting in the dangerous obedience, the new vanity, of the soldier.

It was this quality of obedience in Pitton—the obedience he had passed on to his soldier son—that separated him from Jack. Over the hill, in a kind of no-man's land beside the droveway and the half-abandoned farmyard, Jack did more or less what Pitton did in the wilderness of the manor grounds. But Jack was free in a way Pitton wasn't and now could never be. Perhaps it was Jack's intellectual backwardness, his purely physical nature, that made him content with what he had. And that was not little. Jack was lucky in his circumstances: his cottage, the land he could till, and, above all, his isolation, the silence and solitude he went to sleep in and woke up to. These circumstances, taken together, made his backwardness unimportant, and not the burden it might so easily have been in another place. These circumstances of Jack's, together with the nature of the man, made his life appear like a constant celebration. That labor in his garden, after his paid work on the farm, that exhaustion, the pleasures then of food and the drive to the pub, the long, muzzying drinks, the sight year after year of the sweet or beautiful—and profitable—fruits of his labor: why not, then, the bare back in the summer, as much as the fire in winter?

There was a relish and a boisterousness and a toughness to Jack that neither Pitton nor his son would ever now have. The soldier's boisterousness of which Pitton's son was no doubt capable was perhaps like the boisterousness of the undergraduates in the cellar of my Oxford college before dinner: a form of caste behavior, something acquired, as unnatural as formal manners.

Pitton wouldn't have cared for the brutishness and constriction of Jack's life—farm, cottage, garden, pub—all within a few miles. Pitton was more intelligent, had seen more. He had models where Jack had none. Pitton expected more for himself; he wished to offer more to his wife, of whose beauty (though I never heard him speak of it or hint of it) he would have been proud. But the superior intelligence and knowledge which made Pitton ambitious also made him obedient; and vulnerable; put his life in the hands of others.

So THERE was something in the simple first impression Pitton made on me—observing him enter the grounds by the white gate every morning at nine.

He didn't look like a gardener. With his felt hat and tweed suit, he looked more like a visitor, like a man passing through. He was in fact going to the garden shed, which was also his changing room. He entered in his suit, a visitor; he emerged a gardener, having adapted his garb to the weather and job of the morning. But he had no idea of himself as the last of the legendary sixteen. He had another idea of himself, another idea of romance. And although (as we were to see, when the time came) he valued his job on the manor and the freedom of his job—he was unsupervised, and could work out his contracted hours as he chose; and although it was in his power to turn a blind eye to poachers or even some local gentlemen looking for a little Saturday-afternoon shooting; although, in outsiders' eyes, a little of the grandeur and privilege of the manor attached to Pitton, the manor formed no part of Pitton's idea of romance.

And that was disappointing to me: that on the manor Pitton, like the Phillipses, and like me, was a camper in the ruins, living with what he found, delighted by the evidence of the life of the past—like a barbarian coming upon an ancient Roman villa in Gloucestershire, momentarily delighted by the wonder and ruin of a heating system he no longer understood or needed; like a barbarian in North Africa, brushing away new-desert sand from a mosaic floor with gods now as mysterious and unnecessary as the craft of the mosaic floor itself, once hawked about by merchants traveling with patterns, stones, and journeymen floor-layers—but not tormented in any romantic way by the idea of that life, not wishing to recreate or "restore."

It was Pitton who, after he had cut a way through the orchard and woodland undergrowth to the "garden refuge" area, had shown me the thatched two-story children's house, one of the refinements of the grounds, yet by its appearance never much used by children, more an adult refinement, a piece of period fantasy and elegance. Pitton understood that, and thought the children's house worth showing. But the garden refuge he had created over the years (especially melancholy with faded flowers and discarded flower arrangements—not all from the manor, some from the funerals in the little church—that spoke of death and the rituals of farewell)—this refuge of Pitton's was just behind the children's house. The house, in fact, with its high conical roof served to hide the dump and made it more of a "refuge."

But if Pitton were not as equable as he was, if he couldn't live easily with the idea of ruin, if he had been one of the original sixteen and had been weakened by elegiac fantasies, he might not have been able to do what he did do.

That summer, my first, word came down from his employer, my landlord, that the "hidden garden" was to be opened up and cleaned. Hidden? Was there something in the grounds—apart from the lawn and the wood and the walks at the other side of the house that were for the exclusive use of my landlord—that I didn't know? There was. The "hidden garden," as it turned out, was so successfully hidden that, though I walked past it every day, I had never suspected that there was anything unusual there. It was a trick, like false books on a shelf.

It was at the back of the main garage; and what looked just like the vegetable-garden wall at the back of the garage was, in fact, the outer wall of the hidden garden.

Behind that outer wall and the true wall of the vegetable garden was the hidden garden. It was enclosed on all sides, and entered by a wooden door. This door, which I passed every day, was permanently shut and seemed from the outside to be one of the many doors or gates to the vegetable garden which, with the diminution of staff, the thinning away of the sixteen, had been closed forever. That door was now opened, and Pitton went to work, carting away barrowloads of old wet dead leaves flattened by their own weight, and earth mingled with old beech mast. (I noticed then his precise way with the loaded wheelbarrow, before pushing it off. He stationed himself carefully; and then, holding his arms straight down, after a pause bent his knees, so that in the process of holding and raising the handles of the barrow his back remained more or less straight. It made me think that this was probably how the men who carried sedan chairs in the eighteenth century handled their bodies, to prevent ache or damage.) Barrowload after barrowload Pitton carted to the refuge; and in the hidden garden, below the tall, spindly-branched blossom trees, there came up, almost as new, a little tiled fountain, the tiles pale blue with spangles of gold. A frivolity, a little extra, a gilding of the lily, a little something else to do when all had already been done, something from the twenties or early thirties.

The Phillipses called me to witness. Pitton called me to witness. We exclaimed, all of us, dutifully, at the secretness of the garden. The Phillipses exclaimed that something so beautiful could be so neglected; we all exclaimed that so many people had walked past the place without knowing; and we felt we were a little privileged, seeing what we did. But then no one seemed to know what to do with the hidden garden. The door was closed; the garden and the tiled fountain became secret again; and no doubt soon began to be covered again by the debris of leaves and beech mast and dead beech twigs.

The fantasy of a summer for my landlord. Something one day— some quality of light, some object in the house, some letter—might have reminded him of that garden of his childhood. He wanted to see it. He sent down instructions. Pitton worked for a week. And when he had seen it he forgot about it again. (Had he seen it, though? Had he walked so far from his usual, protected beat? Had he come so close to my cottage and what he would have considered the public part of the grounds? I never heard from Mr. or Mrs. Phillips that my landlord had actually gone to have a look.)

What had disappointed me no longer disappointed me. Pitton couldn't do the job he did, couldn't work with the knowledge that his labor was eventually to be wasted or mocked, couldn't keep a kind of order, couldn't hold back utter vegetable decay, if the glory of the old manor garden and the grounds had been part of his romance, if he had been one of the legendary sixteen. Pitton could do what he did because he had his outside, army or army-officer, fantasy.

And as a result, perhaps because of resentment of this outside life, this self-sufficiency of Pitton's, or perhaps because of resentment of his manner and pretensions, the idea that was put about was that, in the business of gardening, Pitton didn't really "know." He grew vegetables and certain kinds of flowers that were required by the house—and that meant his employer. But somehow, in spite of this, he didn't really know, wasn't a true gardener, a man who possessed the mystery.

And in this rebuke or resentment of Pitton there was contained an idea of the gardener which I felt to be very old, going beyond the idea of the gardener which I had found at my Oxford college, going back to the beginning of worship and the idea of fertility, the idea even of the god of the node: the gardener as the man who caused the unremarkable seed to grow into leaves, stalks, buds, flowers, fruit, called this all up from the seed, where it has lain in small, the gardener as magician, herbalist, in touch with the mystery of seed and root and graft, which (with the mystery of cooking) is one of the earliest mysteries that the child discovers—one of the earliest mysteries that I, my sister, and my cousins discovered when in the hard yellow earth of our Port of Spain yard we, taking example one from the other, and just for the sake of the magic, planted hard dry corn, maize, three seeds in a shallow hole, fenced the hole round with a little palisade of sticks (to protect it from the chickens that ran free in the yard), and then three days later, in the morning, before going to school, discovered the miracle: the maize shoots that morning breaking the earth, the green outer sheath developing quickly into a thin leaf curling back on itself, like a blade of grass, like sugarcane, developing until the child became bored, ceased to watch and protect, and the chickens knocked the stick palisade down and pecked the still tender plant down to nothing.

It was this childhood sensation, this childhood delight in making things grow, that was touched in England when I saw the vegetable allotments at the edge of towns, beside the railway tracks. I attributed to the people who worked in those allotments something of what I felt as a child when I planted my corn seeds; felt it as old, that emotion, that need, surviving here, in England, the first industrial country, surviving in the hearts of dwellers in the ugliest and most repetitive Victorian industrial towns, surviving like the weeds that grow in the artificial light and polluted air of railway terminals, growing in the oily gravel between the rails almost against the buffers.

That instinct to plant, to see crops grow, might have seemed eternal, something to which the human heart would want to return. But in the plantation colony from which I came—a colony created for agriculture, for the growing of a particular crop, created for the great flat fields of sugarcane, which were the point and explanation of everything, the houses, the style of government, the mixed population—in that colony, created by the power and wealth of industrial England, the instinct had been eradicated.

The vegetable fields of Aranguez in Trinidad, on either side of the American highway, had been created by accident, with the debris, the accidental diffusion among laborers, of the learning of the Imperial College of Tropical Agriculture. They looked like the allotments in England, and there was a connection of learning, of science. But the plots of Aranguez at the edge of Port of Spain and the allotments at the edge of English towns spoke of different instincts, needs, different hearts now. The old world, of planting and fertility, the very early world, perhaps existed in the colony, and only for a short time, in the child's heart. Adult eyes saw in agriculture not magic but servitude and ugliness. And that was why the English allotments touched something as small and as far away and as vague as my memory of planting three seeds of corn in the yard of our family house in Port of Spain.

*T*HE IDEA that Pitton didn't "know" was something in the air at the manor. It was an idea that came to me gradually, with knowledge of my surroundings. I do not remember Mr. or Mrs. Phillips offering it as a statement. So I suppose that the idea would have been put to me in a number of indirect ways by the Phillipses before I had settled in and learned to look around me and come to my own judgments.

I assumed, for instance, that it was because of this idea, that Pitton didn't know, that Mrs. Phillips in my first autumn (and really, as I was to understand, not long after she herself had come to work and live at the manor) cut back the old overgrown moss-rose bushes in the overgrown rose garden and reduced them to rampant brier.

When the spring came and the true rose leaves didn't show among the seven-leaved brier stems and the thorny rosebuds didn't appear, she said nothing; she dropped the subject of the roses and the pruning. It was one of my early lessons in the valley in the idea of change, of things declining from the perfection (as I thought) in which I had found them. And though every May for some years afterwards, when I was there, I looked for those buds in spite of the brier, hoping for magic, this silence about the roses was for me a way of coping with the disappearance of the roses. What was perfection to me would have been decay to the people before me, and hardly conceivable to the first designers or gardeners.

Nothing more about the roses, then. But by this time Pitton had been given his "character." And increasingly I felt it as odd that this resentment of Pitton as a man with an insufficient grasp of his mysterious craft, a man without the true vocation, should come from people—the Phillipses in the manor, and Bray, Pitton's immediate neighbor—none of whom could be said to have vocations or trades, people who, for this reason, in this agricultural, nonindustrial part of England were curiously unanchored, floating.

The Phillipses I thought of as people getting by. It was impressive to me, who had lived all my life with anxiety and ambition, to discover that they had no plans for their future, had almost no idea of that future, had planned for nothing, and lived with the assumption that somehow, should things go wrong here, there would always be a kind of job, with quarters, for them somewhere else. It was impressive to me, and I don't mean it ironically: this readiness for change, for living with what came. But it contained no idea of the vocation or achievement. It contained only this idea of getting by, of lasting, of seeing one's days out.

And the same was true of Bray, Pitton's neighbor. Bray was a car-hire man; and though he was more rooted than anyone in the village and was as close to the manor as anyone could be—his father had worked in the manor in the old days—he, who rebuked Pitton for not knowing about gardens, had so little feeling for gardens and even for the valley in which he lived that he had turned all the front part of his house plot into a concrete area for his various, always changing, vehicles.

The Phillipses, who gave Pitton tea every day—the cry of "Fred!" from Mr. Phillips had tones of authority rather than friendship or fellowship—made no direct statements about Pitton to me. Bray wasn't like that. Bray was more open. It was his "independent" style; he was proud of this style. He was open about my landlord; he wished that openness to be noted. He said, raising the topic himself, "Wouldn't have him in the car. Like a bloody bird. Wants to sit in the front. Then he wants to sit in the back. Then he wants to sit in the front again." And of Pitton Bray said more than once, "He's a very arrogant man."

"Arrogant," like "commonest," was one of Bray's words. "Arrogant," was primarily Bray's version of "ignorant"; but it also had the meaning of "arrogant"; and this word, when used by Bray, with its two meanings and aggressive sound, was very strong.

Pitton and Bray lived in adjoining semidetached cottages on the public road. The cottages had slate roofs and walls of flint and red brick, with the brick in regular two-course bands. Both cottages had once belonged to the manor; and like the "picturesque" thatched cottages not far away, like the manor itself, had been built by the manor estate before the First World War. Pitton's cottage still belonged to the manor; the cottage went with the job. But Bray owned his cottage. He had inherited it from his father, who had worked all his life at the manor and had bought the cottage for very little—the sale was in the nature of a benefaction to him—when the manor estate had begun to shrink, the family being active elsewhere.

The smallness, sturdiness, the straight lines and the materials (red or orange-colored brick and flint) had made me think of those cottages as semiurban. But then, getting my eye in, I had seen the style in old farm buildings for many miles around, had seen it as the local way with flint, which was so plentiful here; and I had grown to understand that the cottages had been built as experimental "improved" agricultural cottages. They were as a result more genuinely "period" now than the thatched cottages just down the road. The thatched cottage still stood for an idea of the rural picturesque; and thatching was far from being a vanishing skill; thatchers were at work in all the valleys of Wiltshire. But the building style of the improved cottages—the flint and the bands of brick—was no longer practiced by the local masons. That particular skill with flint was hard to come by; and the social idea, of improving cottages for agricultural workers, no longer had a point.

Similar houses, then, for Bray and Pitton, houses with an easily readable past. But on Bray's side of the party wall and fence there was the idea of proprietorship. Bray owned his house; he wanted that to be known. And to that he added the idea that he was a free man, a man who worked for himself. On Pitton's side there was the idea of style. Pitton kept a tidy garden, with a hedge, a patch of lawn, and small flowering trees. Bray's garden was more a concrete yard for his cars and minibuses. And that was the cause of some trouble between the two men.

Pitton said nothing about Bray. Everything I learned about the running dispute between the two men I learned from Bray—I used his cars. Bray told his stories in his own way. He suppressed his own actions and provocations; he reported only what Pitton did. And the effect of this was to turn Pitton—so well dressed, so steady in the manor grounds, his gait so measured—the effect was to turn this man who was a paragon in public into a madman at home.

Bray would say as he was driving me to the railway station, "Our friend has taken up building these days. Drilling holes in the party wall at three o'clock in the morning. What do you think of that?"

And so Bray would allow one to play for a while with this picture of Pitton as a madman with the electric drill, raging about his house at night, a Mr. Hyde with a modern ray gun, yet somehow sobering up sufficiently to appear neatly at nine, a Dr. Jekyll of the manor grounds, at the white gate of the lawn.

And it would be only at the end of the ride with Bray, or during the next ride, or the ride after that, that I would learn that Bray, for every kind of good reason—his passion for work, his self-reliance, his hatred of the idleness which was undoing the country, the unreliability of other people—for all these very good reasons Bray had been taking down or tuning motorcar engines in his paved yard until well after midnight.

In Bray there was an element of perverseness. He knew that his paved and oil-stained yard and his half-taken-down motorcars offended people. He knew that they were an especial offense to Pitton, who lived next door; he knew, too, that it was inappropriate, a noticeable disfigurement of the valley which he was anxious for his tourist passengers to see. But Bray, though he would have denied it or not found words for it, wished to offend Pitton's idea of correct behavior and style. And there was the added reason that Bray felt he could do as he pleased with his ground and house because they were his and because he—unlike Pitton and unlike nearly every working man he knew—was a free man.

Freedom was important to Bray. And though he presented the car-hire business and the taking of people to the various terminals of the many airports and the picking up from the airports of foreign children, though he presented this as a high skill, almost a vocation, equal to anybody else's, his vocation was really to be a free man, not to be what his father had been, a man "in service," a servant.

Service—a world dead and gone. But not to Bray; his childhood lay there, just as my childhood lay in the vanished world of sugarcane fields and huts and barefoot children; and ditches and hibiscus hedges; and religious ceremonies which I accepted but didn't understand; and the beauty of the lighting of the lamps after the prayer in the evening; and the fear of the rumshops and the quarrels and fierce fights. Just as "estate," "laborers," "gardeners" called up special pictures for me, so Bray lived with pictures of the valley I could only dimly visualize.

He spoke often of the past to me. He spoke of harvesttime and children taking tea to their fathers in the fields; of shepherds and their huts on the downs; of laborers who were granted vast daily allowances of beer; of picturesque clusters of laborers' cottages, now knocked down. So far from concealing his background, he always brought it up, to remind himself (and me or whomever else he was talking to) of how far he had come.

What had Bray's father been? He had said at first the "head gardener," the top man of the legendary sixteen. And perhaps only someone like that would have had the privilege of buying his cottage at a very low price. But later he had also said that his father had been the butler, the chauffeur (and sometimes even the "coachman"—there were wagons in the sheds next to the antique, ivy-covered granary). So it is possible that this claim that his father had been head of the legendary sixteen was only Bray's way of putting down the "arrogant" Pitton.

Whatever his father had done at the manor, Bray was proud of his father; did not reject him. But connected with the father's service at the manor was a memory that touched Bray himself and still caused him pain.

He began to tell me one day of the time he had gone to work at the manor during the holidays from the village school (now no longer existing as a school, existing only as a building, a cottage, a desirable dwelling). It was an important memory; it still caused him pain. He could talk about it to me because I was a stranger; because I could understand; and because I was interested. I had developed a lot since 1950; had learned how to talk, to inquire, and no longer—as on the S.S. *Columbia* and in the Earl's Court boardinghouse—expected truth to leap out at me merely because I was a writer and sensitive. I had discovered in myself—always a stranger, a foreigner, a man who had left his island and community before maturity, before adult social experience—a deep interest in others, a wish to visualize the details and routine of their lives, to see the world through their eyes; and with this interest there often came at some point a sense—almost a sixth sense—of what was uppermost in a person's thoughts.

So Bray began to talk one day of his holiday service in the manor. But something then occurred—perhaps a stop at traffic lights, perhaps some altercation or exchange of greetings with another driver. And then the pain of the memory overcame Bray's wish to tell me his story; and the days he had spent as a servant in the manor remained secret. Perhaps it was his acquiescence in the role that caused him pain; perhaps he saw it as an exploitation of his innocence, his childishness. Children, whose experience is so limited, readily accept an abused condition. Even his play can encourage a child to live with his abused situation: can encourage masochism in someone meant to be quite different.

Thinking back to my own past, my own childhood—the only way we have of understanding another man's condition is through ourselves, our experiences and emotions—I found so many abuses I took for granted. I lived easily with the idea of poverty, the nakedness of children in the streets of the town and the roads of the country. I lived easily with the idea of the brutalizing of children by flogging; the ridiculing of the deformed; the different ideas of authority presented by our Hindu family and then, above that, by the racial-colonial system of our agricultural colony.

No one is born a rebel. Rebellion is something we have to be trained in. And even with the encouragement of my father's rages—political rages, as well as rages about his family and his employers—there was much about our family life and attitudes and our island that I accepted—acceptances which later were to mortify me.

The noblest impulse of all—the wish to be a writer, the wish that ruled my life—was the impulse that was the most imprisoning, the most insidious, and in some ways the most corrupting, because, refined by my half-English half-education and ceasing then to be a pure impulse, it had given me a false idea of the activity of the mind. The noblest impulse, in that colonial setting, had been the most hobbling. To be what I wanted to be, I had to cease to be or to grow out of what I was. To become a writer it was necessary to shed many of the early ideas that went with the ambition and the concept my half-education had given me of the writer.

So the past for me—as colonial and writer—was full of shame and mortifications. Yet as a writer I could train myself to face them. Indeed, they became my subjects.

Bray had no such training, no such need. The prewar depression, the war, the postwar reforms and boom lay between him and his past. The further away he was taken from that past, the more the world changed, the more perhaps it pained him.

Politically he was a conservative. "You know me," he would say. "I'm a down-and-out Tory," running together "downright" and "out-and-out." By that, being a conservative, he meant really that he worked for himself and was a free man; that he had less regard for people (like Pitton) who lacked the will to be free and worked for other people; and that he had no regard at all for people who were parasites on the state, and hated the idea of paying taxes to support these people. With this Toryism, however, and his hatred of the Labour Party and the "commonest," there went a strong republicanism. He depended for his livelihood on people with money; he liked the odd ways of the rich and liked to talk about these ways. But at the same time he hated people who drove Rolls-Royces; he hated landowners, people with titles, the monarchy, and all people who didn't work for a living.

He hated titled people and old families and people of inherited wealth in a way I wouldn't have thought possible for an English person, until

I read William Cobbett. There, in the prejudices and strongheaded-ness and radicalism of one hundred and fifty years before, a radicalism fed by the French Revolution (which in the pages of Cobbett, in the living, breakneck speed of his prose, could still feel close), I found many of the attitudes of Bray. An empire had intervened, a great new tide of wealth and power; but the passions of Bray were, miraculously, like the passions still of a purely agricultural county, the passions con-nected with manors and big farms and dependent workers. Much of this, with Bray, was rooted in his own family connections with the manor, and with some still rankling humiliation connected with his holiday period "in service" there.

Pitton, the gardener with the tied cottage, dressed carefully; he aimed at a kind of country-gentleman style. Bray, the free man, wore a driver's peaked cap. He said (when we were some months into our business relationship, which had developed into something like a vil-lage acquaintance) that he wore the cap because it helped with the police. And he was right, as I saw on many occasions, especially at the airport. The police, uniformed themselves, acknowledged the peaked cap, responded to it, and were easier (in every way) with this badge of a trade.

He also said another time that he wore the cap to distinguish him-self from the ordinary taxi drivers, who spent so much time parked and idle and skylarking. But they, the taxi men, thought the peaked cap servile, mocked Bray for it, as they criticized him for his low charges (seeing servility there as well). And that—Bray's "servility" and gen-eral old-fashionedness—was the reason why Bray—who, because he was punctual and reliable and fair, had built up a bigger clientele than he could singlehandedly manage—that was the reason why Bray couldn't get a driver to work for him for any length of time. Bray asked too much of the drivers he employed; he wished them to work the hours he himself worked; he wished them to dress formally, even to wear a uniform.

Bray himself didn't dress formally. He wore the peaked cap. But everything else he wore went counter to the suggestions, the implied deference, of that cap. He wore a cardigan, mostly; very seldom a jacket.

A cardigan can be unbuttoned or buttoned in many ways; it can suggest formality, casualness, indifference; it can suggest, as Bray often made it suggest, a man called away from fireside and slippers and television. And the peaked cap—it would be set at many different angles: it could express regard or disregard. Set correctly, that cap (together with a buttoned-up cardigan) could suggest not deference so much as a man handling himself with care: a self-respecting more than a respectful man.

The cap helped Bray to assert himself, to pass opinions and judgments on people he came into contact with. It would have been harder for him without the cap; he would have had to find words, set his face in different ways. He would as a result have been constantly embattled (the car-hire or taxi business being what it is). The peaked cap, with its many angles, together with the various ways of wearing the cardigan, enabled Bray to make (and make clear) a whole range of subtle judgments.

In fact, for the very reason that he was reacting against the service manner of his father, Bray had the variable, fluid personality of the servant: the various accents, voices, expressions. Bray, unlike Pitton, had no model. And, depending on himself alone, he gave a distinct impression of oddity. And that variable, passionate personality of Bray's, that many-sided personality, was perhaps fundamentally unstable. He didn't serve the manor. (There might have been some quarrel there, about which I knew nothing: the Phillipses never mentioned it, and the quarrel might have been before their time.) Yet his resentment of Pitton was also partly the resentment of someone he felt to be an intruder. Because he, Bray, felt and claimed that he knew more about the manor and our landlord than Pitton ever could.

Similar houses, improved agricultural cottages, and both with working men who, for all their differences and conflict, aimed at the same thing: dignity.

So tensions surrounded Pitton both where he lived and where he worked. Because at the manor Pitton returned or vented to the full— but on the Phillipses—Bray's resentment of him as an outsider and interloper. Pitton, in spite of his buttoned-up look and lack of words, had his way of passing on his "feelings"; and, as much as the Phillipses might indicate to him that he didn't know, he could pass on to them that they were townies, newcomers in the manor.

So these three sets of people, so physically close, and all in different ways "in service," lived in a net of mutual resentment. An odd thing about them was how differently they dressed. Choice in dress —cheap versions of stylish clothes—was limited by what the shops in Salisbury offered. And though I soon got to know the shop or "outfitters" where Pitton bought his country-gentleman clothes (and they were not particularly cheap), and the "sports" shop (much cheaper) where the Phillipses bought their padded anoraks or zip-up pullovers, and though I couldn't help seeing the clothes as merchandise, not truly personal to the wearer, more as samples of a vast stock, and though the shops in Salisbury were so close to one another, yet this "difference" in their clothes was important to them all.

And all these people were tough—or insensitive, or partly blind to their condition; they needed to be. Bray earned the freedom he was so proud of. He never turned a job down and worked prodigious hours; he had nothing like a connected private life, and seldom had a full night's sleep. The Phillipses were tough—even Mrs. Phillips, "nervous" and liable to headaches—living as they did with nothing put by, and with the knowledge that at any moment they might have to leave and live elsewhere, with other people, other relationships, other conditions.

And Pitton lived not only with the irritations of Bray and the Phillipses, but also with the knowledge that away from the vegetable garden all his labor—not voluntary like Jack's, but paid, his job—was in the wilderness of the manor grounds: repetitive brute labor, with hardly anyone to notice, like the clearing away of the dead leaves of autumn; pointless labor, like the cleaning of the hidden garden, which had then been simply closed up again; labor in grounds awaiting a successor.

His improved agricultural cottage; the garden shed; the manor grounds. This was his little run—a dreadful constriction, if it was all he had. He needed the other idea that he had, the country-gentleman idea. Unsupervised, without fixed hours, he might, without that other idea and the "temperament" it gave him, have become slacker, might have degenerated into a tramp, become a Jack without the zest, the true coarseness, the life.

I had a taste of Pitton's temperament myself in my second summer. I had gone away, done some traveling, and come back almost at the end of the summer. I found that the grass around my cottage had not been cut at all in my absence. A mere fringe of ground around the cottage was technically mine to look after and "keep in good heart." Five minutes' work with the mower, no more. But this little area Pitton had scrupulously left alone, though it spoilt the appearance of the lawn.

Mrs. Phillips said, "People are funny." As though at last I had been given an idea of what they had to put up with.

She would have watched the grass and weeds grow during my absence. She would have waited with some pleasure for my reaction when I got back.

I had no wish, though, to get drawn into the resentments and quarrels at the manor. When I saw Pitton in the grounds I went to him and asked him to lend me his mower. He was abashed. He had set up a little quarrel, a little tension, and had done so for some weeks in the full sight of the Phillipses. And now—at what should have been the climax, quarreling time—he was abashed. What he had done he had done in the sight of the Phillipses. But he didn't know how to quarrel with me, a stranger. It was touching. He began to mumble some explanation, but then thought better of it. He went directly to the shed and brought out the mower and a tin with the fuel mixture. He was solicitous; he even gave me a rag, to wipe the mower casing after I had filled the tank.

When I was finished with the mowing I took care to leave the mower and the fuel tin just outside the locked door of his garden shed—as though letting him know by this dumb show (I hadn't been so careful before when I had used his mower) that I wasn't taking him for granted. And he responded in a way I never expected. On the Thursday afternoon he took my dustbin to the manor courtyard for the Friday-morning dustbin collection. He lifted the filled metal bin by one handle only, using only one hand, and not altering his gait or normal walking pace: a demonstration of his great strength, in spite of his age and paunch and apparent slowness.

So we became friends. And on some afternoons of the late summer and early autumn—sunshine and shadow on the lawn—we worked together. He allowed me to help with the last cutting of the lawn—I always liked cutting the lawn. And I helped with the gathering of the leaves—a pleasant midafternoon activity (for an hour or so), oddly serene, stacking the leaves into a roughly carpentered two-wheeled caged trolley, pushing that through the orchard and past the children's house to the "refuge," removing the front of the trolley, tilting the trolley forward and then spreading out the leaves on the springy, slippery leaf hill.

A few days before Christmas I went to Pitton's house to give him a bottle of whiskey. It was damp and cold; the road ran with wet; the beech trees and the sycamores, though without leaves now, still seemed to keep out the sun. Pitton's gate and the paved path to his front door were in better shape than Bray's. It was only when I was right at Pitton's door that I noticed how badly in need of paint the door and timber surround were; and that the front casement windows were half rotted.

It was a long time before Pitton came to the door. Perhaps he had had to prepare, to dress. And there was an embarrassment about him, a tightening of his face, which let me know that he didn't like being "caught" in his house.

The house was much poorer than I thought. The improved agricultural cottage of sixty-odd years before, however sturdy its external appearance, was a little ragged and knocked-about inside. The narrow hall was shiny with rubbing, hardly a recognizable color. The small front room was scrappily furnished.

Modest furniture which, though old, still made one think of the shops where it had been bought; modest television and hi-fi, which again made one think of cheap shops; cheap unlined curtains. Only the photographs—of Pitton and his wife together, younger; of Mrs. Pitton alone, twenty years before (a photograph with which she was clearly pleased, looking over her shoulder); a photograph of the son —only these photographs made the room, which had been Pitton's for so long, personal.

The casement windows, as I could see more clearly from the inside, were warped; the room was drafty. Why hadn't Pitton done something about the decorations? I know what he would have said. Decorations were the estate's responsibility; the house wasn't his. He was waiting for the estate to decorate his front room and no doubt the rest of his house; he was content to allow time, a portion of his life, to pass in drabness. It was disappointing. Here was the true servility, the true obedience, of the man. It was hard, faced with his gravity, his measured movements, his weighty manner, his self-cherishing, to grasp that other fact about him. So much of the money he earned, then, went on clothes, for himself and Mrs. Pitton, that show to the outside world about which they were both so particular.

I gave him the whiskey. He thanked me, but he didn't look especially pleased; his tight expression didn't go or soften. That expression softened, the muscles of his face grew slacker, only when, making conversation, covering up what I now recognized to be the error of my visit, I mentioned his hi-fi equipment. I said I had nothing like that myself. The tight, embarrassed look on Pitton's face was replaced by a foolish, self-satisfied smile. He was glad—it was amazing—he was glad his possessions had surprised me.

And that foolish smile of Pitton's took me back to early childhood—like a dream here, in this valley, in this house of Pitton's—and to painful memories. Within our extended family our little unit was poor; and I remembered, on the one or two occasions when remote, richer branches came to visit us, how strong the instinct with us was to boast, to show off, to pretend that we were richer than we were letting on. Curious instinct: we didn't boast with people who were as poor as ourselves; we boasted to people who were richer, who could easily see through our vanity. I had seen it in others too; my earliest observations as a child were about the lies of poverty, the lies that poverty forced on people. We were a very poor agricultural colony at the end of a great world depression. Very few people had money;

great estates had to be sold for very little, money being so scarce; and among the laborers there was great distress. Yet as a child I saw people pretending to their employers, to the people who paid them every week, that they, the paid people, were richer than the payer knew; that they, the daily or the weekly paid, people who worked for eight hours or more a day for less than a dollar a day, had secret means and—almost—a whole secret life.

Something of this—some whiff of huts and damp and the swamplands of my childhood—came to me at Christmas, in the Wiltshire valley, in Pitton's improved agricultural cottage. He was poor. I discovered now that he was hurt by his poverty, ashamed of it. I discovered now that his nerves were rawer than those of the Phillipses or Bray. He was much more vulnerable than they were.

THE SHOUT of "Fred!" came from somewhere in the manor at about three o'clock. It had taken me a little time to work out that that was being shouted, the shout having at first seemed like another of the many country noises: the cry of some animal; the far-off cuckoolike shout of the cowman driving the cows back from the water meadows to the milking shed (he was simply shouting, "Go on! Go on!"); farm machines; birds; the flap of pigeons' wings as they fluttered about their perches or roosting places in the thick ivy on the old granary wall; the antiquated milking machine from the farm beyond the churchyard—this machine rose to a scream just before it was turned off, making you aware then, in the comparative silence, of the whine with which you had been living for the previous two hours, a whine which lingered like a ringing in the ears or like the sound of cicadas; the drone and roar of military aircraft.

When I had worked it out, the shout of "Fred!" from Mr. Phillips became quite distinct; and I thought it was part of an old routine, something that had existed long before my time. I soon discovered that it wasn't so. And I was able to give a character and mood to the shout, and to understand the tensions that played around it. Pitton, I then realized, never acknowledged the shout or called back.

It was an afternoon shout. But sometimes—and especially in the spring—it could be heard in the morning. It meant then that Mr. Phillips was mediating between my landlord and Pitton. In the spring my landlord wanted to see flowers; to go shopping; sometimes to combine the two things. He didn't want to visit other gardens (that would have been too disturbing to him, entering other people's houses or territory). He preferred to go to flower shops and garden centers; and he wanted Pitton to go with him.

On these excursions, when Pitton was called away, where did he sit in the manor car? Did he sit in the front, beside Mr. Phillips, the other manor servant? Or did he sit alone in the back, a man apart in another way?

I feel Pitton was taken along for the company and the protection his company (together with the company of Mr. Phillips) offered my landlord. Pitton couldn't have been taken along purely for his advice as a gardener, because the plants bought—which Pitton had to look after—were not always suitable. Azaleas, I remember once, unsuited to our chalk, which Pitton had to plant more or less in pots of sand. I asked him why, and he floundered, became inarticulate, until inspiration came to him and lit up his face and he said, "Minerals." Having planted the azaleas in sand, he had then, every day until the azaleas died, to "feed" them with an expensive "iron" solution, "feeding" being quite an appropriate word, for these small azaleas needed to be fed with droppers, the way birds or young motherless animals might have been fed.

In my third year, my third spring, there were more of these morning shouts than before. And this had to do with a change in my landlord's condition. From being very ill and almost immobile with his acedia—at about the time the Phillipses had gone to the manor to look after him and his house—my landlord was beginning slowly to recover. Some medicine or drug had been found to neutralize the paralyzing nature of his acedia, and this brought into play again the personality (or that part of it) that had survived his long withdrawal and blankness. An operation had then partially restored his sight.

In this reawakening of my landlord to life and his especial world the Phillipses helped a great deal. Mr. Phillips was professional, understanding, a protector, a strong man to whom the sick man, at once employer and dependent, could entrust himself. To the strength of her husband Mrs. Phillips added tenderness and admiration for the artistic side of the employer who wrote poetry and now, in addition, with his restored sight, began to do drawings. These drawings were oddly fluent, practiced, easy, as though they had been done many times before, as though they came from a segment of that past life of my landlord's that he had just recovered: Beardsley-like drawings, of another age, with long tendrillike lines and little stippled areas emphasizing the large areas of white.

Some of these drawings—in reproduction: his continuing or reawakened extravagance—he sent me by Mrs. Phillips now, in place of the old printed sheets of poetry he had sent in my first year.

In his reawakening, his rebirth, my landlord met the Phillipses halfway. He was tender with them, as they reported. They were part of the life he thought he had said good-bye to. The Phillipses accordingly felt needed; perhaps in none of their previous jobs had they been made to feel like that. And they in their turn became softer, less spiky, more secure in their positions in the manor. Their toughness was now partly explained: it was the toughness of people who wanted to be as tough as they had found the world tough, and wished to hold themselves ready for whatever fortune threw at them. The Phillipses, becoming confident in the manor, no longer strangers to the place, became happier; as happy in their way as their employer in the summer. That repeated morning shout of "Fred!" seemed to say it all. As did that glimpse of a happy Mr. Phillips—like an impresario—driving with his employer that day in the manor car, on the road below the old beeches.

That mood lasted into the next summer. Pitton often had to go away on some excursion and sometimes when he came back he had some little piece of news for me. "I've hardly done anything today. I was called away early this morning." He wasn't complaining; he liked the idea of being "called away"; he was recording his pleasure at the new idleness, the new closeness to his employer, and with that closeness the sudden luxury almost of his job: car rides, shopping trips, sight-seeing trips, all on a workday morning. "He said, 'Pitton'—that's how he calls me, you know: he doesn't call me Mr. Pitton." I called him Mr. Pitton; that was why he gave this explanation. " 'Pitton, I think we should go to Woolworth's this morning. I hear they have a good garden department.' Woolworth's," Pitton said, amused but respectful. "Imagine him in Woolworth's."

Of these summer excursions of my landlord I heard second accounts from Mr. Phillips sometimes. And of some of these excursions I had even a third account. This came from Alan, a literary man from London, a distant relation of my landlord, who sometimes came now to spend a weekend at the manor, which he had known, he said, from visits as a child, beginning with the war.

Alan was in his late thirties. He was a small man, as small as I was. His size was one of the things that tormented him. He told me almost as soon as we met—as though to raise the subject before I did—that at school someone, one of the teachers, I believe, had referred to him as "dwarfish." This worry about his physical appearance perhaps explained Alan's clowning, his mighty explosions of laughter, the extravagant cut and colors and shininess of the clothes he wore at parties in London, where from time to time I saw him. The gaiety of these clothes and the boisterousness of his manner contrasted with the nervousness, almost the shiftiness, of his eyes; and contrasted as well with the solitude and soberness of dress and behavior he imposed on himself when he visited the manor, where one sometimes surprised a wrinkled old-lady's look on his face, before the wrinkles became the wrinkles of gaiety.

Alan seemed to spend much time alone when he was at the manor. He was to be seen at odd hours wandering about the grounds, carefully dressed, and usually in country clothes—but there was no audience there for his clothes or his moods. What did he get out of these visits? He said he liked the house, the atmosphere; and he was fascinated by my landlord, whom he found very "period," the period, as Alan said, "before the deluge," "antediluvian."

He had heard from my landlord about the trip with Pitton to Woolworth's. When he told me this he roared with laughter. "He said that Pitton was too ashamed to enter, and had absolutely to be dragged in."

Who had improved the story I had had from Pitton—the story in which Pitton had been simply amused by the trip to the garden department of Woolworth's? Was it my landlord, the reawakened recluse? Or was it Alan?

Alan had no book to his name. He wrote occasional book reviews and did occasional reviews of books and films and other cultural events for the radio. His radio work was better than his printed work, his voice and speech suggesting, and transmitting, a greater intelligence and zest. Such a slight name, though, such a slight achievement for someone nearly forty, someone who had already more or less defined his personality and path and the level of his ambitions.

On the radio his voice and attack and wit suggested that those few minutes in the studio were the merest interlude in a busy, complete, rounded life: a life one might envy. Listening to him, one felt that there was so much there, in the man, the sensibility, the cultivation, the mind; there was so much more that he would have said if he had had the time. That was also the impression—though to a fainter degree—that his printed work gave: the few paragraphs one read appeared to be just a shaving from a larger, more considered view of life and art and history, and even from a more considered view of the book or play being written about. But those little reviews and short radio talks and swift discussions abruptly terminated by a chairman before the news program came on—that was the sum of Alan's work, life. He did no other job.

To know his name, to mention some slight thing he had done, did not—as one might have expected from someone so urbane—get an abashed dismissal from him. It encouraged him to speak of his work. He remembered all the phrases he had made, phrases that had seemed on the radio to bubble out of a natural effervescence, and sometimes fell a little flat in print. He would say, "As I said in that review of the book about Montgomery, the writer seemed to have been dropped on the head as a baby by a military man—" And he would break off and roar at his own joke, just as he roared at the joke—his own, or my landlord's—about Pitton going ashamed and cringing outside the doors of Woolworth's and having to be led in firmly by the long-haired recluse.

"Isn't it nice to have rich friends?" Alan said one weekend. And feeling he had said something frank and funny, he fluttered his eyelashes; and the coquettishness, quite unexpected, revealed another side of his dissatisfaction and incompleteness.

Alan, speaking of rich friends, was thinking more of himself as a writer, the man with patrons and grand houses at his disposal. But we were all embraced that summer, made light-headed, by my landlord's reawakened sense of the luxurious, his reawakened extravagance, his constant wish to seize and heighten the passing moment, to arrest and elaborate on every experience. These were the manners and style, as Alan said, as though to explain his point, of "before the deluge."

Now Mrs. Phillips brought to my cottage new printed drawings, a shopping basket, flowers—elegant gifts which I found difficult to acknowledge, for the man and the nature of his gifts seemed to require a matching light elegance, and I found myself in my letters to him straining for effect, trying to make myself worthy of his generosity, trying to give myself a sensibility equivalent to his own.

One sunny morning, about coffee time, I saw Pitton standing outside the overgrown box-bordered enclosure at the side of the lawn, the enclosure once attached to the house that, as I had heard from Bray, had stood on the site formerly (and possibly had older, religious antecedents).

The weeds in the enclosure had grown tall, stalky with fine white flowers. But Pitton had cut his annual path through the weeds to the orchard, one swath up, one swath down. The path had been cut low, revealing level, tightly knitted grass, the grass in one swath lying at a contrary angle to the grass in the other, the two swaths showing as two distinct colors, one green, one almost gray.

And Pitton now, in the middle of the morning, was standing on the lawn just outside the enclosure, standing still, looking down at the grass. The overgrown box trees made an arch above the entrance to the enclosure. Pitton was framed in this wild green arch; behind him was the two-swathed path between the tall white-flowered weeds, like a passage in a maze. He was leaning forward, looking fixedly down, legs oddly apart, as though he were standing on sloping or uneven ground. His woolen tie—winter and summer Pitton wore a tie—hung straight down; his tie didn't rest on his paunch.

He reminded me of a man I had seen thirteen years before, a forest Indian in a new mission settlement in the Guiana highlands, in South America. The settlement was on the bank of a river, not one of the great continental rivers, but a narrow river of these highlands, with big boulders on the banks, and big smooth boulders, sometimes neatly cracked, in the riverbed itself.

It was a Sunday morning, and the Indian was dressed as formally as Pitton was now dressed. The Indian was in blue serge trousers and a white shirt. He had gone to the Sunday morning service in the mission chapel. The settlement was in a new clearing; the stumps of felled trees still looked raw; the forest still pressed on three sides. And now after that morning service the Indian was on his way back to his forest village, taking the path at the edge of the clearing, just above the river, which in sunlight was the color of pale wine, and at dusk became black. Night here made for anxiety. Daylight was always reassuring.

Something on the path had caught the man's attention, had alarmed him; and he had stopped to consider what he had seen, the thing that didn't belong to the path—a twig perhaps, a leaf, a flower—and perhaps hinted at a terrible danger. For the Indians here there was no such thing as natural death. There was a killer abroad always, the *kanaima*, a man like any other in appearance, never known or suspected to be the killer; and he it was who eventually killed everybody. Stock still, then, the Indian on his way back from the chapel stood on the path above the river in the morning sunlight, in his blue trousers and white shirt, wondering whether (in spite of what the missionaries had told him and his fellows) the thing he had just seen on the path wasn't a sign that the *kanaima*, who got everyone in the end, hadn't finally come for him. It was a narrow path between big sunken boulders; the Indian didn't make room for me when I got to him. I walked around him; he didn't look at me.

It was with a similar stance and abstraction that Pitton stood outside the overgrown enclosure. But he knew he had caught my attention, and he was waiting for me to go to him. When I was almost upon him he lifted and slowly swung his left leg so that he stood upright. A stiff, deliberate movement—it might have been a wooden leg. But the face Pitton lifted to me was alight with passion. I had never seen him so stirred. His eyes were bright, moist, staring; his nostrils were quivering. He was full of news. Bursting with news.

He said, "I've been drinking champagne. He called me to his garden and gave me champagne."

And more than the wine had made Pitton muzzy. It was the sunlight, the occasion, the luxury, the hour of the morning, the unexpected development of this bewildering summer, play piling upon play. If I hadn't come upon him, he would, I feel, have gone home to share his news with his wife.

He said again, getting muzzier by the minute, contemplating the moment, eyes almost wild, "Champagne."

I heard another version of this event about a month later from Alan. The summer was over, more or less. Alan was wandering about the grounds in a matelot outfit, like a sailor figure of one of the earliest poems my landlord had sent me, in my first summer, after the poems about Shiva and Krishna.

Alan said, "He's in great antediluvian form. I hear he's been feeding Pitton pink champagne." And the idea so amused Alan that the full laugh he started on began to choke him. Recovering, he said, "Pink champagne at ten o'clock in the morning. He told me that Pitton was absolutely slain. Absolutely slain."

And I felt now that that other story, about Woolworth's, hadn't been improved on by Alan, but by my landlord. He had stored up the story of Pitton and the champagne, as Pitton himself (and Pitton's wife no doubt) had stored it up. He had stored it up to tell it to visitors like Alan, people who knew and cherished his reputation as a man with a style of before the deluge. Yet the impulse that morning, the need to celebrate the moment, would have been genuine. Later would have come the ideas he had of his own romance; later would have come his wish to make the story, to tell the tale, to spread his legend.

After the long morbid withdrawal, the near death of the soul, he had revived. But what had also revived was the idea of who he was. That was shown in the disproportionately large and thickly lettered signature on his new drawings; it was even bigger than the signature on the printed poems he had sent me about Shiva and Krishna while he was still very low, pressed down into himself. The personality that had survived its illness now had a smaller area for play; it was also a smaller personality. It could play only with people like Alan—there were not many like Alan, not many who knew his, my landlord's, legend now—and Pitton.

"*I*SN'T IT nice to have rich friends?" Alan had said. But that was Alan's own fantasy; that was the vision he preferred to have of the place where he came to stay. The Phillipses knew better. They knew how many things at the manor needed to be done; they knew how little could be done.

The manor had been created at the zenith of imperial power and wealth, a period of high, even extravagant, middle-class domestic architecture. The extravagance of houses like the manor lay partly in the elaborateness of the modern systems—plumbing, heating, lighting—that had been built into them at the time of the building. Whatever their architectural style or whimsies, and though in certain particulars (thatched roof, use of flintstones) they might aim at local, rustic effects, houses like the manor were a little like steamships. They had been built with that confidence; not just the confidence of wealth, but also the confidence of architects and technicians in the systems they were putting in. And it was that industrial or technical confidence—the confidence which in other manifestations had created the wealth that had built the manor—that now made the manor an expensive place to look after. The manor had been built like a steamship. But like a steamship, it was liable to breakdown and obsolescence. A boiler exploded in the manor one day; another time a bit of the roof was blown off. Each accident would have cost thousands.

The plumbing and drainage systems were obsolete. When late at night water was used in some quantity at the manor and the cistern there began to fill again, the metal pipes in my cottage hummed, in the dead silence; during the day that humming noise was masked by other sounds. The metal pipes that had been buried in my cottage walls (such had been the confidence of the original builders in their materials and systems) had also built in such damp in the walls that the pipes were shadowed on the surface of the walls by lines or tracks of gray-black mold, which was like the fur a rat leaves in its nest or hiding place.

Seventy years and more of rain, rolling chalk and flint and mud off the downs, had clogged the drains in some places. The lawn was not the simple level ground it seemed. It concealed Edwardian drainage pipes, which were now broken underground no one knew exactly where. In the winter of the great flood a small hole, like a rabbit hole, suddenly opened in the lawn during a morning of heavy rain; the hole seemed to cave in on itself, melt into itself; and then out of that melting hole a brown torrent—at first looking only like a kind of animal activity: a mole kicking up earth very fast—gushed for half an hour.

From time to time we had a visit from the agent. This was a reminder that we were not exempt from the world where others lived; that there was a practical side to affairs: earnings, accounts, a need to balance income and expenditure.

It was from the Phillipses that in the beginning I first heard of these visits. In those days, before the Phillipses had become confident, they appeared to look upon these visits by the agent as inspections and they prepared accordingly. They didn't overdo the zeal, but it was possible, from a certain amount of activity in the manor courtyard, and sometimes even from hints dropped to me about the drift of leaves against my north wall (impossible absolutely to clear: that wall was the natural resting place of beech leaves for two or three hundred yards around), it was possible to tell that a visit from "the agent" was expected.

But then the agent often turned out to be a very young man, a junior, someone fresh from school or college, someone who had just joined the firm and was using our estate to cut his teeth in the land-agenting business. Agents here handled mile upon mile of fishing rights, beat upon beat; thousands of acres of farmland, thousands of acres of woodland. Our few acres of wasteland, virtually untilled, though a world to us, offered no land agent a challenge or even a training. And it often happened that the young men who came, moving on quickly to higher or bigger things within their firm or another firm, never came again. It was hardly worthwhile, therefore, cultivating them or even getting to know their names. And from looking upon the visits of "the agent" as inspections we began—or at any rate the Phillipses began—to look upon them as occasions to ask for things, repairs here, a lick of paint there. And from making ourselves spruce to attract commendations (which might be reported at a higher level somewhere far away) we sought to look as ragged as we could.

After that wonderful summer of the motorcar drives and the flowers and the champagne we began to get very ragged indeed. Three of the beeches at the edge of the lawn were judged to be dangerous, liable to fall into the manor courtyard. And within a week they were cut down and their branches cut up and corded, some stacked in one of the outbuildings, some carted away by the tree cutters as part of their fee. So all at once, within a week, I lost some of the green shade, the green gloom by which I had felt embraced whenever I returned to the manor from any journey, however short or long.

Only the yews and beeches at the front of the house separated me from the road; and though the beech trees—big as they were—were not really a form of sound protection, I fancied after those three beeches went that the road noises were louder, especially after five—so that, for the first time here, I became aware of the end-of-day traffic. And I fancied I heard the military airplanes more clearly too.

How fragile my little world was here! Just leaves and branches.

Just leaves and branches created the colors and the enclosure I lived within. Remove them—a morning's work with a chain saw—and the public road would be just there, less than a hundred yards away, and all would be open and exposed.

How often, with Pitton's mower, I had cut the thin, pale-green, straggly grass under those beeches, going right up to the end of the lawn, next to the overgrown yews, going right up to where the ground was not grass or lawn so much as old twigs and beech mast and old, light-starved dust. It was never satisfying to use the mower there; but it was necessary, because it completed the job, gave the complete, swept, cared-for effect all over, so that for a day or two after a grass-cutting it was a pleasure for me to look at what I had done, the swaths I had created myself in rich grass and poor grass, from end to end of the lawn.

Now, in the openness after the three beeches had been felled, grass began even in the autumn to appear on that twiggy, dusty soil. And all that winter and spring, until the grass began truly to grow again, there remained, quite literally, impressions of the felled beeches on the lawn. The tree fellers had made them fall at a particular angle, so that in the new openness, the new light around the manor courtyard, the beeches, though they had ceased to exist, seemed for half a year to cast ghostly shadows.

The decision to cut the beeches was a prudent one. The gales were severer than usual in the spring. So severe that I stood in my cottage kitchen to watch (through a low window) the effect on the beeches in front and (through the glass at the top of my kitchen door) the trees at the back. It was strange, but for myself, in my cottage, I never ever feared. And I actually saw the two great aspens at the back of the manor garden snap, twice, a tearing-off near the top and then a fierce, short snapping-back lower down. So that, understanding the principle of the damage, it was a little like watching a human or animal limb break. I hadn't planted those trees; but I saw them destroyed.

In the spring and summer the three aspens, planted perhaps ten feet apart, had created the effect of a great green twinkling fan above the garden wall. Now two of the three aspens had been snapped like twigs and showed—but on a magnified scale—that sort of twig-snapped damage. And their debris lay between the water meadow and the vegetable-garden wall, just beyond the brier wilderness of the old rose bed.

It needed more than Pitton and his hand saw to clear the mess. I tried to help him. But even when we worked on a smallish bough, there always came a moment when the saw stuck in the wet, sappy wood and became very hot.

Pitton would say, "It's tying. We'd better stop."

"Tying, Mr. Pitton?"

I liked the word. I had never heard it before; but it was suggestive and felt right. Pitton became embarrassed, as embarrassed as he had been when I had asked him what was in the sand that was good for the azaleas he had been asked to plant. As embarrassed as he had been when he told me my landlord had liked the pe-*onies* (rhyming with "ponies") in front of my cottage and, while feeling constrained to use the affected Edwardian pronunciation of my landlord, had wished at the same time to show—without disrespect or disloyalty—that he also knew the other, more common and correct pronunciation.

The fallen trees were a great obstruction now if I wanted to go on the river walk. The jagged white wood of the aspen stumps—fifteen or twenty feet high—slowly lost its rawness; with the spring and summer there were even new shoots.

The planter or the designer of the garden would have carried in his or her mind's eye the fan effect the three trees were intended to have when the seedlings or saplings had been planted ten feet apart. Far apart they would have seemed then, and for the next five years or so; but still too close together, as it turned out: the trees at the sides, as they had grown, had leaned away from the vertical. The fan effect had been seen by me. I had seen the three trees grow by many feet every year. I had also seen what the planter of the garden would not have cared to think about: the very second, not longer, when the two side trees snapped. The trees would have spanned, or been contained within, my landlord's life. He must have seen that two of the aspens were no longer there; he must have seen the mighty debris in the back garden. But I had no word from Mr. or Mrs. Phillips that my landlord had seen or made any comment.

It seemed suitable, so ragged had we become since the autumn, that in the early summer we should have had a visit one day, in mid-morning, not from one but two men from the agent's. And this time not just the standard very young men. There was one of those, but with him there was an older man, a taller, heavier man in his late forties or early fifties.

I saw the two men on the lawn with Mr. Phillips—Mr. Phillips shorter than the other two, but much more muscular, in his zip-up windcheater; the young man in his navy-blue blazer; the heavier older man from the agent's in a well-worn gray suit, a country shirt, and an old-fashioned polka-dotted handkerchief stuffed into his breast pocket.

They looked at the granary. They opened the garages or wagon sheds next to the granary. They opened the farmhouse and looked at that. They wandered away, down the box-hedged enclosure; and a little while later reappeared. The young man in the blazer came in to see me. The older man went on with Mr. Phillips along the lane to the manor, past the overgrown yew hedge and the new openness where once the tree beeches had cast shade.

Talking about the dereliction he had seen in the back garden, the young man said, "It's a cruel thing to say. But the best thing would be to cut down all the beeches and plant afresh."

It was a cruel thing to say. It would do away with the place and setting I lived in. But the young man wasn't speaking with any great conviction or concern. His eyes were quite bright with pleasure. He had been slightly oppressed by being all morning in the company of his superior, the man in the gray suit; and now, in the cottage, he—younger than he looked from a distance—was oddly skittish and playful and relaxed. Not at all agent material, I would have thought. And it turned out, very soon, that his heart wasn't in the business.

His comment about the trees was just something he had said because—perhaps—he had heard it said in various circumstances by other people in the agency. As was his comment, looking at the paddock where the dairyman from the neighboring farm had kept his pony, and where the once famous old racehorse had come to die: "You could put a couple of beeves in there and fatten them up."

A couple of beeves—was that really his language, his style? It wasn't; and that self-awareness or self-knowledge lay so close to the surface of his thoughts that it required only the beginning of conversation to bring it out. His father was a gamekeeper on a proper estate not far away. Through the recommendation of his father's employer he had been taken on for a trial period by the agency; and he had accepted the offer—this thin young man with the smiling, blank, unformed face—to please both his father and his father's employer. But his heart was elsewhere: he didn't know exactly where. He would have liked service life, would have dearly liked to be an officer. But some physical disability—and perhaps also some examination failure—had kept him out of that.

He said, "You're never one of them."

Them? Who were his "them"? The "them" he was concerned with turned out to be the other young men from the agent's. At the end of the day they simply went home. There was no question of going to a pub with "them" or of "them" asking him home.

And simply, in his skittish, restless, shallow way, he bared his personality in a few minutes. And there was almost nothing more he had to say when the big man in the gray suit came to call with Mr. Phillips. The young man in the blazer then stopped talking and continued to smile in his friendly, empty way.

The big man sat down in my shabby armchair and he seemed genuinely tired, genuinely happy to sit down, happy to sip the coffee he was offered. He tried to suggest that, without looking, he really was looking; but I didn't feel he was looking now; I felt he had seen enough already. He was puffy, a recent puffiness over a body that had once been sturdy and active. He was in his late forties; his breathing was difficult; and his hair was thin and flat and lackluster. The polka-dotted handkerchief in his breast pocket was an odd touch of gaiety.

He was not interested in me, my past, or what I did. He had ceased already to be interested in Mr. Phillips. He was already, though sitting in my armchair, far away, with himself, his solitude. What could interest such a man? What kinds of things had once pricked his curiosity or caused him surprise? Perhaps now—he gave that impression—he was a little melancholy that active life had gone by so quickly already. Perhaps he had been moved by the dereliction of what he had seen in the manor and in the manor grounds; perhaps it had chimed in with his own mood, reinforced that mood.

He said, no doubt having been briefed by Mr. Phillips, "Nice spot for writing."

I said, "It's nice. But I know it can't last."

He said quietly, "No one can be certain of anything." And the words, though so ordinary, seemed to be spoken less to me than to himself and about himself.

All at once the inspection—if it had been that—was over. All three men left. They walked back to the manor along the lane between the cottage and the vegetable garden. The man in the gray suit walked heavily, carefully, making me aware of the hard lane, with chippings of stone or heavy limestone beaten into the surface; with water-carried drifts of beech mast and leaf debris in the ruts made by motor tires. They walked past the hidden garden Pitton had some summers before spent a week clearing—Mr. Phillips muscular and steady and already half-protective towards the heavy, breathless man in the gray suit on his left; and with the slender, frivolous, even slightly skipping, gamekeeper's son in his blazer on the right.

*A*BOUT HALF an hour or so later, before lunch, Mrs. Phillips came to see me. She was wearing her blue padded cardigan or jacket that bloated her and suggested someone wearing an emergency life jacket—as in an illustration in an airline card about emergency exits and what to do when the aircraft came down in water. The dark skin below her eyes, the darkness and pouches of her nerves, had lost some of its gathers and fussy lines; had lost even some of its darkness. Though she still had the manner of an invalid, someone who needed to be looked after, she had long ago begun to heal. Her hair had gone thin, had

begun to go back from her forehead, giving her the high white forehead of a lady in an Elizabethan painting. So there was in her face a
mixture of coarseness and delicacy.

She stood in the kitchen doorway, not coming in. Behind her, the
stony lane, the abandoned cold frames, the vegetable-garden wall with
the tiled coping, and the blackthorns that had grown up in the past
five years on both sides of the wall: flourishing on the other, sunny side
of the wall, rising above the wall; but thin and long-stalked on my
side, the side I could see, growing in a poor corner and dragged up
mainly by light, it seemed. Those blackthorn seedlings, the flowers and
then the fruit, had worried the Phillipses. Though they had lived here,
in the region, all their life (and Mr. Phillips's father had been born just
a few miles away), their knowledge of country things was restricted.
Far away, rising now from what more than ever had become a water-
meadow wilderness, against the big southern sky which I loved looking at, there was the damaged, the mutilated, aspen fan, with the jagged torn stumps of the two side aspens clearly showing. It would be
fifteen or twenty years before aspen greenery such as I had known
would again shade and give scale to the view.

Mrs. Phillips said, "I thought I should let you know."

This was her nurse's manner, which she shared with Mr. Phillips
and perhaps to some extent copied from him. The other side of this
manner, with Mr. Phillips, was his authority, his power, his irritability. With Mrs. Phillips it was her invalid's manner, the thin dark skin
darkening and gathering below her eyes, the thin veins getting blue
and prominent, seeming about to rupture, suggesting with the very
many fussy shallow lines on her forehead infinite suffering and fragility.

She said, "I thought I should let you know. I know you are close
to him. They're letting Mr. Pitton go." The "mister" was for my sake;
that was how I called him and referred to him. She and Mr. Phillips
called him Fred. "Of course," she said, a little more jauntily, "it's been
coming for some time."

And that was true, though I had never wanted to face the facts or
to inquire too carefully into them, half wishing to believe in magic, in

things going on as I had found them, believing—like Alan, to some extent—in the great wealth of my landlord and the ability of the people who looked after his affairs to perform great financial feats. But I knew that Pitton and his house were costing money; and the Phillipses were costing money; and the manor itself was very expensive to maintain, even in the way it was. And I could see that the estate— more a nature reserve than workable land—provided little revenue.

The great inflation of the mid-seventies would have cut cruelly into whatever income my landlord had. And the manor required too much attention. It wasn't a place that could simply be let go. It wasn't like my cottage; its scale was more than human; it exaggerated human needs. People had to be trained to use buildings like the manor; and that was why—like the ancient Roman villa at Chedworth in Gloucestershire—these buildings were perishable. People could easily do without them.

When the boiler exploded at the manor, and the ceramic or concrete or asbestos casing of the tall metal chimney against one wall had shattered into a thousand jagged fragments all over the manor courtyard, I heard—either from the Phillipses or from Michael Allen, the young central heating man, who came with his van and spent many days in the courtyard—that the annual heating costs at the manor were four to five thousand pounds. That might have been an exaggeration. Men like Michael Allen, entering rich houses for the first time because of their skills and trades, might have liked to exaggerate the importance of their county or gentry clients. Still, five thousand pounds as a heating bill—it showed how unstable prices, and our world, had become.

In 1857, in *Madame Bovary*, Flaubert could write of the peddler's six-percent interest charge as extortionate, bloodletting. Now we lived easily with that kind of charge. In 1955, when I was very young and new to London and trying to write, I wanted nothing more than five hundred pounds a year; and, more modest than Virginia Woolf thirty years before, I would have undertaken to pay for my own rented room out of those five hundred pounds. In 1962, at a lunch in a London club with a humorous writer and a cartoonist, I put my needs—the two other men had asked—at two thousand pounds a year: I had moved up from the rented room to the rented, self-contained flat. This figure had scandalized my fellow lunchers, older men, as far too low. And indeed, just three years later, when I had bought a house and taken on a mortgage, I would have considered five thousand pounds a year as just about fair. Now that was a figure that could be talked about as a heating charge. Not many fortunes would have been able to stand that kind of expense, one among many; and my landlord had retired from the world in 1949 or 1950, some years before I had thought five hundred pounds a year enough for my needs.

I watched for Pitton. He had the knack—sometimes it seemed, in spite of the steadiness and gravity of his movements, like a little game he played with himself—of reaching the white gate at the end of the lawn more or less on the stroke of one o'clock.

He would appear on the lawn in front of my cottage, his morning's work done, four or five minutes before the hour. He would do what he had to do in the garden shed—put away tools, reassume formal clothes (if that was necessary) for the short walk along the public road to his house; lock up the shed; and then, adjusting his pace to the time in hand, start on the walk to the gate. Sometimes he would enter the lawn from the vegetable garden, through an old wooden gate (over-specified, pulled out of true now by its own sturdiness and weight) in the garden wall. Sometimes, coming out of the summer bush as clean as a cat, he walked up from the overgrown orchard through the overgrown box-hedged enclosure.

This morning he came out of the box-hedged enclosure. He had only in the last week cut his first summer path through the tall weeds there, one swath up, one swath down. He was not wearing his plastic raincoat or his Wellingtons. He was quite formally dressed, without a jacket, but with a country shirt and his woolen tie. He didn't have to change. What he had to do in the garden shed didn't take long. His walk to the gate was his very slow, arm-dangling walk. Not the way he walked when he pushed open the gate at nine in the morning; not the way he walked when he worked. This very slow walk was the way Pitton walked when his work was over, when his time had become his own again. And there was nothing in his walk now that hinted at the end of a routine; nothing in his pre-lunch ritual that suggested an agitated man, a man in possession of the news Mrs. Phillips had given me half an hour before.

At two o'clock he was back. He unlatched the white gate that separated the short, dark, yew-hung lane from the open manor lawn; latched it behind him; and his walk, though unhurried, suggested a man who was at work again.

I thought that there had been a mistake; that Mrs. Phillips had misheard, or had passed on to me as a decision something that had been only an idea, something that had perhaps been discussed and dropped. Pitton was so untroubled: I thought he knew better than Mrs. Phillips.

An hour and a half later, after my walk on the downs, past Jack's cottage, up between the barrows to the view of Stonehenge, an hour and a half later, coming back to the grounds, I heard the shout of "Fred!" from Mr. Phillips, shouting to Pitton from the manor, shouting to Pitton somewhere in the back garden. There was no reply. This was normal. And then at five there was the ritual of Pitton's departure—locking up the garden shed, and expressing in his very slow walk to the front gate the end of the day's labors.

But he didn't appear at the gate at nine the next morning. He didn't appear at half past nine or at ten. It was later, in the middle of the morning, just before eleven, that I saw him. And he was banging imperiously at my kitchen door, the only door I used, the door that faced the abandoned cold frames, the heavy timber-framed glass covers stacked up against the high garden wall, the nettles growing tall behind and between the glass, and, over the wall, some distance away, near the river willows, the tall middle aspen and the mangled but already sprouting stumps of the other two.

The foolish pride he had displayed when I had seen him in his house and complimented him on his hi-fi equipment; the pretense that he had a rich source of money quite separate from his gardener's wages; the passion, the staring, enlarged eyes, the quivering nostrils on the pink-champagne morning when he had stood awkwardly bent, the tie dangling from his neck, in front of the overgrown box trees and waited for me to come to him—all of that, the folly, the pride, the wildness, the passion, was in his face. But instead of the surprise of champagne there was the bewilderment of anger, an anger that seemed to have taken him to a depth of feeling for which he was not prepared, anger that seemed to have taken him close to madness.

He said: "You heard? You heard?"

He was wearing no tie. The shirt of the day before, but no tie. I saw him without a tie only on Sundays sometimes, in the summer, when the ice-cream van passed before lunch and tinkled its chimes, and we both went out to buy ice cream.

He wanted someone to witness and share his outrage; he could not bear to be with himself. But he had no gift of words, had never had. All the passion came out in his face—it was like the champagne surprise, but twisted, and taken several notches higher—and in his abrupt movements.

I opened the door wide for him to come inside. But he, as though recognizing that he had nothing more to say, stayed outside. Abruptly he turned away and walked fast and jerkily—as though with some sudden clear purpose—down the lane between my cottage and the yew hedge and the "forester's hut" on one side and the half-cottage against the garden wall on the other side, the half-cottage in which I stored coal and wood and other things. A little way beyond this half-cottage—and how well, from using the lawn mower in that neglected corner, I knew the uneven ground, partly built up from wood ash, and knew the tufts of rough grass—there was the tall gate in the vegetable-garden wall.

This was Pitton's gate. It was chained and padlocked every evening, and Pitton had the key. The gate, as old as the manor, had a heavy timber frame, with solid boards in its lower half and vertical iron bars in its upper half. It had been pulled out of true by its own weight and sturdiness. Whenever Pitton opened the gate he had to lift it slightly; and the part of the vertical iron bar which he had held in this strong lifting way four or five or six times a working day was smoother and much darker than the rest of the iron, which was rusted and rough and dry.

To this gate Pitton went, walking fast, jerkily. His own gate, opening into his own territory. But he didn't have the key. That was in the garden shed. He crossed the lawn in his new hurried way to the garden shed built onto the side of the "farmhouse." Beside the green-painted, faded door there was an old climbing rose. Pitton pruned it each year; it produced only a few roses, but they were all big, cabbagy things, pale pink. Pitton had the key to the garden shed on him. It was attached to a chain; the chain was fixed to a loop in his waistband. He pushed the green door open. The shed was dark inside. He forgot about the key to the garden gate. He left the shed door wide open and walked across the lawn—that part which still bore the impression, like ghostly shadows, of the three felled beeches—to the openness of the manor courtyard.

The wide open door of the garden shed, left just like that, was unlike Pitton. A while later he walked past my cottage again to the heavy gate in the garden wall. Forgetting again that he didn't have the key to the padlock; that he had gone for it to the garden shed and got distracted.

He was disorientated, his frenzy expressed in these brisk, jerky little journeys, half yielding to his old routine, his wish to look after his garden, to do the jobs he had planned to do that morning; and then awaking afresh to his loss. Like an ant whose nest had just been smashed, he moved about hither and thither. At some stage he closed the door of the garden shed; and then he went away—but not by the white gate.

At lunchtime Mrs. Phillips came to see me. She had a reproving hospital manner. She said, as though speaking to one patient about another who had behaved badly, "Your Mr. Pitton was quite another person this morning. He came and sounded off about everything under the sun. Accusing us of everything he could think of. As though we had anything to do with anything. He knew very well what was going to happen. He knew everything yesterday. I don't know why he pretended not to know. It was just pretense, you know. He didn't say a thing, not in the morning, not at lunchtime, not when he had his tea with us. That was typical Pitton."

She spoke as though Pitton's refusal the previous day to acknowledge his notice or his news—when she would have been waiting for his reaction—was wicked, and deserved the punishment it got. She spoke as though this wickedness of Pitton's made everything explicable, absolved us all of the need to feel concerned for Pitton and frightened for ourselves.

And it was strange, Pitton's silence of the previous day. Had he not understood, had he not taken in what had been said to him? Had he simply not listened? Had the words of the man in the gray suit been roundabout? Had the news been too shocking for Pitton to believe it? Or was it his own form of magic? I remembered how when Jack had fallen ill and his garden had grown wild, and the chimney was smoking in the summer, and Jack was in his bedroom trying to get warm, trying to unfreeze the blocks of ice that his lungs must have felt like, I remembered how Jack's wife had denied that anything was wrong with the garden; and her manner had even suggested that I had said something discourteous and wrong.

So QUITE suddenly, from one day to the next, part of the routine of the manor I had grown into, part of my new life and comfort, my private, living book of hours, was snapped.

I never saw Pitton unlatching the wide white gate at the end of the lawn at nine again, or walking back to it at one and then at five with the special slow step of a man who had done his morning's and then his day's labor. Were there personal things he had left behind in the garden shed—Wellingtons, a plastic raincoat, a jacket? Did he come back for these things later, or did he abandon them, with the garden-shed key? The key he had carried in that intimate way, on a chain that ran from a loop in his waistband to his right trouser pocket. That key he had to give up to Mr. Phillips.

And thereafter at odd hours the washed-out green-painted garden-shed door (beside the thick-stalked rose bush, now almost a small tree, that Pitton had pruned year by year) thereafter for long periods during the day that door remained open—Pitton's shed exposed, Pitton's territory no longer Pitton's (neither shed, nor key, nor tools, nor the heavy, tilting gate to the vegetable garden). That open garden-shed door, which Pitton had been so particular to keep closed—I could see it from the window of my room, and it was unsettling. I wished to close it; it was like the wish to straighten a mirror or picture hanging crooked on a wall. That open door, together with other changes—it was as though the man concerned had died in some unsanctified way, and everything that had been his could now be treated without ceremony.

When Jack—over the hill—had fallen ill, his flower and fruit garden had grown wild; and his vegetable garden—created in the waste ground between the farmyard metal dump below the beeches and the beginning of the cultivated down—had gone to seed. Pitton's vegetable garden didn't go to seed. It was tended through the summer and its produce was gathered in. Many strangers now came to the manor grounds, to do irregularly, in bits and pieces, the job that Pitton had done with unhurried system, the job around which he had built his mornings and his afternoons, his week, his year, marking the end of each stage with his own kind of ritual. This fragmentation of his job was like a further downgrading of the man, downgrading him now, and downgrading all he had done and been in the past, all his careful routine.

Some of the strangers in the manor were casual workers, paid by the hour or the day and obtained by the Phillipses from I don't know where, perhaps from the places Mr. Phillips had worked in before. Some were friends. One, who soon ceased to be a stranger, was Mr. Phillips's widowed father.

He was much smaller than his son, and slighter. Physically he was of another generation, another world: one could see in him the physique of agricultural workers in old photographs. Since the death of his wife, Mr. Phillips's mother, the old man had been solitary. This opening up of the manor grounds to him (where he had been only an occasional visitor on Saturday afternoons), and the opportunity for a little light work, was a blessing to the old man.

He lived much in the past, and liked to talk of the past. He was sociable. Solitude was not something he had chosen. It was like old age: something he had had to learn to live with. He had been born not far away and had lived all his life in the county. He told me at our first meeting, just outside my kitchen door, that he had started life as a carrier's boy—the carrier for whom he worked making a living by carrying goods and parcels for people living along the eight miles between Amesbury and Salisbury. The old man spoke of this job, his first, as of something indescribably rich and rewarding, an enchantment.

He dressed neatly, in jacket and tie, like Pitton, and unlike his son, who preferred more casual and "sporty" clothes. And again unlike his son, the old man wore very pale colors: it was as though the chalk of the downs by which he had been surrounded all his life had affected his taste in colors, had made him see tints where another person might have seen something neutral. The old man often came now simply to walk about the grounds; and he dressed for these walks in the manor bush as though for an urban promenade—in this he was like Pitton, in my earliest memory of Pitton. Sometimes, with the suit or the sports jacket and tie, the old man also walked with a staff, of a sort I had never seen before: shoulder-high, with a prong or fork at the top in which the thumb was rested: the carrier's boy now walking freely, privileged as the father of his son, walking with his old-fashioned staff in the overgrown grounds of a big house that was being built while he was a carrier's boy. Did the old man make the connection?

The summer jobs were done. The fallen aspens—about whose wide, tangled spread of broken branches grass and weeds had grown tall and dark, a separate area of vegetation—the fallen aspens were cut up with a chain saw and the cut logs piled up in the back garden. Grass now grew tall around the log piles, just as grass and the plants they attracted grew into a bush around the trunk fragments that were too big to cut up and stayed more or less where they had fallen, soon looking old, like old debris, suggesting the further advance onto the back lawn of the water-meadow wilderness. The grass of that lawn was cut— the area of the aspen fall never recovered, never returned to grass, and was abandoned to weeds and marsh growth—and the lawn in front of my cottage was cut. And the vegetable garden was looked after.

This garden was hidden from my cottage by a high wall. Beyond the half-cottage that was my outbuilding there was, set in this wall, the heavy gate with the metal bars. This gate hung unevenly, but Pitton had developed the knack of closing it. His successors didn't have this knack. The gate, unlatched, dragged more and more and was eventually left open: Pitton's garden, the scene of his secret labors, was now quite exposed.

Astonishing now, when I went in to look, astonishing as always, the different sense of space, the openness on the other side of the garden wall. The wall on that side was warm, sun-bleached; old fruit trees had been trained and pinned against it. The wall on my side was damp, always in shadow, only summer weeds growing in the poor soil at its base. The wall that I saw from my cottage was a northern wall. The wall on the other side was Mediterranean: part of the grandeur of the original walled-garden design, with its paths, its nursery beds, its vegetable areas, its formal orchard. Pitton had been able to keep only part of the garden going; but he had honored its formality, design, and dignity. Now, after the bonanza of his vegetable garden, his successors were creating only an allotment.

A cycle in the life of the manor had come to an end. There might one day be the beginning of a new cycle. But for the moment or for some years ahead the great walled garden, calling for the labor of many hands, had returned to a modest human scale, had become the setting for a small allotment.

The wide white gate at the end of the lawn—the gate that had been Pitton's gate—was padlocked, for security. And since the estates along the river were so little protected, so open, and the area now attracted many communities of dropouts and vagrants, a new tide of idleness washing back and forth over the empty spaces of south-western England, for greater security a mass of cut branches, rapidly going brown and dry and dead, was piled up against the gate.

I had replaced the idea of decay, the idea of the ideal which can be the cause of so much grief, by the idea of flux. But now, in spite of myself, the associations of the manor altered for me. I saw Pitton's hand in many places—in the "refuge"; in the vast leaf-grave he (and I, working together on some afternoons) had gathered for compost (now no longer needed); in that open garden-shed door; and in the heavy door in the garden wall that could no longer close. Yet I also knew that what had caused me delight, when I first came to the manor, would have caused grief to someone who had been there before me; just as what caused me grief now spoke of pure pleasure to old Mr. Phillips, with his suit and his staff, happy in the wild grounds and the small allotment.

The memories of Pitton, those lingering signs of his work, work to which the man himself would now never add, were like the memories of a man who had died. And yet he was still with us, still living in his improved agricultural cottage next to Bray. It was because of that cottage—the cottage that went with his job—that he had to go. The cottage had become valuable—sturdily built, not period in the accepted way but old enough and genuine enough in style to be interesting; and of manageable size. It was worth many thousands, a hundred times the two or three hundred pounds that Bray's father had paid for his cottage; and the estate needed the money.

But Pitton didn't believe this. I met him one Saturday morning in Salisbury. He was at his most country-gentleman in appearance—the suit, the shirt, the shoes, the hat, the carefully studied outfit which consumed his money. Pitton's Salisbury hat! So stylish, so elegant and gentlemanly the gesture with which he half lifted it off his head in greeting! The imitation was now so old, the gesture so habitual, that perhaps no idea of style attached to it in Pitton's mind any longer.

The face the uplifted hat revealed ran counter to the stylishness of the gesture: it was still the face of shock he had shown me when I had opened the kitchen door in answer to his imperious, angry knocking. Still that expression on his face: as though our meeting—which by chance took place in a pedestrian shopping street not far from the shop where Pitton bought his clothes, and where clothes like Pitton's could be seen in the window still—as though our meeting revived all the twisted emotions in him that could find no resolution or outlet in words.

He had been told, he said, that the estate wanted his house in order to sell it. But he didn't believe that story. Who would want to buy a house next to Bray? It was an agricultural cottage, a tied cottage, something for a gardener, something that no one had particularly taken care of. And just as when I had gone to his house that Christmastime he had suggested that he had a source of income other than his gardener's wages, so now when he spoke of the house where he had lived for twenty-five years and more, it was to suggest that if it had been another kind of house he would have looked after it differently; and it was almost as if he were suggesting that his real house was somewhere else. Yet he didn't want to leave his agricultural cottage. And though many months had passed since he had stopped working at the manor, he wasn't really trying to find another job. It was as though he had begun to feel that if he didn't start looking for another job he mightn't after all have to find another job.

He was confused, pulled in many directions, helpless. He seemed to be proving the point made by Mrs. Phillips. She had been continuing to look for some explanation of Pitton's dismissal that would make it easier for everyone to bear; and she had settled on the idea that in his last year at the manor Pitton had gone very strange, that he had been finally undermined by the solitude of his labor—a pretense of work, a kind of half idling—in the wilderness, and that he had "gone to pieces."

In her previous job, Mrs. Phillips said, she had seen any number of people who had gone to pieces; it wasn't only people you read about in the newspapers who went to pieces. I had thought that Mrs. Phillips was straining too hard to find an explanation. But then, meeting Pitton at the bus stop in the valley and meeting him sometimes in Salisbury, and talking about his problems, which he kept on insisting were insoluble, I thought it was possible that Mrs. Phillips was responding to the odd mixture in his personality of passion and servility and affectation and pride and independence.

He didn't want to be a gardener again, he told me. He could do the job at the manor; but he couldn't do it anywhere else or for anybody else—it was too undignified. Nor did he want a town job. The country gentleman in him, or rather the free country laborer in him, feared the anonymity, the nothingness of the town worker.

I would meet Pitton at the bus stop in the valley. We would talk then until the bus came. We never talked on the bus. We sat on different seats. We also continued to meet in Salisbury; and sometimes we met in the village on the public road when I was coming back from my walk over the downs. Our talks were circular. He would put ideas to me about what he might do; I would encourage him; and then he would reject my encouragement, returning to the idea of the "grudge" against him.

Pitton's difficulty—as I understood when I put myself in his place, and examined myself and my own fears—was that he had lost touch with the idea of work. In fact, after the manor, the freedom there, the routine he had created, the calm he had established for himself, his relationship with the seasons, the year, time itself, what he feared was not work but employment—and perhaps not employment so much as the idea of the employer.

In the end, quietly, ashamedly, he took a job. He drove a laundry van. I knew about it only when I saw him driving the van, the laundry leather moneybag added to his country-gentleman clothes and slung over his shoulder and chest like a bandolier. And in the end he left his cottage and was given a council flat in the town, on the old London coach road.

It could not have been pleasant for him in the cottage towards the end, when he had been under pressure to leave, to release the property and the capital it represented to the estate. I expected that he would have been happy at having found another place to live, and quite a reasonable one. But, with the passion and twisted emotions that had now become permanent with him, he complained. The flat was shabby.

In what way? It hadn't been decorated. They expected him to do his own decorating; that was the way he was being treated.

It was always hard—so convincing was Pitton's manner—to understand that he was an obedient soul, the father of an obedient soldier; that—with all his passion—servility, or dependence, ran deep in his nature.

*B*RAY SAID, "So our friend has moved out."
I was sitting beside him in his car, and he spoke out of the corner of his mouth, the corner that was on my side.

Bray said, "An arrogant man."

Below his driver's cap Bray's eyes, at once concentrating on the road and expressing an inward pleasure, were like slits, sloping sharply down to the sides of his face. And then, speaking of the manor family as though they were all still there, as though the manor organization of which his father had formed part still existed, Bray said, "They're a funny family." There was tribute in his words, and also pride.

He reached for a book on the shelf below the dashboard and passed it to me, with the semiabstraction of a man concentrating on the road and also with the clumsiness of a man not used to handling books. He said, mysteriously, "Have a look at this when you get home." As though the book, the mysterious object, would explain much; as though the book would free him, Bray, of the need to say more.

The book was by my landlord. It was nearly fifty years old, something from the 1920s. It was a short story in verse, with many illustrations. The paper was good, the book was expensively bound in cloth; and though it carried the name of a reputable London publisher of the period, it was clear that the production of such a slight work in this lavish way had been subsidized or paid for by the author.

The story was simple. A young woman gets tired of the English social round—many opportunities there for drawings of the costumes of the 1920s. She decides to become a missionary in Africa. Goodbyes are said; the lovers who are left behind pine in different ways. A

ship; the ocean; the African coast; a forest river. The young missionary is captured by Africans, natives. She has fantasies of sexual assault
by the African chief to whose compound she is taken; fantasies as well
of the harem and of black eunuchs. Instead, she is cooked in a cannibal
pot and eaten; and all that remains of her, all that one of her London
lovers finds, is a twenties costume draped on a wooden cross, like a
scarecrow.

This was the joke knowledge of the world the young boy of eighteen had arrived at; this was the knowledge (which would have appeared like sophistication) that had been fed by the manor and the
grounds. And perhaps later knowledge had not gone beyond the joke:
outside England and Europe, a fantasy Africa, a fantasy Peru or India
or Malaya. And perhaps passion too had never gone beyond the tit-
illation of the Beardsley-like drawings of this book. And that was the
most amazing thing about the book Bray had preserved and cherished:
the drawings.

They were in the very style of the drawings which Mrs. Phillips
had brought over as gifts from my landlord during the previous summer, of the shopping expeditions and the champagne. He had struck
his form and won admiration for his style at an early age; had early
arrived at his idea of who he was, his worth and his sensibility; and
he had stalled there. Perhaps he had stalled in what might be considered a state of perfection. But that perfection—that absence of restlessness and creative abrasion, that view from his back windows of a
complete, untouched, untroubled world—had turned to morbidity,
acedia, a death of the soul.

That morbidity had been like a long sleep. Then he had miraculously awakened, and he had found his world still about him. He knew
that the spaciousness of earlier days had gone. But he was prepared,
as he had always been prepared, to live with what he found—that was
how, projecting myself onto him, I read him.

He liked ivy. When the trees in his garden collapsed he did not
complain. He had enjoyed the ivy for many years, and now he would
have to content himself with other things. So it was with people; when

their time came, it came. He had made no comment—from what I heard from the Phillipses—about the fall of the aspens, which he must have seen for fifty years at least. So, understanding now that there was no longer a gardener, he never—from what the Phillipses said—asked for Pitton, with whom the previous summer he had played and about whom he had made up his stories, to tell to the people remaining to him, like Alan. (Like a child of two or three who might play every day with its grandmother; but then, should that grandmother suddenly die, might never ask after her.)

I saw Pitton driving his laundry van sometimes. Hard to recognize in him the man whose routine, whose appearance at the white gate, had been part of the new life and comfort and healing I had found in the valley.

Sometimes we met on a Saturday in Salisbury. Once he came up behind me and called me by my name. Strange behavior, from a buttoned-up, wordless man. But I had known him in his glory; I had helped in the grand garden of the manor, helped with the grass, the dead beech leaves. And I had called him Mr. Pitton.

He grew shabbier. Fragments of his country-gentleman clothes survived on him, in other combinations; but his style changed. The laundryman who did the valley round and knew Pitton said of him, but gently and understandingly, "He's a little grumpy."

But then Pitton changed. The valley laundryman—tolerant, as content with the rhythm of his weekly round, the rhythm of his year, his annual two-week holidays, as content with the passing of time as Pitton had once been—the valley laundryman understood this change in Pitton, too, and said of Pitton's improving behavior, his lessening grumpiness, "You get used to it."

There was more to it than that. Pitton, in this last decade of active life, grew out of what he had been. He got to know more people, at work and on the council estate where he lived. Where he had feared anonymity, he found community and a little strength. He saw his former life as from a distance. He had always sought—in his clothes, his pride in his wife's looks, his odd poor-man's pretense about the other source of income—to maintain this distance from what he was. Now there was no need. Gradually he stopped acknowledging me from the laundry van. One day in Salisbury, in that pedestrian shopping street where he had tried to fill me with his own panic, one day he saw me. And then—the new man—he didn't "see" me.

ROOKS

*A*LAN SAID, "So Pitton left. Tremendous figure of my childhood."

That was Alan the writer, the man with the childhood, the man with the sensibility. I understood this idea of the writer because it was so like my own when I had first come to England. Then I would have envied Alan the material available to him: my landlord, the manor, the setting, his deep knowledge of the setting; the London parties I occasionally saw him at. But Alan seemed to have as much trouble with his idea of the writer and his material as I had had with mine.

At first he used to hint that he was at work on a book—hinting that the part of him that one saw, the part he was displaying in the manor grounds or at a London party was just a fraction of his personality or even a disguise; that the true personality would be revealed in that book he was writing. His radio reviews and discussions and his short printed pieces had the same suggestion, that he was fully engaged elsewhere, in some bigger venture.

But no book came from Alan. No novel or autobiographical novel (setting the record straight, showing the truth behind the shiny bright clothes and the clowning manner); no critical study of contemporary literature (which he sometimes spoke about); no Isherwood-like book about postwar Germany, which he spoke about at other times. Eventually, with me, he stopped hinting that he was writing. But he still talked like a writer and behaved like a writer.

And that writer's personality of Alan's was partly genuine, and no more fraudulent than my own character, my idea of myself as a writer, had been in 1950. Just as, in my writing in those days, I was hiding my experience from myself, hiding myself from my experience, to that extent falsifying things, yet at the same time revealing them to anyone who looked beyond the conventional words and forms and attitudes I was aiming at, so all the literary sides of his character that Alan exhibited, all the books he said he was writing, hinted at truths that were as hard for him to face as certain things had been for me.

That Isherwood-like book about postwar Germany hinted at the dissatisfactions and torments of his emotional life and his involvement with a young German for whose sake he had gone to live in Germany for some time. He spoke of this attachment obliquely at the beginning, as though testing my reaction to a confession of passion from him (half a clown); as though testing my reaction to sexual inversion. Either my reaction didn't satisfy him, or he changed his mind; or his attitude to this unhappy affair altered as he began to talk about it to me, a stranger. He dropped the subject; the sketch of the young German remained unfinished; and Alan's references to Germany thereafter were straightforwardly political or cultural.

And there was his autobiographical novel, the story of his childhood and the development of his sensibility. It was to be an absolute compendium of such books. His wish (as I understood too well) was to say to the world: "I too have witnessed these things and felt these emotions." But below his wish to do all that had already been done, to display knowledge of all the settings (or their equivalents) that had occurred in similar books, there was something in his childhood or upbringing or family life which had deeply wounded him, had committed him to solitude, uncertainty, an imperfect life.

His literary approach to his experience, the self-regard that would have gone with its "frankness" (on approved topics, no doubt—homosexuality, masturbation, social climbing), perhaps hid the cause of his incompleteness from himself. And often in London, considering his overskittishness at parties, his startling, self-mocking dress, his nervousness in the presence of people he admired, his extravagant flattery of those persons, often in London, considering him, I felt I was considering an aspect of myself from some years back. And I had an intimation that those over-bright moments of Alan's would have been followed in the solitude of his rooms or flat by self-disgust, rage, wretchedness. And I could see how the solitude of the manor, the walks in the ruined garden, would have been (in addition to its literary suitability) a kind of therapy for him. Therapy over and above his pleasure at having "rich friends" (because writers, as Cyril Connolly had said, should have rich friends); over and above his pleasure at saying to me (because it was old-fashioned, "before the deluge"): "I telephone and have Phillips meet me at the station"—not saying "Mr. Phillips" or "Stanley" or "Stan."

And there was the house itself. It had a staff, and it still worked as a big house, more or less. It offered a room and a bathroom with refurbished plumbing. It offered from the back windows (as I supposed: I hadn't seen it) a view of the garden, the river, the water meadows on both sides of the river, with the empty downs beyond: an untouched view, a view without other houses or people, a calming view. For Alan it would have been a house without any kind of strain, making no demand on him, not requiring him to act or maintain a particular personality.

There was my landlord. For me it would have been a strain to be in the house with him, a strain to meet him, and to note however involuntarily his idiosyncrasies and affectations; it would have undone the magic. But my landlord—in addition to his literary value to Alan as "material," someone from an earlier age—was the one person to whom Alan stood almost in a position of authority. To my landlord —recently recovered from his acedia—Alan was still an adventurer in the titillating world from which he, my landlord, had withdrawn. My landlord was the one person to whom Alan could bring news. And yet their meetings would have been few and wouldn't have lasted long.

From Mr. Phillips I heard that my landlord tired quickly of conversation and people, social encounters; that he could suddenly become restless and dismiss even old friends. I heard—indirectly—from the Phillipses that Alan usually ate alone in the manor. (And the picture that came to my mind was not of a tray being taken to Alan's room, but of a dim ceiling bulb lighting a modest spread on an old lace tablecloth in a musty room smelling of old cedar and wood preservative.)

So the solitude I saw was indeed solitude. And if Alan thought it "creepy" that I could live in the place for so long without getting to know my landlord, I thought it strange—until I understood the particular solace the place offered him—that he should want to visit, for the reasons he gave: to be in the place important to his childhood, for the sake of the novel he was working on or planning, and also (for the sake of another book) to be in the presence of my landlord, to study his speech and mannerisms, the mannerisms of a more gracious age, the age before the deluge (not the age that had finished in 1914, this time, but the age according to Alan that had finished in 1940), the age when houses like my landlord's were still important, not only socially but also in the making of literary and artistic reputations.

Alan suggested that in spite of his apparent idleness, his rambling about the orchard and gardens, his readiness to come to my cottage at any time, his visits to the manor were periods of work; that he was taking away volumes of "notes." Sometimes he let me into the secret of the notes he was making or had made. My landlord had said to him once: "Would you like some toast? Shall I get Phillips to bring you some toast in a chafing dish?" And Alan had roared with laughter as much as he had roared at the story about Pitton and the pink champagne. "A chafing dish!" he said. "Have you heard anybody speak of a chafing dish?"

So that I felt not only that Alan (like me, twenty-five years before in Earl's Court) had a good idea of what as a writer he expected to find; but also that my landlord, even in his shrunken world, and through the darkness of his acedia, still had an idea of what was expected of him.

But there was Alan's solitude, so visible in the manor, so clear in the melancholy of his knobby little face when he was caught unawares. That solitude was real enough, as real as the pain of his childhood; as real as the acedia of my landlord and the physical dereliction this acedia had created all around him. That solitude of Alan's as he walked about the garden and grounds was like a demonstration of the psychological damage he had suffered once upon a time. There was a part of him that hurt, a part where he could never be reached and where he was always alone; and the nature of his education, his too-literary approach to his experience, his admiration of certain writers and artists of the century, his wish to do again, but for himself, what they had done, all this conspired to conceal things from himself. The solitude of the manor grounds was a solace. Outside that was threat and the vision of his own inadequacy.

He made up for this by flattery of the people he admired and whose strength he wished he had. Like a child offering sweets to his fellows in order to buy peace, Alan told many people he was making notes about them for his big book about contemporary literature. He was keeping his eye on so many people, noting their conversation, keeping their letters; he was going to write about so many people. And it was hard, once Alan had told you he was making "notes" about you, to ignore him, hard not to start acting up (even like my landlord) to an intelligent, friendly man who might indeed be making notes about all the things you were saying.

He balanced this by a contempt for those writers in whom he saw versions of himself—mimics, people doing what others had done in social chronicles and wishing to show that they could do it too. Towards these writers, whose faults he saw very clearly, he was merciless. One such writer—he was physically bigger than Alan, but was also something of a dandy in clothes—whom I saw in London told me: "The venomous little insect came galumphing across the room at Clarissa's and said to me, 'My dear, you must stay in this Saturday and listen to *The Critics*. I've slaughtered you.' Ha-ha."

But there were not many people like that, people to whom Alan expressed open hostility. The public objects of Alan's dislike were mainly certain kinds of buildings, paintings, gardens, flowers. And here even my landlord was not exempt. My landlord liked gladioli. Pitton grew them for him in the garden. Alan hated them for their gaudiness and size. He said, closing his eyes, a shudder going right through him, "They should be that high"—bending and holding his open palm down to the level of his shin. He could shudder with distaste like this when he spoke of these things—flowers, pictures, buildings—as though making up, in the violence of his aesthetic responses, for all the coyness he imposed on himself with other people, all the talk about "notes" and the writing he was preparing to do about them ("All this is going down in the diary," he would say, or, personalizing it, "This is for Diary," or, "Diary will take due note"), all the sweets he offered the world to buy peace. It was this aesthetic violence—at bottom quite genuine, reflecting a genuine sensibility, a true concern for the life of the mind—that gave his radio talks and discussions their bite and attack and suggested that they were the merest glimpse of a fuller life and more prodigious personality.

It happened sometimes that months passed without our meeting —he might not come down, or I might be away when he did come down. One day, quite unusually, he telephoned me from London; and I was aware only then that I hadn't seen him for perhaps a year or more. There were the sounds of music in the background. The music was very loud; it made me ask where he was telephoning from. It was from his flat. He said, "You talk like my neighbors. Of course I am blasting away." And he gave his great choking laugh.

The old Alan, it would have seemed. But it wasn't. He was drunk; and as he began to speak, it became clear that he was very drunk. Alcohol and music: the supports of solitude. This was new to me: not the solitude, but the drinking. I had never thought of Alan as a drinking man. But even drunkenness didn't alter Alan's character or show the other side of the man; drunkenness didn't liberate him. It exaggerated, made ludicrous, his appeasing public character. Hardly able to control his words, he was seeking only to send messages of love, to flatter, to speak to me about my work.

And he was asking nothing in return. For there was, as it were, no means of getting back to the person from whom all this issued. The person that wished to buy peace from the world was beyond the reach of the world, was hardly known, it might be said, to Alan himself. It didn't matter how much one flattered back; it didn't matter how much love one sent back; one could never touch the true person.

Some months later he reappeared at the manor. He had greatly changed. His eyes, once so seemingly unreliable and shifty, had become dead, lackluster; there was a very old sadness there. The knobby little face had become white and soft; it had become like the face of a frail old woman. And it was as if this transformation gave a glimpse of the ambiguity in the personality, perhaps just one of the many ambiguities that had tormented Alan.

Especially noticeable to me was the skin of his cheeks. It was very white and seemed to have become very thin, seemed to flutter above the flesh (as though there was some vacancy between skin and flesh) whenever Alan spoke or closed his mouth too firmly. This thin, delicate skin made me think of the outer petal of a blown rose; it seemed to have something of the texture. It made me think also of the faded black plastic sheeting that covered the old cottage-shaped hayrick on the droveway, plastic sheeting so beaten about by wind and rain that it had not only lost its luster and snap but appeared also to have developed within its thinness little blisters and air pockets.

The man had changed. And—he was in my cottage, sitting in my wing chair, half reclined, looking small, the upholstered wings above his head, his knees neatly together—it was a little as if (this was the idea that came to me) the man that one knew had been subjected almost to a moral attack by the unacknowledged personality within; that the man had been pulled down by this inner personality, which now sat like a watchful guardian on the man's shoulder and was the only entity with whom Alan could now have a true dialogue. Of the old personality there remained only the clothes that made the upholstery of the chair look grimy. These clothes were as carefully chosen as ever; but the man within was so quiet, so little ebullient, his movements were so slow and considered, that the clothes did not suggest the old personality.

From the Phillipses I later heard about the drunken telephone calls Alan had made to the manor at about the time—or perhaps a little before—he had telephoned me. The first three or four had been taken. But then—perhaps Alan had pushed his luck too far, had begun to make the telephone calls at odd hours, perhaps had said things he hadn't said to me—my landlord had become alarmed. Alan's disturbance, so manifest, had given my landlord fresh glimpses of his own acedia again, his own hell. To fear that kind of illness was, in effect, to start being ill again. And for a while my landlord had had a relapse.

Alan's telephone calls had been refused; Mr. Phillips had ordered Alan not to telephone again. Alan had been forbidden to come to the house. All Mr. Phillips's protective feelings towards his employer, the sick man, were awakened; the prohibition on Alan's visits was lifted only when Mr. Phillips was sure that Alan had stopped drinking.

But the man who had reappeared in the manor was ravaged. That old lady's face was the face of a man beyond cure. And though he refused the glass of wine I offered (quite innocently, not knowing at the time his recent history), though he refused, while insisting (with beautiful courtesy, almost as though he were my host) that I should have a glass myself, his apparent cure was—as with some other bad diseases—only a remission, enabling him, perhaps cruelly, perhaps in a spirit of reconciliation, to look at the world he was leaving and to say his good-byes.

He said good-bye. He never came back. I heard him once or twice on the radio—as bubbling as ever. If only he could have lived there, at that pitch, in something like a radio-studio atmosphere, something of that artificial social arrangement, instead of having to go home and be alone. And then one day I heard—some days after the event—that he had taken some pills one night after a bout of hard drinking and died. It was a theatrical kind of death. Theater would not have been far from Alan's mind that evening. It might so easily have gone the other way. Somebody might have telephoned, or he might have telephoned somebody, gone to a party in brilliant clothes, been witty or flattering or outrageous, would have ridden over the theatrical moment of suicide. But his solitude would almost certainly have brought him there again.

The news was kept from my landlord. Mr. Phillips thought it would be bad for him to be told. But somehow my landlord found out. For him it was one person less in his shrinking world; another person not to be mentioned again.

Of Alan's books and "notes" there was of course almost nothing. Out of his love for the life of the mind, and the artist's eye and hand, he had flattered very many people. And it was this flattery that was his odd memorial for a week or so. A number of people who wrote about Alan after his death wrote with that part of their personalities that had almost been created by Alan's flattery. Their obituaries were curiously self-regarding; as much as to Alan—who came out in these notices as an eccentric, an anachronism, someone from "before the deluge" (the words were actually used in one piece)—these people paid tribute to themselves for having known and befriended Alan, for having spotted his talent and sensibility, having been singled out by him for his confidences, his confessions of sadness. No one spoke of his flattery. And more than one person, it turned out, had been telephoned by Alan in distress just a few days before he had died.

Mr. Phillips, mentioning Alan's death, permitted himself a look of sadness, a twinge of regret. But then almost immediately his face clouded with the irritability which I thought of as his usual public expression. This irritability was like Bray's peaked cap; it enabled Mr. Phillips to express many things. He could wear his irritability dead straight; or he could wear it mockingly or self-mockingly. He could use it to express authority, or to be an aggrieved worker; or it could be the irritability of a man protecting his good fortune, not wishing to exult.

Now his irritability bridged his human response to the death of Alan and his professional pride as a male nurse and as protector of the manor. He had spotted Alan immediately, he said. He had spotted Alan's depressive nature. He had been right to forbid Alan the house. The drunkenness would simply not have done. Its effect on my landlord would have been calamitous; and then Alan could so easily have done in the manor what he had done at home. Think of the trouble, the confusion, the further effect on my landlord, holding on to the remnants of his own lucidity and health.

That was how he, Alan, was remembered at the place which he thought of as his special retreat. "I telephone Phillips and have him meet me at the station." That was how (in one mood) Alan thought or wanted to think of his time and position at the manor. It was half a social idea, half a literary idea: the being met "at the station," with all its old-fashioned country-house–weekend suggestions; the use of the name Phillips without the "mister"—though Alan called Mr. Phillips Stanley or Stan and Mr. Phillips called him Alan.

*M*R. PHILLIPS's old father said to me, "So your friend Alan died. Nice man. I hardly knew him. I saw him a few times. He was always very pleasant."

He, old Mr. Phillips, the small, neat man, had been walking in the grounds with his tall pronged staff (the sign that he had come to the grounds to walk and not to work). He was carefully dressed, in his very pale colors—no pattern in the fabric of his tie, jacket, or shirt, this absence of pattern together with the broad lapels, collars, and ties of the period adding to the pallor of the clothes, suggesting chalk below the tints, the way the chalk of the downs modified the color of young grass or corn and in dry weather whitened a plowed field.

The old man said, "Whenever I hear of something like this I think of my cousin. He died when he was eight. In 1911, coronation year."

We were standing outside my cottage, below the beeches. The old man slightly lifted his face. He was smiling; his eyes were watering. I knew the expression. The smile wasn't a smile, the tears were not tears. It was just what happened to his face whenever he began to talk about his childhood or early life.

But he couldn't tell me about his cousin just then. We were both distracted by a great squawking noise. The noise was made by a flock of rooks circling overhead. Big black beaks, big black flapping wings.

I had never seen them here before. I had got used to starlings arriving suddenly in screeching flocks, settling like black leaves on trees. But rooks in this number I hadn't seen. They flew around slowly, squawking, as if assessing us. In my first year, on one of my early, exploratory walks, I had seen two or three downs away, on a wooded hill on the other side of Jack's cottage, spread-eagled husks of these birds nailed to a fence by Jack's very old and bent father-in-law.

Old Mr. Phillips said, "They've lost their nests right through the valley. They lost their nests when the elms died. They're prospecting. They need tall trees. They'll choose the beeches. You know what they say about rooks. They bring money to a house. Money is coming to somebody in the manor. Who do you think it's going to be? Of course it's an old wise tale." "Old wise tale"—it was what he said; and the idiom, as he spoke it, with its irony and tolerance, sounded original rather than a corruption. "If you think they're birds of death you can't stand the noise. If you think it's money, you don't mind."

And in that noise of the squawking, prospecting rooks, the old man told me about the death he had not forgotten, the first death against which he measured all other deaths, the grief that was more painful than any other and was still with him more than sixty-five years later.

He and his cousin were skylarking. They ran behind a horse-drawn van belonging to a local firm. They jumped on the nose bags that were slung on the rear axle. The driver didn't see them. They rode on the nose bags for a mile or two, eating apples. Then they got bored. They got off. A motorcar, unusual for those days, came along the road, kicking up white dust, dust that lay an inch or two thick on the unpaved country road. Both boys were involved in the white dust cloud. Bizarrely, then, another car came along and old Mr. Phillips saw his cousin knocked down. It was the only thing he could see, and he was frightened. He ran to the riverbank and hid in a bed of withies until midafternoon. From there he saw the dust cloud settle. He saw his aunt, his cousin's mother, come. He saw the boy taken away in an ambulance. "To the military hospital—the army was here even in those days."

There the boy died. No one thought of flogging old Mr. Phillips—

that worry had been with him. In his aunt's house that evening he saw the body of his cousin—with whom he had been riding that morning—laid out.

"These things strike you afterwards," the old man said. The funeral was the next day. "His little coffin," old Mr. Phillips said, and now real tears for that death more than sixty-five years before were running down his face.

Then he pulled himself up, altered his tone. "No, not little. Fair-sized coffin. My aunt asked me and the other boys to collect moss. That was how I spent the day of the funeral. Gathering moss. It was to put in the grave, to soften the whiteness of the chalk in the sun. It's what the undertakers still do. They hang a mat, green and looking like grass, down the sides of the grave. Of course they come back later, after the mourners have gone, and take it away."

The wet riverbanks, the downs: everyone saw different things. Old Mr. Phillips, with his memories of chalk and moss; my landlord, loving ivy; the builders of the manor garden; Alan; Jack; me.

THE ROOKS, prospecting, made such a racket that I wondered how I would endure it—another sound to be added to the noise of airplanes at certain hours in the day; the artillery barrages on some nights from the firing ranges (the sound of which made one conceive of air as a substance, elastic up to a point, and beyond that point liable to puncture); the end-of-day traffic increasing year by year and coming to my cottage through a thinning screen of beeches and yews.

But the racket of that day was unusual. The squawks of the big birds, flapping slowly around, were like the squawks of discussion; when the discussion and the prospecting were over the birds went away. And when the first party of settlers, the first nest-builders, came, they built only one nest. It was as though they were testing the trees, the site, the people. The rocky or pebbled lane below the beeches was littered with lengths of pliable twigs, material for the nest, fallen and useless, suggesting that for every twig successfully knitted into the nest three or four or five had been lost. At last it appeared, on the upper part of a beech: one rooks' nest.

There was a pause then, long enough to make one feel that there would be no more rooks' nests in those winter-stripped beeches. But then, very quickly, there appeared a second; and a third; and then many more, big dark burrs high up, beyond the reach of predators, and soon to be hidden by the foliage of the spring and summer. From the train to London, through Wiltshire and Hampshire, I saw the same colonization going on, rooks' nests appearing where there hadn't been any.

The elms had finally died in the valley. Many, before they had finally died, had been felled, cut up; others had died standing up, remaining bare, going grayer against the summer green. And the valley road became suddenly open. Curves once overhung with green, mysterious and full of depth, showed plain; tilled downs, without a border of elms and wild growth between the elms, sloped down simply to the asphalt road. House plots showed plain, and houses and their ancillary little corrugated sheds looked naked. The shallow river and its wet banks remained enchanting; but the land on either side became ordinary.

And time altered for me. At first, as in childhood, it had stretched. The first spring had contained so much that was clear and sharp—the moss rose, the single blue iris, the peonies under my window. I had waited for the year to repeat. Then memories began to be jumbled; time began to race; the years began to stack together; it began to be hard for me to date things.

Bray, the car-hire man, once the neighbor of Pitton, the gardener (whose house had been bought, for a price that had a sobering effect on Bray, by a young surveyor with a Salisbury practice), Bray began to talk to me of religion. Was that before or after the rooks came? Before or after the discovery of the young vagrant who had been camping for some time in the manor grounds?

He had been living, this man, in the children's house in the overgrown orchard, near Pitton's garden "refuge." There had been wanderers in previous summers; but this man was one of the many new itinerants—not gypsies now, but young city people, some of them criminals—who moved about Wiltshire and Somerset in old cars and vans and caravans looking for festivals, communities, camping sites. The discovery of this man created alarm. It would have been easy for others to follow him, and for knowledge of the children's house to spread. So at last, sixty or seventy years after it had been built, the children's house, seldom used by the children for whom it had been intended, and still more or less whole, even though its thatch had slipped in one place, was closed, its door and windows nailed up and barred with timber planks. And, as a further deterrent, Mr. Phillips had the round building wound about with barbed wire.

Like the closing of the wide white gate at the end of the lawn after Pitton left, and the piling up of dead branches on the inside of the gate, to keep the gate closed, this abandoning of the children's house was an event. But I couldn't date it. The order that Pitton had imposed not only on the grounds but also on my idea of the seasons, that order had gone. I no longer had that order to set events against, events which now, as time raced, became jumbled—even the coming of the rooks, even the talk from Bray of religion.

A S M U C H as any comparable area of Egypt or India, the region (once a vast burial place) was full of sacred sites: the circles of wood or stone, the great burial mounds, the medieval cathedrals and abbeys, and the churches that were often no less grand. And faith hadn't stopped there. Scattered about these monuments, cultural shrines, and side by side with them sometimes, were relics of more recent ways of worship.

In the center of Salisbury, across a narrow pedestrian lane from a well-known cake shop, there was a magnificently windowed Gothic church. On the wall of the chancel at the far end, and just below the roof, there was a primitive painting of Doomsday: the colors of the painting magenta and green, both faded: with naked medieval figures in heaven on the left, hell on the right, the quality of the painting and the knowledge of anatomy appearing to match the quality of medieval

mind and soul: men naked in a world beyond their control, the wings
of the consoling angels as fearful and unnatural as the bird or reptile
swallowing the damned. Opposite this monument of medieval piety
was the busy cake shop, the inner room of which had been a Victorian
Sunday school. A carved stone slab, like an escutcheon, recorded this
fact and the date of the foundation of the school in Victorian Gothic
characters. Gâteaux and quiche and coffee at varnished pine tables in
a room where not long before children had learned Bible stories and
hymns and respect.

In one of the river valleys outside Salisbury, at the top of a footpath running up from the river, there was still a small, one-roomed
"mission hut." It was a rough shed of timber and corrugated iron and
had perhaps been built just before the First World War. There had
been as much pride and religion in its plainness then as there had been
medieval awe in medieval grandeur. Now the hut was without a function. Further along the road on this side of the river there was a red-
brick building with Victorian Gothic windows. This building was still
marked at the top WESLEYAN CHAPEL. It had ceased to be that a long
time ago; it was now a private house, the Victorian Gothic arches and
lettering part of its unusual "character" as a dwelling place.

Quite different—and not only because it was still in use as a
church—was the renovated parish church near the manor and my cottage. This church was an age away from the religious anxiety of the
Doomsday painting of St. Thomas's in Salisbury: the sense of an arbitrary world, full of terrors, where men were naked and helpless and
only God gave protection. The parish church had been renovated at
the time the great Victorian houses and manors of the region were
being built. And it was of that confident period: as much as a faith, it
celebrated a culture, a national pride, a power, men very much in control of their destinies.

That was still its atmosphere, though the people it attracted were
now, in terms of wealth, lesser than the Victorian magnates, less predominating, and though their houses were like the small change of
the great Victorian dwellings. The very scantiness of the parish-church
congregation—enough now for only one service a month rather than

one a week—supported the idea of an enclosed, excluding cultural celebration: the sound of car doors, the gentle chatter before and after the service, with hymn singing in the interim to the sounds of an organ (still there in the little church, still working!) muffled by the thick renovated walls of stone and flint in a checkered pattern.

No room for Jack there, Jack who celebrated life while he lived. No room for Mr. Phillips or for the strange, townish people who came now to do a few hours' rough work in the manor garden. And no room, I would have thought, for the old Bray, the man of puzzling views, a mixture of high conservatism and wild republicanism, a worship of the rich (the users of his cars) with a hatred of inherited wealth and titles. The old Wesleyan chapel (as a private dwelling extended, with matching Gothic windows), the empty mission hut, the Victorian Sunday school now part of the cake shop—that was the nineteenth-century popular religion which, lingering into the twentieth, had partly made people like Bray, the religion of constriction and discipline rather than celebration. That was the constriction that Bray, and thousands like him, had grown out of; that was why those relics of recent Christianity dotted the region. So many kinds of religion here, so many relics.

But now—Bray talked of religion. It crept up on me, the talk. I wasn't aware of how seriously he was speaking when he spoke of "the good book." I barely took it in, heard it simply as part of his chattering everyday irony. I sat beside him in his car, had a sideways glimpse of his peaked cap and the slope and slit of his eyes, eyes squinting at the road. The squint-and-slit, the set of his face, and what I knew of his temperament led me to feel that he was joking.

I had associated his appearance and manner for too long with the man who spoke glibly and cynically about politicians, certain members of the royal family, trades unions, businessmen in the news or in the courts, and every other kind of passing topic. Like the new pound note, for instance, introduced by a Labour government and rejected by him purely for that reason: "I call it Mickey Mouse money." He had probably heard somebody say that. With Bray it was the combination of the views that was original. The views themselves—as I found again and again—were borrowed from radio or television programs, popular newspapers.

As soon as I understood that he was speaking in earnest, my vision of him changed. In the same features, the same way of speaking, I saw not the glibness of his cynicism but personal feeling and, soon, passion.

I thought later that there would have been another reason why it took me some time to understand that Bray was speaking seriously when he spoke of religion. It was that he was learning himself, that he was being inducted into some new doctrine which he had accepted without fully understanding, and had then had to learn about. A new doctrine: because the religion Bray had embraced was not the religion of the Victorian relics which he and thousands with him had rejected. The religion that emerged from his talk, the religion into which he was sinking week by week, had to do with healing, or more specifically a healer: a wise person (the sex of the person concealed by Bray); a Bible opened at random during a "service"; the words on the pages interpreted; the kneeling believers receiving each a personal message, personal guidance. A healer; "meetings" around a Bible as a sacred object; shared food; a hint of companionship, even conviviality, in piety.

This talk of meetings made me think of a "spiritualist" gathering I had gone to in a north London suburb twenty years before, out of interest (seeing the sensational meetings so matter-of-factly advertised outside the red-brick building) and also in the hope of finding copy for a five-minute radio talk for one of the magazine programs of the BBC overseas services.

It was in an upstairs room, reached directly by steps from the pavement; the lamp above the entrance was marked simply HALL. Most of the people waiting inside were regulars. Among them were some children, healthy, playful, a little restless. They sat in the front row. The medium was a heavy, ordinary, middle-aged woman. She apologized for being late; she said she had had to travel from somewhere south of the river. Very briskly, then, she started. There were messages for all of us. There was even one for me, from my grandfather, who was very far away, the medium said, and whose voice came only faintly to her.

But most terrible were the messages for the children, three or four of them, so handsome and well cared for, with their restless feet. These messages were preceded by the medium clutching at her throat and saying that she was choking, could hardly breathe. And the woman with the children, clearly their mother, gravely and without anguish, leaning forward (she sat in the row behind the children), nodded, as if to corroborate the identity of the spirit who was transmitting this message. Her husband, the father of the children, had been hanged. And I never got to know (I never asked the person who had told me) whether the father had been hanged by the state—in England or abroad—or had hanged himself. Every fortnight now the hanged man's family came to have this communion with him—which no doubt explained their composure: they were believers. There was a simple message for each child—help Mummy, be good at school; and each child waited for his or her message; and became grave when the message came. What memories they would retain of these visits! New characters, new passions, were being given them, to separate them from their fellows. Twenty, thirty years from then, those characters (in adult bodies and with adult needs) would act out those passions.

Something of that chill of twenty years before came to me when Bray talked to me of his meetings. He himself was as composed as the children and wife of the hanged man twenty years before. They had been driven by a dreadful need, clear for all to see. What was the need that had driven Bray?

He was so full of talk, so opinionated, so full of noise, that I hadn't stopped to think about the satisfactions or otherwise of his life. A married daughter lived in Devon, where she had moved after her husband had found "a piece of ground" (Bray's words); she never came back to visit. Bray gave many reasons when he first mentioned the fact; but then he gave none. What did she have to come back to? And thinking of Bray in this way, attempting to see him from the point of view of the daughter who had resolved to stay away, I had another idea of the man, saw how overpowering he might be, how constricting life in his house could be. And this new idea of Bray was added to the idea of the man with memories of the fields full of laborers at harvesttime, of allowances of beer, of children taking tea to their fathers and grand-fathers; the man with his undisclosed memory of taint from his short holiday job as a boy in the manor; his wish to be independent, com-bined with his unwitting possession, as a servant, someone trained to please, of three or four characters.

I had sensed a little of his instability. But what had now befallen him? From what I heard, in those meetings (in some town on the south coast) and in this sharing of food, this communion, Bray had joined people whom the radical conservative in him despised: workers, people looking for employment, the kind of person he, Bray, the self-employed man, celebrating his freedom after his father's and grand-father's lifetime of servitude, looked down on. The man who scoffed at Pitton, exulted in his fall, now showed sympathy for people like Pitton, people for whom in England, even in this well-to-do part of England, there was no longer room: people coming down from the Midlands and finding themselves dispossessed, without lodgings or security, people (unlike the naked souls in the Doomsday painting in St. Thomas's) who knew what it was to be in charge of their fates, but felt they had lost control.

The more I heard about Bray's meetings the more I thought of that London meeting of twenty years before. And the scene recon-structed itself in one detail after another, down to the lamp painted HALL shining palely in the quiet street, quiet at night in that part of residential London in those days, with few people out and very few cars. So ordinary and dull the street, so desperate the people up there, in the room at the top of the tall flight of stairs.

"It's as with everything else," Bray said. "You can take out only what you put in. The more you put in, the more you take out. The good book is always open for you."

From Mrs. Bray I heard more. She was someone I hardly knew. I knew her mainly as a voice on the telephone. She answered the tele-phone when Bray was out and made the bookings for him; he telephoned her regularly when he was out. She was brisk (Bray's instructions, to save his customers telephone charges); she was efficient. No extra talk there. A cheerful little voice on the telephone; its possessor hardly seen. She lived in her house—there was no garden: Bray's paved yard left little space for anything like that. She was driven into Salisbury or Andover by Bray to do her shopping; she seldom took the bus. Sometimes Bray, in the car, greeted her in Salisbury. Then I saw her: a very small, thin woman, a wisp of a woman, hardly there—as though life with Bray, the driver, the mechanic, the man with strong views, the hard worker, the perverse neglecter of the valley's beauty, had worn her down. It was from her, now, that I heard more of Bray's religion and "meetings."

"I can't answer for him these days. He's at one of his meetings, I expect. He's emptied the deep-freeze. That's how I know. That's not the way you treat a deep-freeze. I don't understand him. If you have a deep-freeze, you build it up. You don't keep emptying it."

I had heard about the deep-freeze from Bray. It was important to him. I didn't have one myself and he delighted in telling me about the rituals connected with it. The bulk buying (and at reduced prices from certain shops, apparently), the cooking and the storing of great batches—the deep-freeze made food the center of a new kind of ritual, provided a new kind of shopping, a new kind of excursion, restored an idea of plenty and harvesttime and celebration.

Mrs. Bray had her own ideas. Towards the deep-freeze she was more squirrellike, hoarding, wishing to keep the granary full. And when one day I met her at the bus stop—unusually: she was usually driven by Bray to Salisbury or Amesbury or Andover or to some special discount supermarket on the outskirts of Southampton—she was still inflamed about the deep-freeze. So small, so thin, so inflamed.

She said, the rooks cawing and flapping above us: "If you have a deep-freeze, you build it up. You don't keep emptying it." She spoke as though, in an ideal world, she would keep her deep-freeze full forever and never touch it. She spoke as though—in spite of the manifest hardships, the absence of Bray and a car—the replenishing of the deep-freeze was the purpose of her trip to Salisbury. She repeated, "You build it up."

At the end of the road—no longer hidden at its far end by the elms and the growth at the roadside between the elms—the red bus appeared.

She waited until the bus almost stopped. She said, "It's that fancy woman of his."

The words burst out of her. As though the arrival of the bus, the sudden darkening of the bus-stop area, the folding door opening back, the noise of the engine, had provided her with the correct dramatic moment for the disclosure, the abandoning of civility and talking about things she didn't absolutely have on her mind. And having taken her inflamed mood up several degrees, she stamped into the bus, slapped her coins down on the driver's little stand, and generally did as much as she could to draw attention to herself and her anger.

She sat in one of the front seats—such fuss, such commotion from such a small person—and paid no further attention to me. And I wondered whether in 1950, when I was eighteen and new to England, new to adult life, I wondered whether, seeing a woman of that age in a bus behaving in such a way, I would have thought it even likely that the anger of a woman so old and small and white-haired would have had to do with her husband's "fancy woman."

The words, coming from that little lady, were shocking to me. I had known her for so long as a friendly, brisk voice on the telephone, knowing my voice and taking pleasure in anticipating my name before I spoke it. "Can do," "Will do," "Thank you, sir"—those were the words (spoken swiftly on the telephone, to prevent me from having to put in new coins) I associated with her. "Fancy woman" was awful—demeaning to her, demeaning to the woman she was talking about (if such a woman existed), demeaning to her husband, demeaning (the way obscenities of speech are demeaning) to all of us.

And it was of this other woman that I now heard from Mrs. Bray, on the telephone, at the bus stop (where she began to appear more often), and in the shopping streets of Salisbury. How had Bray met this other woman? Who would be attracted to Bray? I had never thought of Bray as a partner for anyone; but that was a man's way of looking. In this business of sensing or seeing partners, a woman would live in a different world.

In the beginning I had had my doubts about the existence of this woman. But then, quite quickly, from Mrs. Bray's circumstantial stories, I believed there was a woman; and from Mrs. Bray's stories I could see the point up to which Bray had directly and innocently spoken about the woman, speaking of the oddity of the meeting with her as he might have spoken of any other oddity connected with his taxi work.

She had arrived late one night at Salisbury railway station on a slow train from the south. (Only a few details, in Mrs. Bray's stories, of the age and appearance of this woman; and I had no idea whether all these details had formed part of Bray's story as he had told it to Mrs. Bray.) She had told the ticket collector that she had no ticket; no money; no place to spend the night. He or a colleague had telephoned the police; they (the curious, taken-for-granted humanity of the British state and its officials) arranged for the woman to be put up in a bed-and-breakfast place for the night; a decision about what was to be done with her was to be taken by higher officers the next day. The bed-and-breakfast place was run by a man supplementing his poor income from his original business, a picture framing–junkshop–antique shop.

It was at the request of the police (or a policeman), then, that Bray (the fair, the reliable, and ready for a job at any time of day or night) had gone to the railway station and taken the woman to the bed-and-breakfast place. That must have made an impression on him— the bright lights of the station, its near-emptiness, the solitude of the woman.

But it was the next day that his feelings were engaged, when in the morning he had gone to the place to take the woman to the police station. As she came down the short paved path from the front door he saw (as he had told Mrs. Bray) the rotten, spotty complexion of the woman, the over-big tweed overcoat (clearly somebody else's) she had on, the general manner of the dropouts' or "traveling people" of the neighborhood whom he so disliked. But then suddenly (as he had told Mrs. Bray), when she had come out past the wicket gate onto the pavement, she had turned on him with anger, sarcasm, scorn. And she—narrow, close-set eyes—had said, almost shouted, to him: "But I have no money, you know."

Mrs. Bray reported the woman's sarcasm with a sarcasm of her own. But it was possible, even with this, to see how Bray would have been taken aback and to see how, in the very aggression of the woman, the spirit she showed at that particular moment, he would have found an attraction, would have fallen for her weakness, her need, her dependence on him at that moment. She had then said to him with a continuation of her hostility and pride (which clearly at the same time contained an appeal to someone she had seen faltering): "You know where they'll be sending me back to, don't you?" Not jail; if it had been, Bray wouldn't have responded. It was a kind of county home for people with nervous disorders. And in that grown woman there was something of the child who still expected its pleas to move adults, to move others.

That was what Bray had told Mrs. Bray. There his direct, early story stopped. And the reason was that for that wounded, appealing child in that woman's body, for that soul imprisoned behind those eyes, Bray had felt an immense passion, and all the protectiveness of his nature. Whenever I thought of the woman and Bray, I thought of those sentences. Mrs. Bray spoke them often: the only intimacy of the couple to which she had been admitted. "But I have no money, you know." "You know where they'll be sending me back to, don't you?"

He didn't take her to the police station, didn't get her involved in any paperwork there. He offered to keep her at the bed-and-breakfast place. He knew the man, the junkshop man who had begun his business as a picture framer and called his shop a gallery.

This man had been like so many others, shopkeepers or would-be shopkeepers, who had been attracted to Salisbury for the sake of its civility and wealth and countryside, but hadn't sufficiently studied the pattern of its traffic, the location of the car parks, the very roundabout one-way-street system, or understood the way shoppers moved about the town center.

A shop might be just two or three minutes' walk from the market square, but could be off the main shopping track. Many little businesses failed—quickly, visibly. Especially pathetic were the shops that—not understanding that people with important shopping to do usually did it in London—aimed at style. How dismal those boutiques and women's dress shops quickly became, the hysteria of their owners showing in their windows! Not in the turbulence or disorder of their display but in the opposite, a melancholy unassertiveness, not the unassertiveness of good taste or old-fashionedness, but something more like a nervous condition, as though the window wished it didn't have to be seen, this unassertiveness of the window like an expression of the owner's wish to abandon the project, run away.

No longer the swag of the fisherman's net with plastic starfish or painted wooden fish or real shells; or the bits of driftwood; or the autumn leaves. Nothing like that now; more like a laundry sale, a sale of unreclaimed items: just the garments, the skirts and the blouses, things unloved, even by the keeper of the shop—who could be glimpsed sometimes, when the light was right and the window did not reflect the street, in the middle of her dwindling, much-handled stock: vacant, grumpy, unwelcoming, she who at the beginning had been all charm and a wish to please, offering civilities (a cup of coffee, perhaps, or classical music) over and above the civilities of simple trade, now seemingly anxious to drive everyone away, to fail utterly, to have no possible encouragement or excuse for reopening her shop. All just a few yards away from boom and success and the tramp of tourist feet.

It was above a shop like this, a picture framer's, a "gallery," that Bray's woman stayed. There wasn't the demand in Salisbury for the amount of picture framing the shop needed; and the shop didn't have the stock of frames or mounts to attract such business as was going. Brackets of ten or twelve picture-frame styles, elegantly sliced off at the diagonal, hung over pegs: like little decorated gallows, those picture-frame samples, quickly lost amid the secondhand furniture and household goods, the junk-or-antique trade, to which the shop had turned, until even this had been subsumed in the bed-and-breakfast business that the hard-pressed owner had started on the two upper floors.

It was here, through the woman or girl, or through the bed-and-breakfast man, that Bray had got to find out about the healer and the meetings. And as fast as he had learned about the healing, so he had talked to me about what he had learned. In the beginning he hadn't talked with great knowledge. That was one reason why I took some time to understand that he was talking seriously.

Gradually then there came out an account of his new religious life: the healing sessions, the "good book" opened at random for each one in turn, and its words interpreted. Gradually there came out too the new idea of community he had found and surrendered to: the discovery of people wounded in their minds and hearts, for whom the material world had proved too much, had passed out of control. Not the arbitrary medieval world of the Doomsday painting in St. Thomas's: that was a world men had never understood or thought they could control. In that world men could get by only by appeasing, making sacrifice, performing rituals. In this healing world of Bray's it was different: as in the ancient Roman world at the very beginning of Christianity, the grief and the communion came from the feeling that the world had once been under control, but was so no longer.

And at the center of this tenderness and compassion was the woman he had seen at the railway station, who had the very next day thrown herself on his mercy, the woman who was totally dependent on him. Of her appearance I gathered nothing more than I had already heard: the over-big tweed coat, the lank hair, the unhappy, close-set eyes, the bad skin. This was what Bray had reported to Mrs. Bray the first day and the next; that was all Mrs. Bray had to go by; that was all she had to embroider on.

I thought that part of the woman's attraction for Bray would have been the absence of an overt allure. Allure in the woman might have made Bray uneasy, might have made him feel he was being used; it might have given him the idea that there were or could have been other men in the picture. In the woman he had found there was only a child's need in a cruel world; and to that need Bray would have thought that he alone was responsive. And from time to time in those aggressive, unhappy eyes there might have been an acknowledgment of Bray's ability to protect.

Mrs. Bray said of Bray, "If I told the taxi union or the council where he got his fancy woman from, I suppose they would take away his license."

I didn't think her power would run that far; I didn't think she thought so herself; and I don't believe she wanted any harm to come to Bray. It was his new serenity that enraged her. As far as he was concerned, he behaved as though there were no quarrels at home. And perhaps there were none; perhaps Mrs. Bray's rages were for people like me, who might have known about Bray's other life. But it was only from Mrs. Bray that I heard about the woman. From Bray I heard only about the healing and the meetings. His meetings took up more of his time. There were certain afternoons and evenings now when he was not free; but apart from that his taxi-driving, car-hire life continued as before.

He said to me one day in the car, after a silence which he had allowed to happen, perhaps to give greater effect to his words: "I've taken up tithing."

He spoke the words with pride, boastfulness, pleasure. It was like the time he had spoken from the corner of his mouth about Pitton's departure and from the dashboard shelf had handed me, with an air of mystery and favor, the book my landlord had published in the 1920s.

Tithing! Such an old word. The tenth of one's produce for the church. Such a subject for radical protest. Perhaps even in the Middle Ages, when men lived in the world of the St. Thomas's Doomsday painting, it had been resisted. But now Bray, a hater of privilege and taxation, boasted of offering his tithe to his healer—spoke of tithing as though he had toiled up to the top of the hill and seen the fine view.

He said, "And that has to be before tax, you understand. I give a tenth of my gross. It hurts. Of course it hurts. It's meant to hurt. You have to make the sacrifice." And then, not knowing that from his wife I had been given an idea of the person he was talking about, he said,

"There's someone I know. Started a little secondhand business. Didn't do well. Began taking in foreign students. French, German. We get a lot of those here. But that didn't do well either. The agencies wanted the students to stay with families. He was ready to put his head in the oven. Then he began tithing. It hurt. It was like the last straw. But he kept at it. And you know what? In the last two months the social security have been sending him people. For the first time for a couple of years he's making regular money. As Churchill said during the war, there's a tide in the affairs of men. It goes out. But it also comes back in. It's the same with tithing. You get back only what you put in. It has to hurt. Then you get double."

So, beneath the noisy rooks—whose arrival portended death or money, according to the old wise tales, as Mr. Phillips's father said—serenity came to Bray. He still took down engines in the mess of his paved yard (but he was more circumspect with his surveyor neighbor than he had been with Pitton); he still wore his formal-informal uniform of peaked cap and cardigan; he still talked a lot in the car. But his old readiness to snap and cavil and rant was abated or, rather, it ran into, meshed in with, his religious talk. He was a man at ease with himself, a man with a secret, an inner vision.

He was indifferent to the frenzies of Mrs. Bray. But perhaps, as I suspected, that frenzy was for outsiders: an act, a character, that made it easier for her (for so long living hidden away in her house) to go out among people. And because there was no change in this public character of Mrs. Bray's, because I could see always what her talk would lead up to, I dreaded meeting her (once no more than a gentle old voice on the telephone) just as some time before I had dreaded meeting Pitton, whose early gardening rituals it had enchanted me to observe.

*A*BIG car stopped for me at the bus stop one day. It was a new neighbor. Newer than the surveyor. And this stopping, this offer of a lift to Salisbury, was his way of introducing himself. A big car, a middle-aged man, perhaps in his late fifties; a big house (I had heard it had been put up for sale, but hadn't heard who had bought it, didn't even know until now that it had been sold). The accent of the neighbor was still a country accent; he wanted me to know that he was a local man, that he had known the valley a long time, and that he was already (though new in the house) familiar with the people.

He said, "I gave Mrs. Bray a lift last week. She's very fierce these days. Do you know John Bray? Why does he charge so little? He'll have to work till he dies. He provides a good service. He's dependable; he has a lot of regulars; people like him. I've often told him that as a car-hire man he should charge as much as the market will bear. But he goes his own way."

We passed an old farm, ruined old walls, muddy yard.

My new neighbor said, "My mother grew up in that house. Different people now, of course."

It was his way, not an unpleasant way, of claiming the valley, claiming kinship with the people of the valley. I thought of Mr. Phillips's father, going watery-eyed at the thought of his early days, the beginning of the century, in the valley, and his first job as a carrier's boy; his boy's adventure of hiding in "a bed of withies" when the motorcar had knocked down his cousin. There was, in my neighbor's talk, a wish to be linked to that kind of past, the past contained as well in Bray's memories of harvesttime and children taking tea to their grandfathers in the fields. But at the same time there was an element in my neighbor—his big quiet car, being driven without hurry beside the river—of the rich man unbending.

"How's Mrs. Phillips?"

I didn't know there had been anything particularly wrong with her. I was aware only that, like my landlord after his two glorious outgoing summers, Mrs. Phillips had retreated, was less in evidence. But I hadn't inquired why.

My neighbor said, "I believe her nerves are getting the better of her."

Mrs. Bray's rages, Bray's fares, Mrs. Phillips's increased nerves— I was impressed by the minuteness of my new neighbor's knowledge;

and I believe he intended me to be impressed. In my mind—with the speeding up of the years, consequent on my own aging as well as on my repeating experience of the seasons in the valley (less and less new knowledge added every year), and with the dislocation of memory caused by recent events (like the departure of Pitton)—in my mind, he, my neighbor, had only just arrived in the valley.

We came to the village with the bridge over the river. My neighbor turned off the main valley road and steered his big car gently over the narrow railed bridge.

He said, "I often take this road. There are some pretty little bits." He was at once proprietorial and celebratory, as celebratory of the valley and the river as I had been in my early years. For me, though, the years had begun to stack away, the seasons had begun to repeat. Not so for him. Yet he was an older man and had deep roots here. Perhaps it was that depth of knowledge, added to proprietorship, the ownership of the big house, that had given him his special, almost reverential, view.

The bridge was the only one over the river in the valley. The site of both bridge and village would have been old; and though there were no barrows or tumuli here, and the village buildings were mostly of this century, there was a feeling here of the past, not of temples or mysteries, but of human habitation, agriculture, fields or pasture existing over the centuries within the limits of the wet meadows.

The feeling was especially strong in the large field beside which we were now driving. I had never seen this field plowed. Its roadside hedge was marked with enormous oaks, thick straight trunks widely and evenly spaced, these oaks (which might have been allowed to grow out of the hedge) suggesting a planting done more than a hundred years before (and with what security, what a conviction that this corner of the earth would continue to be as the planter of the hedge and the oaks had known it).

In my second or third year in the valley, during a winter of great floods, when the river had overflowed its banks at many places and cut new, fast-moving, noisy channels through the water meadows up and down the valley, all this field with the great boundary oaks had been flooded, creating the effect sometimes, according to the light, of a great white lake; and the swans and the moorhens and coots and the smaller wild ducks and other river birds, leaving the familiar river course, had paddled about this field as long as the lake lasted, as if in addition to the joy of finding a big new feeding ground, there was also the excitement of being on water in a place where normally there was only land. The flood, receding after a few days, had left the field sodden, with little drifts of black mud caught in the grass, and ruffled-looking, as though the movement of the water had pushed the grass about in the wrong way. Every winter since then, whenever the black and yellow council noticeboard, FLOODS, was placed beside the road, I had waited for this drama to repeat.

The road ran along a ledge in the down, following the curve of the down. The river was on the right, now closer, now farther away, now almost level with the road, now some way below it. A narrow river, winding in a wide valley—it offered many different views. This drive was quite different from the drive on the other bank; it might have been another river.

The road twisted up sharply; the river fell away; fields separated it from the road. Then there was a bushy, overgrown lane that ran diagonally between the fields down to the lushness of the river.

My neighbor said, "I used to cycle around here when I was a boy. I loved coming to the top of this hill in order to go coasting down that lane. It ends in a footbridge over the river."

When he was a boy: forty-five years before, perhaps, in the 1930s, with the war coming. Quiet roads, almost empty skies; no constant military roar, as now; no sight, miles away to the west and miles up, of the vapor trails one after the other of commercial airliners, vapor trails usually like disappearing chalk marks, but in exceptional atmospheric conditions coming together to make a thick white arc of cloud from end to end of the horizon, clearly showing the curvature of the earth.

My neighbor nodded towards the pair of run-down red-brick cottages in the lane. They were the only buildings in the lane.

He said, "I often think it would be nice to live there. Shepherds used to live there in the old days, when there were more sheep about."

This was my first glimpse of the cottages I was to move to when I left my cottage in the manor grounds. But I didn't remember when I was negotiating for the cottages that I had seen them in the company of my new neighbor; that he had pointed them out to me. At the time I paid little attention to the cottages. I was more interested in my neighbor, seeing in his wish to live in a pair of agricultural cottages another sign of his "unbending," another sign of the softness that hinted at other strengths held in reserve.

I remembered the drive and the cottages much later, after I had moved and was living in the lane.

A car came down the lane one Saturday afternoon. It overshot the cottages and then with difficulty (the lane beyond the cottages was very narrow, barely the width of a car) it reversed into my entrance and parked there. The car was driven by a young man; his passenger was a very old woman.

The old woman got out and walked down the lane, past the cottages, then back up the lane. She peeped through the hedge. The young man explained: his grandmother was visiting old places in her life, and she had come to look for the cottage where as a child she used to come to stay with her shepherd grandfather. She remembered a lane narrowing down to a footpath and then a footbridge over the river; that was the way she used to go in the mornings to get milk from the farm on the other side of the river. The lane she had come to seemed right, the young man said; but his grandmother didn't recognize her grandfather's cottage.

And I was horribly embarrassed. Embarrassed to have done what I had done with the cottages, all the things that had disorientated the old lady and made her question where she was: the new entrance and drive; the remodeling of what the old lady would have remembered as the back of the cottages into the front of the renovated house; the extension to the house that had done away with the half of the building her grandfather had lived in; the landscaped garden that had replaced the fruit-and-vegetable cottage garden the old lady probably remembered. (But there would also have been years of unburnable household refuse, some of which had been passed down to me, banking up the hedge mounds; and the garden, choked with bush when I took over, would have gone through many changes, many cycles, before that.)

Embarrassed, in the presence of the old lady, by what I had done, I was also embarrassed to be what I was, an intruder, not from another village or county, but from another hemisphere; embarrassed to have destroyed or spoilt the past for the old lady, as the past had been destroyed for me in other places, in my old island, and even here, in the valley of my second life, in my cottage in the manor grounds, where bit by bit the place that had thrilled and welcomed and reawakened me had changed and changed, until the time had come for me to leave.

And it wasn't until the old lady (with her memories of seventy years before) had come to my new house that I remembered the drive and the detour with my new neighbor; his talk of the people and the beauty of various "bits"; and his pointing out to me the cottages in the lane which at that time were still more or less like the cottages the old lady had known as a child but which, when she came to visit them, she found she had lost for good.

*I*T WASN'T for Mrs. Phillips that the ambulance came; it wasn't for my landlord. It was for Mr. Phillips. He collapsed in the manor one day and was dead before the ambulance came.

And all at once it was understood—even by me, in my cottage—how much the manor relied upon him, his energy, his strength, his protectiveness. He was a protector, by instinct and training; he called up the weakness, the need to be protected, in the people he attracted; he was not capable of, would not have understood, a relationship between equals. For people who did not need him he showed only his grumpy, irritable side, which was his way of dismissing such people.

When I had first come to my cottage and, in my stranger's accepting mood, had added Mr. Phillips to my mental catalog of English "types," and seen him as exemplifying his role as country-house servant, he had in fact barely arrived, was almost as much a newcomer as I, was still testing out the job and his response to the semisolitude of the manor, and still hardly knew my landlord.

He had grown into the job and made it his own; and over the years he had developed a regard for my landlord, for the softness, the vulnerability, the pride, the obstinacy, all the things that made my landlord a man apart, and which might have been expected to make a man like Mr. Phillips impatient. He had developed especially a regard for the artistic side of my landlord. Though as politically irascible as Bray and as ready to adopt the "punchy" simplicities of the popular newspapers, Mr. Phillips didn't scoff at my landlord's artistic side, any more than Bray scoffed at it, Bray who one day, as though offering me the key to my landlord's character, had with the clumsy gesture of a man not used to handling books handed me the illustrated verse tale my landlord had published in the 1920s. It was extraordinary, in both these tough, practical men, who almost certainly hated "modern" art: this idea of the artist or the man of artistic temperament as a man apart. Perhaps—like other ideas: the mad scientist, for instance, derived from the old figure of the obsessed and sinful alchemist—this idea of the artist, the man seeking to recreate the world, went right back to the time when all art or learning was religious, an expression of the divine, serving the divine.

I benefited from this regard of Mr. Phillips for the artistic side of my landlord. The regard was extended to me. It was part of the security of my second life in the valley, one of the accidents that made it possible. And now all at once that security was gone.

It was decided, by Mrs. Phillips, that just as Alan's death had been kept by Mr. Phillips from my landlord, so now Mr. Phillips's death was to be kept from him. She didn't think he would take the news quietly; and she feared that she would not be able to manage my landlord if his behavior became in any way extreme. And so, though withdrawn for some time with her nerves, Mrs. Phillips stepped forward once again now and sought to take charge of things: Mrs. Phillips with the thin blue veins in the dark, finely gathered skin below her eyes, and the more prominent veins at her temples and below her thin hair that spoke of stress and pain.

She took to telephoning me; on the telephone now she became long-winded and repetitive. She told me again and again that Mr. Phillips was her second husband and though she meant no disrespect to his memory and didn't want anyone to think that her love was less, the grief for Mr. Phillips had repeated, had been like a continuation of, the grief for her first husband; that the grief she had felt for him, Mr. Phillips, had been further absorbed by all the things she had had to do after he had collapsed, and all the trouble at keeping the news from my landlord.

She was repetitive. But she was reporting on a continuing discovery about herself and the development of her grief; the grief was like something with a life of its own. She was also perhaps saying—perhaps only to herself—that she intended to stay on at the manor, to try to do the job she and Mr. Phillips had done together.

And it was only several stages on in my response to the event and to Mrs. Phillips's telephone conversations that I saw that a new uncertainty had suddenly come to Mrs. Phillips's life. I had been shocked when I had first learned that the Phillipses had made no plans for their future, had not laid anything by. Then I had admired them for their adventurousness, their readiness to move on, to make their home in another place. Of course, they could be adventurous in this way because they never doubted that there would always be some new position for them—and it could be said that that kind of expectation was in itself a kind of security.

I don't think they had even contemplated retiring. They knew very well that they had taken up an old-fashioned job; but they saw it as a kind of withdrawal; and they had probably seen themselves going on in this way until they were old. Now the active partner had been taken away; and Mrs. Phillips's prospects, if she left the manor, seemed to me fearful.

No doubt I exaggerated. I didn't know the Phillipses' friends, didn't know how they lived or joked together. Especially I didn't know about their work, their world of work, and what adjustments they made as workers to preserve their pride. I remembered only how, out of her own security at the manor, Mrs. Phillips had been ready to see Pitton cast out; how much at a loss Pitton had been when he had to leave, how passive he had become, refusing to look for work, out of his unspoken dread of the figure of the employer.

But what was true about Mrs. Phillips's grief was not true about old Mr. Phillips's grief. He had coped with the deaths of his father, mother, sister, wife. The death of his cousin in 1911—as he had told me more than once—had prepared him for all their deaths. Now to his great surprise, in his mid-seventies and near the end of his life, he had found in the unexpected death of his son a grief that had surpassed that earlier grief. He was broken, Mrs. Phillips told me. The grounds of the manor that had given him such pleasure after Pitton had gone —he could no longer bear to be there. And he no longer came to work in the vegetable garden; or, formally dressed in a suit or jacket and trousers in the very pale colors he liked, to walk with his pronged staff.

It was as though he too had died. As though it was of this death —his son's—that he had spoken when we had seen the first rooks squawking and flapping about the manor beeches.

*I*VY WAS beautiful. It was to be allowed to grow up trees. The trees eventually died and collapsed, but they had provided their pleasure for many years; and there were other trees to look at, other trees to see out my landlord's time. So too it had been with people. They had been around; when the time came they had gone away; and then there had been other people. But it wasn't like that with Mr. Phillips. He had been too important to my landlord. My landlord had awakened from his long acedia to the tenderness and regard of Mr. Phillips; and the death of this strong, protective man couldn't be hidden beyond a fortnight.

My landlord was enraged when he found out, enraged that he had been encouraged to think and talk of a man as living when the man had died. He quarreled and made scenes. He knocked down glasses, overturned full ashtrays, pushed meal trays off his bed, generally tried to make a mess. Grief was beyond him, was too frightening for him. He could express only resentment, and his resentment focused on Mrs. Phillips.

She thought it was unfair. What she had done, as she told me on the telephone, had been done for his sake. She thought it was selfish: in his rages there was no consideration for her own feelings about her husband's death. And she thought it was childish. She said, "Nothing he can do is going to bring Stan back."

In the early days she had been full of regard for the manor and its master. For the artistic side of my landlord, which was like another emanation of his privilege, she had had a corresponding reverence. She had had something like awe for the little gifts she had brought to me from my landlord—a poem in verse or prose, a drawing, a dainty little basket, a sandalwood fan, some sticks of Indian incense. Sometimes in those early days she had even typed out (perhaps without being asked) the prose poems or prose writings, the act of typing making her job more than that of a housekeeper. What she typed mightn't have been always comprehensible; but that added to the mystery and the beauty for her.

She had passed on to Mr. Phillips her reverence for the artistic side of my landlord. But while Mr. Phillips had allowed this reverence to grow, Mrs. Phillips's own reverence had lessened. She had become more matter-of-fact about everything. Gaining security in the manor, she had lost her original feeling of awe; gaining security, she had looked inwards, concentrated on her nerves, surrendered (like her employer) more and more to the protection of her husband.

Now that her husband had gone, she had lost her security. The manor job, which had been so easy for so long, became suddenly hard; the manor became full of tension. And in her dealings with my landlord she went right back to her nurse's attitude. But she was without the strength now to back up that attitude. The man was childish, she said; he wanted attention for the sake of attention. She would have known how to deal with that once; now she didn't. The job began to wear her out.

The vegetable allotment within the walled garden was abandoned. But there still came to the grounds some of the strange men whom Mr. Phillips had called in to do occasional pieces of work. While Mr. Phillips lived these men had walked and moved quickly, like people not anxious to draw attention to themselves, done their jobs and gone away. But now there was no authority; and there was a change in the attitude of these men. They walked more slowly; they walked past the windows of my cottage; they raised their voices.

On my way back one afternoon from the river walk I saw two men in the overgrown garden. They had billhooks. They were near the old pile of sawn aspen logs. One man was small, much smaller than Alan (who had worried so much about his size). This man had a sly, dangerous face; in his eyes there was a look that made me feel he had been caught out and resented it. The other man was taller, though not much taller, dark-haired, with dark skin around his dark eyes.

The taller man said, without being asked anything, "We are taking away the rotten logs. Margaret knows. She gave permission." Margaret was Mrs. Phillips.

It was my policy not to interfere with people I saw in the grounds; not to act as a watchman. But the billhooks, and the dancing blue eyes of the small man, worried me.

I said to the man who had spoken, "What is your name?"

He straightened up. He almost held his hands at his sides. He said, "Mr. Tomm. With two *m*'s. German."

"German?"

"I'm a German. Mr. Tomm."

Was this how he always introduced himself? Was being a German (he had an English Midlands accent) the most important thing to him, and something he felt he ought to get out of the way as soon as possible? Or was he joking?

He said, "My father was a prisoner of war. He worked on a farm near Oxford. He stayed on and married the old carter's daughter. My father died five years ago. My mother died last Christmas in Birmingham. I used to live up there. But I lost my job and my wife left me. That's why I'm here." He made a scything, grass-cutting gesture with the billhook. "I love gardening. It's all I want to do. I get it from my mother."

I looked at the small man, to see what he was making of the story. He, the small man, was considering me intently. His little cheeks were working; he wasn't going to talk to me. On his small, delicate fore-arms I saw tattoos done in green and red and blue-black. These col-ored tattoos, done with modern tools, were a new craze in the locality, spreading without publicity or overt promotion; Bray had told me about them. In tattoos at least the small man was keeping up with his bigger fellows.

The talker said, "I'm going through a bad patch."

I left them. Just outside the box-bordered enclosure, quite wild now, there was a small pickup van reversed against the entrance, not far from my cottage. For rotten logs alone? I felt that other things—gar-den statues, urns, stone pots, even greenhouse doors—were at risk; that those two men were scavengers rather than serious thieves.

Mrs. Phillips seemed bemused when I telephoned. But she knew the name of the German. "He used to work for Stan. He's a German, you know."

Not many days after, the pickup van came again. The German got out, and a bigger, fat, unshaved man with reddish blond hair reaching down to his shoulders. The fat man wore bell-bottomed jeans and in his hand he held an empty rolled-up nylon sack that was almost the color of his hair. He didn't look at me, the fat man, was quite indif-ferent to me. His eyes were small and preoccupied; his lower lip was thick and red and wet.

The German said, "He's my brother. He has nowhere to stay. Last week he got a job with accommodation in an old lady's house. The solicitor arranged it. But they wanted him to be a servant. The old lady used to start ringing for tea at five in the morning. He's going through a bad patch."

In the days of Pitton, the known and half-tolerated intruders in the gardens and water meadows had been local gentlemen looking for a little Saturday-afternoon shooting. Now there was no Pitton; his day and his order seemed as far away and as unreachable as the original grandeur of the garden had seemed to me when I had just arrived and, among the relics of that grandeur, found only Pitton. There was no Mr. Phillips now, neither old nor young. And the people who came to work in what remained of the garden had become marauders, vandals.

The very kind of people who, in the great days of the manor, would have given of their best as carpenters, masons, bricklayers, might have had ideas of beauty and workmanship and looked for acknowledgment of their skill and craft and pains, people of this very sort now, sensing an absence of authority, an organization in decay, seemed to be animated by an opposite instinct: to hasten decay, to loot, to reduce to junk. And it was possible to understand how an ancient Roman factory-villa in this province of Britain could suddenly, after two or three centuries, simply with a letting-go by authority, and not with the disappearance of a working population, crumble into ruin, the secrets of the building and its modest technologies, for so long so ordinary, lost.

And Mrs. Phillips didn't really know what was happening in the grounds around her. She had no means of judging men, judging faces. Depending on herself now, she was continually surprised by people. That stored subjective knowledge of character and physiognomy which most people have—which begins simply enough, with the association of a particular kind of character with a particular kind of face, an association of greed, for instance, with a fat face, to put it at its simplest—that stored knowledge was denied her.

It was part of her incompetence, her new unhappiness. And it came out again when she tried to get help, when she advertised for women to help in the manor and was surprised again and again to get people like herself, women adrift, incompetent, themselves without the ability to judge people, looking as much for emotional refuge as for a position, solitary women with their precious things (full of associations for them alone) but without men or families, women who for various reasons had been squeezed out of a communal or shared life.

The first of these ladies came upon me like a vision one lunchtime when I was going out to the bus stop. She was below the yews and she was in brilliant green; and the face she turned to me was touched with green and blue and red, green on her eyelids. The colors of the paint on the old lady's face were like the colors of a Toulouse-Lautrec drawing; made her appear to belong to another age. Green was the absinthe color: it brought to mind pictures by other artists of forlorn absinthe drinkers; it made me think of bars. And probably a bar or hotel somewhere on the south coast was the lady's background, her last refuge, her previous life.

How long she must have spent arranging that violently colored face, dusted with glitter even for lunchtime on this summer's day! Where—and to whom?—was she going now on her day off? So dreadfully coquettish, so anxious to please, so instinctively obsequious in the presence of a man—everything about her caricatured by age, and the caricature further set off by the rural setting, the yews, the beeches, the country road.

What had Mrs. Phillips seen in this woman? How had she thought that this woman, rather than the other applicants she must have had, would have helped with looking after the house and my landlord?

Soon enough there were the complaints. Soon enough, complaining of the "staff," Mrs. Phillips put herself once more on the side of my landlord, made common cause with him—almost in the way that Mr. Phillips had done—against the crude, uncomprehending world.

"He rang and asked for a glass of sherry. She went to his room with a bottle in one hand and a glass in the other, and looking as though she herself had had a drop too much. A bottle in one hand and a glass in the other—I ask you. He didn't like it. 'A little formality, Margaret,' he said to me. 'A little formality. It's all I ask. A drink isn't just a drink. It's an occasion.' And I think he's entitled to a little formality. I told her, you know. Take in nothing without a tray. I told her."

Poor lady in green! She did something else wrong very soon afterwards—I believe Mrs. Phillips said she again took up a bottle and glass without a tray: she was too old to learn. And she didn't last out her period of probation. I didn't see her go. That glimpse of her, green (the brilliant green of her dress) in the dark-green shade of yews and beeches, on the black asphalt lane to the public road and the bus stop, that glimpse of her in her brief rural exile (as she made it appear) was all that I saw.

One or two of her successors I saw. Many I didn't. I just heard about them, heard the more sensational stories, from Mrs. Phillips. The arrival of one created consternation: a large removal van drove up to the manor courtyard with her "things." None lasted. One wished to do nothing; one wished to take over and give instructions; one re-arranged furniture in a number of rooms. Perhaps among them there was one who might have done very well, but had to go for that reason—Mrs. Phillips not wishing to train or nurture a rival and possible successor.

The whole situation with the "help" or "staff" became too much; the sharing of the kitchen and quarters became too much. It was decided that there were to be separate quarters for people from outside. One or two of the closed rooms of the manor were opened up. A decorator appeared.

And I felt that my time in my cottage—with the preparation of quarters for new staff, who might not always be single women, who might have families or friends with the privilege of roaming the grounds—I felt that my time in my cottage was coming to an end. Accidents, a whole series of accidents, had kept me protected in what was an exposed situation. Now that protection was coming to an end. The rooks building and cawing above in the beeches—perhaps this was what they had also portended.

The decorator—he seemed like an agent or instrument of change, but he wasn't, any more than old Mr. Phillips had been when he had started working and walking in the manor grounds after Pitton's departure—the decorator was a short, plump man, pink-complexioned, or seeming very pink in his white overall.

I grew to recognize the rhythm of his day, how he paced himself through his solitary physical labor. From time to time, for fixed periods, fifteen minutes in the morning and afternoon, an hour in the middle of the day, he withdrew from his scrapers and rollers and brushes and paint tins and sat in his car, holding the racing page of his paper over the steering wheel, drinking milky tea from his flask in the morning and afternoon breaks, eating sandwiches in the midday break, not being in a hurry then to open his sandwich tin, first giving himself another fifteen minutes or so with the racing page of his paper, and then, having unfolded the greaseproof wrapping of his neat parcel, eating slowly, steadily, without haste, but also without relish.

His car at first he parked on the lane just outside my cottage back door. When, using more gestures than words, I showed him what he had done, he without speaking moved nearer the manor courtyard to a spot where he was hidden from the manor and from me.

His car was like his castle. Out of it, he was at work, in somebody else's place; in it, he was at home. He looked serene, self-sufficient. In the top pocket of his overall (over a very thick, hand-knitted blue pullover) he had an empty, open, flip-top cigarette packet. This was his ashtray; the gesture with which he flicked ash into this packet was practiced. It was clearly an old habit or procedure, part of his tidiness as a decorator. The tidiness, the concentration required for painting, the way sometimes his face went close to his painting hand, the silence in which he worked for ninety minutes or so at a time, his solitude—this gave him a disturbing presence, made him seem more than his job and his appearance, the pinkness of his skin and the whiteness of his overall. And I found, when I began to talk to him, that he had a curious voice: it was soft, evenly pitched, childlike, passive.

He took his cigarette-packet ashtray seriously. I said I liked the idea. He didn't dismiss it or make a joke about it. He spoke very seriously about it. He told me when the idea had come to him and how it had come; people always remarked on it, he said.

And as we talked at various times over the days—he was ready to talk: his solitude was like something imposed on him, something he didn't mind setting aside—I found that he took everything about himself seriously, that he regarded himself with a kind of awe. There was something else: he seemed to be looking at himself from a distance, all his habits, his rituals. He was awed by what he saw: he didn't understand what he saw.

Even this sitting at intervals in his car—that was puzzling to him, because that was when he also took his pills. He took his pills and studied the racing page, because his dream was to be a full-time gambler, a serious gambler. Not betting like a pensioner on outsiders, but betting on favorites all the time: it was the only way to make a living out of gambling. He needed his pills; he took two sorts four times a day. He could do nothing without his pills; he went nowhere without his pills. The pills kept him going. And it was through Mr. Phillips, long ago, that he had discovered the pills. That was the connection with Mrs. Phillips, though, as he said, he didn't know Margaret so well.

Before the pills he used to burst out crying in public, for no reason; he used to just begin to cry. He didn't know why. He was well off, better off than many people he knew. He had a house, a wife, a car. At first people at work didn't know he was crying; they thought he was just allergic to gloss paint or the new synthetic varnishes. But one day the tears got the better of him, and he had to go to the hospital.

He found himself in a ward where the beds had no sheets, only mattresses and blankets. There was very little space between the beds. The nurse was a man. Even through his tears he recognized the oddity of that. The man who was the nurse, Stan, Mr. Phillips, gave him some pills; and he fell asleep. He had never slept so soundly; he woke up feeling so well he was grateful to Stan ever after. That was how he had got hooked on the pills.

And Stan helped him more. "He was so good to me. He said to me one day, 'Look, if you don't pull yourself together, I'm going to have you registered as disabled. You might think there's going to be more benefit for you from the social security because of that, but I'm telling you: there's *nothing* in it for you. There's no extra benefit. Ask the almoner.' And he was right. There was nothing in it for me. So I pulled myself together. So sad about Stan. I used to think that if I really had a big win on the horses I would go to Stan and give it all to him. All. Just like that." He made a lifting gesture, as though, as in a cartoon, money came in coin in sacks. "I thought I would go and say, 'Stan, this is the biggest thing I've done. I want you to take it, because you've been so good to me.' "

His eyes began to water. But they remained expressionless, steady. His face didn't change color; his voice never lost its childlike quality.

"I've lost everything now. House, furniture, wife. But that was when the crying left me. When I left my wife. When I left her I left all my troubles behind. I found her with the man on the Wednesday. I hit her. By Friday they had me out of the house."

This was the story he told over many days, saving up this detail for last. And even in this detail much had been left out. Much, for instance, would have gone on before that Wednesday discovery. But that was the way he saw the event; that was what had worked on him.

Sitting in his car, flicking ash into the cigarette packet in the top pocket of his overall, he gave a dry sob, like a little convulsion.

He said, "It's not for her. It's for Stan."

*T*HE WEATHER was cool, end-of-summer, early autumn. Good weather for external painting, the decorator said: the paint had a better consistency, the charged brush moved more easily. It was one of the few bright pieces of knowledge—knowledge external to himself—that he possessed. But the air that was good for the decorator's brush was also full of end-of-summer dust and exhalations of various kinds.

On my walk one afternoon, just beyond what had been Jack's garden, between the old-metal and timber and barbed-wire farmyard debris below the beeches on one side of the way, and the deep, rubbish-burning chalk pit on the other side (the branches of the now tall silver birches singed a month or so before by a fire that had been fed too richly), I began to choke.

I walked round the old farmyard, continuing in the droveway, breathing through my mouth as deeply as I could, to clear the constriction.

To the right was the wide low slope, where in the old days the black and white cattle, especially when seen against the sky, brought to mind the condensed-milk labels we had known as children in Trinidad; and brought to mind especially a coloring competition for schoolchildren that the distributors of the condensed milk had organized one year. The drawing or outline to be colored was an enlarged version of the label itself. What pleasure, to get as many sheets with the outline as one wanted! What landscapes came to the mind of a child to whom cattle like those in the picture and smooth grassy hillsides like those in the picture (clearly without snakes) were not known!

Always on a sunny day on this walk, and especially if at the top of the slope some of the cattle stood against the sky, there was a corner of my fantasy in which I felt that some minute, remote yearning—as remote as a flitting, all-but-forgotten cinema memory from early childhood—had been satisfied, and I was in the original of that condensed-milk label drawing.

To the left, across the wide, long-grassed droveway, was a stretch of pasture now behind barbed wire. All down the pasture on the other side was a plantation of pines, now tall. Dark and thick that pine wood had seemed until one day the stubbled field behind had been set ablaze; and the thin screen of the dark pine trunks had been seen against the fire, roaring like a jungle waterfall I had once heard, giving me the idea that all matter was one, and that all disturbances, whether of fire or water or air, were the same. Just as the firing ranges beyond Stonehenge suggested by their boom that air could be punctured, and just as the military aircraft, more destructive of sky and air each year, had grown to sound like giant railway trains circling about in the sky on resonant iron rails: a magnification of the railway sound which, when I heard it coming from behind the high brick wall at the end of the Earl's Court garden in 1950, heard it very early in the morning and late at night, had seemed to me to hold the drama and the promise of the bigger metropolitan life I had traveled to find.

Between the cattle slope and the pine screen the constriction in my chest vanished, as suddenly as it had come. I walked on to where the fenced pasture and the pine screen ended; to where, in a dip between slopes, the great rolls of hay had been stacked years before and never used and never taken away. Too black those rolls now, too mossy green in places, too close to pure rot, for them to be thought of as giant Swiss-roll cakes; too black for them to be thought of as larger newsprint rolls for the newspaper presses. Litter, debris, that black grass now, but part of the view, like the long shallow valley behind, open, never tilled, strewn with chalk and flint and looking like a valley in a higher, wilder place, strewn with dirty lumps of old snow. Beyond that, on the droveway, the land sloped up to the lark hills, the barrows and tumuli with their tufts of coarse grass and their stunted, wind-swept trees.

I knew the walk by heart, like a piece of music. I didn't go all the way to the top of the down. It wasn't necessary. I knew what I would see from there, in that light. I turned back; all the views of the walk unrolled again.

Later that evening, in my cottage, the choking fit returned. I felt my bronchial tubes contract and tighten. I waited for the fit to pass. But it didn't; everything tightened, seized up. Within a few hours I was seriously ill, but oddly light-headed. And it was in this light-headed mood—but seeing everything with great clarity, noticing with sur-prise and pleasure the unusualness of the view of the valley through the dark windows of the ambulance—that I was taken to the Infirmary in the town.

I had seen the building for years and had known it was the Infir-mary, the hospital, but had never thought about it, in spite of the com-ings and goings on the asphalt forecourt. I had seen it only as a building. I had seen remnants of the eighteenth-century brick (having learned to see age in red or reddish brick, which in 1950 I had found very ordinary, the material of little houses). I had seen the elegant Geor-gian letters of the legend—stating the voluntary nature of the Infir-mary and giving the date, 1767—carved right along a band of stone near the top of the flat facade.

The Infirmary was on the road to the railway station. It was past the bridge: here the rivers of the chalk valleys all around met and ran together, the water always clear, giving an extraordinary brilliance to scattered pieces of litter, the water seeming (like glass paperweights or like photographs) to have the power to isolate ordinary or well-known objects and force their details on the eye.

Ten years before, illness had heightened, had given a special quality to, my discovery of spring in the manor garden. The illness of that time—brought on by mental fatigue and travel—had been, to me, though it had lasted for many weeks, like the passing tropical fevers of my childhood, fevers associated with the rainy season, fevers which I thought ran their course too soon and which I longed for again. These fevers of childhood had been welcome because, with their great relaxing internal warmth, they pleasingly distorted the sense of touch and the sense of hearing, made the world remote, then very close, played tricks with time, seeming to awaken me at many different times to the same event; and with this drama and novelty (and the special foods and "broths") fevers always gave a feeling of home and protection.

With something like that kind of fever (and all that it implied, for the first time in England, of protection and ease) I had seen the peony below my window (in my half-waking delirium the tight red bud had grown tall on its stalk and tapped on my window in the wind); and the single blue iris among the nettles; and the thorny, scented moss roses; and the rotting bridges over the black creeks to the glory of the river, "freshing out."

It was with real illness now, a more than passing incapacity, a fatigue that seemed to have gone beyond the body to the core and motor of my being, a fatigue that made it necessary for me to judge very carefully first how many minutes I could be up and about for, and then how many hundred yards I could walk without burning up my strength and falling ill again, it was with true illness that when I came back from the Infirmary I began, after some time, to take short turns in the sodden, ruined manor garden. Indifferent to winter for many years after I had come to England, never feeling the need for an overcoat or gloves or even a pullover, I now had a sensation of internal coldness such as I had never had before; I felt chilled in my lungs.

Grass and weeds were tall and wet, black at the roots with different kinds of vegetable rot. Autumn had once had an enchantment of its own, with the trees and bushes "burning down" in their different ways, with different tints, with the wild mushrooms imitating the color and the shape of the dead leaves they grew among; with last year's dead aspen leaves like lace or tropical fan coral, the soft matter rotted away between the ribs or veins or supporting structure of each leaf, which yet preserved its curl and resilience. I had slowly learned the names of shrubs and trees. That knowledge, helping me visually to disentangle one plant from another in a mass of vegetation, quickly becoming more than a knowledge of names, had added to my appreciation. It was like learning a language, after living among its sounds. Now, with the growth of weeds and the advance of marsh plants, and the disappearance of the rose bed, to be in the garden was like being in the midst of undifferentiated bush. The sections of the fallen aspen trunks that had been too big to saw up or remove had disappeared below bush.

The colors of the autumn in the garden were now brown and black. I had learned to see the brown of dead leaves and stalks as a color in its own right; I had collected grasses and reeds and taken pleasure in the slow change of their color from green to biscuit brown. I had even taken pleasure in the browned tints of flowers that had dried in vases without losing their petals; I had been unwilling to throw away such flowers. On autumn or winter mornings I had gone out to see brown leaves and stalks outlined with white frost. Now the hand of man had been withdrawn from the garden; everything had grown unchecked during the summer; and I felt only the cold and saw the tall grass and the wet and saw black and brown. On these short walks in the ruined manor garden, going a little farther each time, past the aspens, then past the great evergreen tree, then approaching the big white-framed greenhouse, after all this time as solid and whole-looking as it had ever been, on these walks brown became again for me what it had been in Trinidad: not a true color, the color of dead vegetation, not a thing one found beauty in, trash.

And it was against this brown that one day, going past the greenhouse to where on my earliest walks towards the river I had found a gate (which still worked when I first came upon it) and bridges over the black, leaf-filled creeks, it was against this black and brown that I saw a new post-and-rail timber fence, the new wood blond and red, like the color of the hair of the unshaved fat man the German had said was his brother, like the color of the nylon sack the unshaved fat man was carrying, to take away the rotten logs or whatever it was he had intended to pillage.

I hadn't heard about this fence or the sale of land it implied. The ground all about was wild; even if I had the energy it would have been hard to go beyond the first creek. But I could see that the line of the new fence ran diagonally across the line of the old path and bridges that led from the garden to the river. A surveyor's line, drawn on a land map; not a line that made allowances for the way the land had been used.

I had trained myself to the idea of change, to avoid grief; not to see decay. It had been necessary, because the setting of this second life had begun to change almost as soon as I had awakened to its benignity. The moss roses had been cut down; the open droveway had been bisected by a barbed-wire fence; fields had been enclosed. Jack's garden had been destroyed in stages and finally concreted over. The wide gate at the end of the lawn outside my cottage had been closed after Pitton left, and cut branches had blocked the way there. And then barbed wire—of all chilling things—had been wound around what had been built as a children's play house in the orchard.

I had lived with the idea of change, had seen it as a constant, had seen a world in flux, had seen human life as a series of cycles that sometimes ran together. But philosophy failed me now. Land is not land alone, something that simply is itself. Land partakes of what we breathe into it, is touched by our moods and memories. And this end of a cycle, in my life, and in the life of the manor, mixed up with the feeling of age which my illness was forcing on me, caused me grief.

I liked the neighbor. I had nothing against him—he had unwittingly shown me where I was to move. He was reverential about what he wished to acquire; the valley and the land were his in a special way as well. His mother had lived as a girl in a farmhouse (now partly in ruin) beside the river. No lack of reverence there; and I had always known that there was no means of preserving a landscape which—in its particular purity for me—existed for me after that first spring only in my heart. From that first spring I had known that such a moment was going to come. But now that it had come, it was shocking. And as at a death, everything here that had been a source of pleasure and surprise, everything that had welcomed me and healed me, became a cause for pain.

*T*HE MANOR help came, lived for a while in the two redecorated rooms, each woman in her own way and with her own hallowed things; and then went away. But someone at last seemed to suit; and Mrs. Phillips felt secure enough to start taking up the threads of her private life again.

The private life, the one she had shared with Mr. Phillips, had been full of public pleasures—pubs, clubs, hotel bars, modest country-town restaurants with dance floors or cabarets—pleasures which, more than house or the sense of place or job or vocation, had given stability and rhythm to the Phillipses' year. This rhythm, overriding her grief, now claimed her; and in the early spring, at what had been one of her and Mr. Phillips's two holiday times, she went off for a fortnight with old friends.

In her absence, her assistant came out of the manor shadows, showed herself, and explored the grounds without constraint. A thin woman of about fifty, as pleased with the solitude and spaciousness of the manor grounds as that other woman or girl had been all those years before, the one who had tied the tails of her shirt above her bare midriff. A different kind of dress on this older woman: she wore an expensive tweed skirt. She had invested much in this skirt. She was like Pitton, I thought: living up to the place and, though a servant, slightly in competition with it. How she changed the place for me! I felt myself, after all these years, under inspection again.

When Mrs. Phillips came back, the strange lady withdrew, became timorous, nervous, as though unwilling for her relationship with Mrs. Phillips to be seen too clearly by me.

The holiday had done Mrs. Phillips much good. Her forehead was smoother; the skin below her eyes was less dark, less gathered up; and her voice was lighter. This lightness of voice was especially noticeable on the telephone. She sounded quite mischievous when, two weeks after she had come back from her holiday, she telephoned to say she had a gift for me and wanted to bring it over.

She was in her sporty quilted anorak. She held a walking stick lightly in both her hands, holding the stick horizontally; and when she held it in one hand it was with the gesture of someone not used to a walking stick, not knowing how to hold it or walk with it.

She said, "I went to see Stan's father on Sunday. He wants you to have his stick."

It was the pronged stick, the staff in the prong of which he rested his thumb as he walked in the grounds of the manor. He was the first person I had seen using this kind of stick. I was myself a user of sticks on my walks. From my father—who had made them for pleasure in Trinidad, from certain forest trees—I had inherited a feeling for walking sticks; and in my early days as a traveler I had always tried to bring back a stick from the country I was traveling in.

His pronged staff was the first thing old Mr. Phillips and I had talked about. He knew that when he walked with it in the manor grounds he had my attention. And now it was his gift. Examining it as a new object, a gift, I found it was shorter than I had remembered. I had remembered it as tall as the old man's shoulder; it was in fact the height of the stick fighter's staff, as high as the lower rib of the user. The bark of the prong and of the wood an inch or so below the prong had been peeled. And just below that piece of stylishness was another: a brass-colored metal band. I hadn't noticed that before, in the staff the old man used; and the staff that Mrs. Phillips had brought was so shiny with new varnish that I thought the old man might have bought a new one for me. But the inch-long black cap at the bottom of the staff, a cap in rubber or some composite material, was worn, front and back.

It was the old man's staff; he had prettied it up because he intended it to be a gift.

I said to Mrs. Phillips, "I will keep it as long as I live."

Just a few years before, this would have seemed to me a big thing to say. Now the words, as soon as they were spoken, made me feel that the protection I offered the old man's gift was hardly protection at all; that just as certain memories of down and river, chalk and moss, were to die with the old man, be untransmittable, so, even if I could bequeath the stick to some considerate inheritor, I could not pass on its associations. Without those associations, the stick, like the blond-and-dark disc of the ivy-choked cherry tree which I had had smoothed down and varnished, a souvenir and a record of the later life of the manor garden, would become no more than an object.

Mrs. Phillips said, "Funny old man."

Strange words; strange distance between herself and the old man. The distance showed in her face as well: the smoother skin, the new clarity of the eyes, the lack of fatigue. And there was, in the tone of her speech, a reviving irony and love of life.

She said, "I think I should tell you before you hear it from somebody else. You know how gossip flies about the valley. I've given my notice."

So the gift of the stick acquired another association. Mrs. Phillips's bringing it over—that almost mischievous voice on the telephone, that distancing of herself from old Mr. Phillips, who had until recently walked with such privilege in the manor grounds—that gift was like the winding down of her manor life. How easily she seemed to do it! As soon as I had got to know the Phillipses, had stopped seeing them as exemplars of their job, I had admired them for their adventurousness, their getting by with so little, their readiness to move on. Yet now Mrs. Phillips's news added a touch of desolation to the beauty of the gift she had brought.

She said, "I don't have to tell you. It hasn't been much of a life here since Stan died. Stan could have managed. I can't do it by myself. He's very difficult." This was a reference to my landlord. "And it isn't going to get better. That's what makes it hard. It isn't the kind of thing where you feel that what you do is going to make things better."

She began to move towards the door. She paused; she looked through the high glass panes of the kitchen door at the broken aspens, growing vigorously again from their stumps.

She said, and her tone was intimate, half questioning, half looking for reassurance—I might have been a relation: "I met someone on holiday. He joined our group for dinner one day. So many matchmakers among one's friends. You wouldn't believe. Anyway. I thought I'd let you know before the gossip reaches you. Stan and I agreed on that. Whoever remained should marry again."

It was strange. She had never been so easy with me, so without strain, the strain first of all of her strangeness in the manor, her uncertainty with me, then the strain of her illness, then the strain of her solitude. And perhaps, as I thought now, the strain of her life with Mr. Phillips, the man of great strength. And I, as if in response to her new personality, had never felt so close to her.

*T*HE NEWS, as Mrs. Phillips said, spread fast about the valley. It got to Bray. His first thoughts were for my landlord, the master of the manor. He said, and it was as though he was speaking of himself as well, "Old age is a brutal thing. I suppose they'll just sell up. In the end there'll be nothing left."

I said, "It's lasted all his life. Not many people can say that. That's happiness."

He stayed with his own thoughts. "When you are young you can fight back. When you're old they can do anything they want with you."

His slit eyes narrowed; a tear ran down his soft, middle-aged cheek. In spite of his talk, the dignity of the house had always mattered to him. He had always taken an interest in its affairs. The dignity of the house had given value to his independence; it was what he measured his own dignity against. The deepest part of him, the part with the hidden memories, the memories that would die with him, was his servant's character.

Squinting at the road, the tears running down his cheeks, Bray said, "She's left. She became very ill and had to go back to the home."

It was the first time he had mentioned the woman he had seen at Salisbury railway station at midnight, the solitary woman in the big tweed coat in the bright lights of the nearly empty station.

THE CEREMONY OF FAREWELL

*I*N MY late thirties the dream of disappointment and exhaustion had been the dream of the exploding head: the dream of a noise in my head so loud and long that I felt with the brain that survived that the brain could not survive; that this was death. Now, in my early fifties, after my illness, after I had left the manor cottage and put an end to that section of my life, I began to be awakened by thoughts of death, the end of things; and sometimes not even by thoughts so specific, not even by fear rational or fantastic, but by a great melancholy. This melancholy penetrated my mind while I slept; and then, when I awakened in response to its prompting, I was so poisoned by it, made so much not a doer (as men must be, every day of their lives), that it took the best part of the day to shake it off. And that wasted or dark day added to the gloom preparing for the night.

I had thought for years about a book like *The Enigma of Arrival*. The Mediterranean fantasy that had come to me a day or so after I had arrived in the valley—the story of the traveler, the strange city, the spent life—had been modified over the years. The fantasy and the ancient-world setting had been dropped. The story had become more personal: my journey, the writer's journey, the writer defined by his writing discoveries, his ways of seeing, rather than by his personal adventures, writer and man separating at the beginning of the journey and coming together again in a second life just before the end.

My theme, the narrative to carry it, my characters—for some years I felt they were sitting on my shoulder, waiting to declare themselves and to possess me. But it was only out of this new awareness of death that I began at last to write. Death was the motif; it had perhaps been the motif all along. Death and the way of handling it—that was the motif of the story of Jack.

It was a journalistic assignment that got me started. In August 1984 I had gone to the Republican Convention in Dallas for the *New York Review of Books*. I had found nothing to write about. The occasion was overstaged, scripted in advance, and in itself empty; and I was oppressed by the idea of thousands of busy journalists simply finding new words for stories that had in effect been already written for them. It was only back in Wiltshire, away from the oppressiveness and hand-outs of the convention center, that I began to be able to acknowledge what I had responded to: not the formal, staged occasion, but the things around the occasion. And suddenly, where there had been nothing to write about, there was a great deal: the experience of a week, all new, which, without the writing, would have vanished and been lost to me. With the discovery of that experience came the language and the tone appropriate to the experience.

It was out of that excitement, finding experience where I thought there had been nothing, and out of that reawakened delight in language, that I began immediately afterwards to write my book. I let my hand move. I wrote the first pages of many different books; stopped, started again. Then from apparently far away the memory of Jack, peripheral to my life, came to me; and with it the conviction that to write of Jack was the best way to get started, to summon up the material of *The Enigma of Arrival*, to set the scene and themes, to indicate the time-spread of the book I was intending to write. For some weeks I made many starts, allowing my hand to run; starting at different points.

There were interruptions. A bad molar. It was extracted—quite suddenly, it seemed. An extraction wasn't at all what I had been expecting when I went to the dentist, who usually saved things; and there came to me a sense of decay, uneffaceable, as I felt, through the anesthetic, the dentist's strong fingers pushing at the painless tooth; a sense of death. Two days later, with a salty rawness in my mouth, there was a prize-giving lunch for an old writer friend in London—this occasion mixed up with looking for a new flat in London, and the special gloom of looking at old flats, other lives, other views. Then Mrs. Gandhi was shot dead by her bodyguard in Delhi. Immediately after that there was a visit to Germany for my publisher in that country: the shock of East Berlin, still in parts destroyed after forty years, seedlings grown into trees high on the wrecked masonry of some buildings, a vision of a world undoing itself: new to me: I should have gone long before to look. On the morning of my last day in Germany, in West Berlin, I went to the Egyptian Museum. I returned to Wiltshire to the news that my younger sister, Sati, had had a brain hemorrhage in Trinidad that day: just at the time I was leaving the museum. She was in a coma; she was not to recover. For more than thirty years, since the death of my father in 1953, I had lived without grief. I took the news coldly, therefore; then I had hiccups; then I became concerned.

When I had left Trinidad in 1950, when the little Pan American Airways System plane had taken me away, Sati was seven weeks short of her sixteenth birthday. When I next saw her and heard her voice she was nearly twenty-two, and married. Trinidad had since become almost an imaginary place for me; but she had lived all her life there, apart from short holidays abroad. She had lived through my father's illness in 1952 and death in 1953; the political changes, the racial politics from 1956, the dangers of the street, the near-revolution and anarchy of 1970. She had also lived through the oil boom; she had known ease for many years; she could think of her life as a success.

Three days after her death, at the time she was being cremated in Trinidad, I spread her photographs in front of me on the low coffee table in the sitting room of my new house in Wiltshire. I had been intending for years to sort out these family photographs, put them in albums. There had always seemed to be time. In these photographs, while she had lived, I had not noticed her age. Now I saw that many of the photographs—her little honeymoon snapshots especially—were of a young girl with slender arms. That girl was now someone whose life had been lived; death had, painfully, touched these snapshots with youth. I looked at the pictures I had laid out and thought about Sati harder than I had ever thought about her. After thirty-five or forty minutes—the cremation going on in Trinidad, as I thought—I felt purged. I had had no rules to follow; but I felt I had done the right thing. I had concentrated on that person, that life, that unique character; I had honored the person who had lived.

Two days later I went to Trinidad. The family had wanted me to be with them. My brother had gone on the day of our sister's cremation. He had arrived six hours after the cremation; he had asked then to be taken to the cremation site. My elder sister drove him. It was night; the pyre after six hours was still glowing. My brother walked up alone to the glow, and my sister, from the car, watched him looking at the glowing pyre.

Two weeks before, my brother had been in Delhi for Mrs. Gandhi's cremation. In London, then, he had written a major article; now, that writing barely finished, he had come to Trinidad. Modern airplanes had made these big journeys possible; had exposed him to these deaths. In 1950, when I left Trinidad, airplane travel was still unusual. To go abroad could be to fracture one's life: it was six years before I saw or heard members of my family again; I lost six years of their lives. There was no question, in 1953, when my father died, of my returning home. My brother it was, then aged eight, who performed and witnessed the terrible final rites of cremation. The event marked him. That death and cremation were his private wound. And now there was this cremation of his sister: still a pyre and a glow after his airplane flight from London. Soon an airplane took him back to London. And airplanes took other members of the family to other places.

I stayed on in Trinidad for the religious ceremony that took place some days later and was complementary to the cremation. Sati had not been religious; like my father, she had had no feeling for ritual.

But at her death her family wished to have all the Hindu rites performed for her, to leave nothing undone.

The pundit, a big man, was late for this ceremony. He had been late for the cremation as well, I had heard. He said something now about being busy and harassed, about misreading his watch; and settled down to his duties. The materials he needed were ready for him. A shallow earth altar had been laid out on a board on the terrazzo of Sati's veranda. To me the ritual in this setting—the suburban house and garden, the suburban street—was new and strange. My memories were old; I associated this kind of ritual with more country scenes.

The pundit in his silk tunic sat cross-legged on one side of the altar. Sati's younger son sat facing him on the other side. Sati's son was in jeans and jumper—and this informality of dress was also new to me. The earth rites the pundit began to perform on the veranda appeared to mimic Sati's cremation; but these rites suggested fertility and growth rather than the returning of the body by way of fire to the earth, the elements. Sacrifice and feeding—that was the theme. Always, in Aryan scriptures, this emphasis on sacrifice!

There was a complicated physical side to the ceremony, as with so many Hindu ceremonies: knowing where on the altar to put the sacrificial flowers, knowing how to sing the verses and when, knowing how and when and where to pour various substances: the whole mechanical side of priesthood. The pundit led Sati's son through the complications, telling him what offerings to make to the sacred fire, to say *swa-ha* when the offerings were placed with a downward gesture of the fingers, to say *shruddha* when the fingers were flicked back from the open palm to scatter the offering onto the fire.

Then the pundit began to do a little more. He became aware of the people on the veranda who were his audience and he began, while instructing Sati's son, partly to address us in a general religious way. He told Sati's son it was necessary for him to cool his lusts; he began to use texts and words that might have served on many other solemn occasions. Something else was new to me: the pundit was being "ecumenical" in a way he wouldn't have been when I was a child, equating Hinduism—speculative, many-sided, with animist roots—with the revealed faiths of Christianity and Mohammedanism. Indeed the pundit said at one stage—talking indirectly to us as though we were a Trinidad public assembly and many of us were of other faiths—that the Gita was like the Koran and the Bible. It was the pundit's way of saying that we too had a Book; it was his way, in a changed Trinidad, of defending our faith and ways.

In spite of his jeans, Sati's son was serious. He was humble in the presence of the pundit, not a formally educated man, for whom—on another day, in another setting—he might have had little time. He seemed to be looking to the pundit for consolation, a support greater than the support of ritual. He was listening to everything the pundit said. The pundit, continuing to add moral and religious teaching to the complicated ritual he was performing with earth and flowers and flour and clarified butter and milk, said that our past lives dictated the present. Sati's son asked in what way Sati's past had dictated the cruelty of her death. The pundit didn't answer. But Sati's son, if he had been more of a Hindu, if he had more of a Hindu cast of mind, would have understood the idea of karma, and wouldn't have asked the question. He would have yielded to the mystery of the ritual and accepted the pundit's words as part of the ritual.

The pundit went on with the physical side of his business. That was what people looked to a pundit for; that was what they wished to see carried out as correctly as possible—this pressing together of balls of rice and then of balls of earth, this arranging of flowers and pouring of milk on heaps of this and that, this constant feeding of the sacred fire.

Afterwards the pundit had lunch. In the old days he would have eaten sitting cross-legged on blankets or flour sacks or sugar sacks spread on the top with cotton. He would have been carefully fed and constantly waited on. Now—sumptuously served, but all at once—he ate sitting at a table in the veranda. He ate by himself. He ate great quantities of food, using his hands as he had used them earlier with the earth and the rice and the sacrificial offerings of the earth altar.

Sati's husband and her son sat with the pundit while he ate. They asked him, while he ate, and as though being a pundit he knew, what were the chances of an afterlife for Sati. It was not strictly a Hindu question; and it sounded strange, after the rite we had witnessed.

Sati's husband said, "I would like to see her again." His voice sounded whole; but there were tears in his eyes.

The pundit didn't give a straight reply. The Hindu idea of reincarnation, the idea of men being released from the cycle of rebirth after a series of good lives—if that was in the pundit's mind, it would have been too hard to pass on to people who were so grief-stricken.

Sati's son asked, "Will she come back?"

Sati's husband asked, "Will we be together again?"

The pundit said, "But you wouldn't know it is her."

It was the pundit's interpretation of the idea of reincarnation. And it was no comfort at all. It reduced Sati's husband to despair.

I asked to see the Gita the pundit had been using during the ceremony. It was from a South Indian press. After each verse there was an English translation. The pundit, in between his ritual doings and his chanting of a few well-known Sanskrit verses, had made use of the English translations from this Gita.

The pundit said he gave away Gitas. Then, using an ecumenical word (as I thought), he said he "shared" Gitas. People gave him Gitas; he gave people Gitas. One devout man bought Gitas a dozen at a time and passed them on to him; he passed them on to others.

And then, his pundit's duties done, his lunch over, the pundit became social, expansive, as, from my childhood, I had known pundits to be when they had done their duties.

He began to tell a story. I couldn't understand the story. An important man in the community had asked him one day: "What do you think is the best Hindu scripture?" He, the pundit, had replied, "The Gita." The man had then said to somebody else present, "He says the Gita is the best Hindu scripture." There should have been more to the story. But there was no more. Either that was the end of the story so far as the pundit was concerned—a mentioning of famous local people, a bearing of witness in the presence of famous people. Or he had found that the story was leading him into areas he didn't want to go to; or he had forgotten the point of the story. Or in fact the point was as he had made it: that he thought the Gita was the most important Hindu scripture. (Though, at the very end, just before he left, he said that his pundit's duties left him little time to read the Gita.)

And to add to the intellectual randomness of the occasion, the pundit began without prompting to speak, and with passion, about the internal Hindu controversy between the conservatives, on whose side the pundit was, and the reformists, who the pundit thought were hypocrites. I had thought that this issue had died in Trinidad fifty years before and was part almost of our pastoral past, when the life of our community was more self-contained. I could not imagine it surviving racial politics and the stresses of independence. But the pundit spoke of it as something that still mattered.

The pundit was a relation, a first cousin. And the great irony—or appropriateness—of the situation was like this. I had discovered through the adventure of writing—curiosity and knowledge feeding off one another, committing one not only to travel but also to different explorations of the past—I had discovered that my father had been intended by his grandmother and mother to be a pundit. My father hadn't become a pundit. He had instead become a journalist; and his literary ambitions had seeded the literary ambitions of his two sons. But it was because of his family's wish to make him a pundit that my father, in circumstances of desperate poverty before the first war, had been given an education; while my father's brother had been sent to the fields as a child to work for eight cents a day. The two branches of the family had ever after divided. My father's brother had made himself into a small cane farmer; at the end of his life he was far better off than my journalist father had been at the end of his. My father had died in 1953, impoverished after a long illness; my father's brother had contributed to the cremation expenses. But there had been little contact between our families. Physically, even, we were different. We (except for my brother) were small people; my father's brother's sons were six-footers. And now, after the ups and downs of fortune, a pundit had arisen in the family; and this pundit, the heavy six-footer who had performed the rites on my sister's veranda, came from my father's brother's family. This pundit had served my father's family, attended at the first death among my father's children. Some of the pundit's demeanor would have been explained by the family relationship, his wish to assert himself among us.

The other, internal irony was that my father, though devoted to Hindu speculative thought, had disliked ritual and had always, even in the 1920s, belonged to the reformist group the pundit didn't care for and dismissed now as hypocrites. My sister Sati had no liking for ritual either. But at her death there was in her family a wish to give sanctity to the occasion, a wish for old rites, for things that were felt specifically to represent us and our past. So the pundit had been called in; and on the terrazzo floor of my sister's veranda symbolical cere- monies had been played out on an earth altar, laid with a miniature pyre of fragrant pitch pine and flowers and sugar which, when soaked with clarified butter and set alight, made a sweet caramel smell.

We were immemorially people of the countryside, far from the courts of princes, living according to rituals we didn't always under- stand and yet were unwilling to dishonor because that would cut us off from the past, the sacred earth, the gods. Those earth rites went back far. They would always have been partly mysterious. But we couldn't surrender to them now. We had become self-aware. Forty years before, we would not have been so self-aware. We would have accepted; we would have felt ourselves to be more whole, more in tune with the land and the spirit of the earth.

It would have been easier to accept, too, because forty years be- fore, it would have been all so much poorer, so much closer to the Indian past: houses, roads, vehicles, clothes. Now money had touched us all—like a branch of a tree or a twig dipped in gold, according to some designer's extravagant whim, and made to keep the shape of the twig or the leaf. Generations of a new kind of education had separated us from our past; and travel; and history. And the money that had come to our island, from oil and natural gas.

That money, that unexpected bounty, had ravaged and remade the landscape where we had had our beginnings in the New World. When I was a child the hills of the Northern Range which I looked at when

I traveled up to Port of Spain on the ten-mile-an-hour train were
bare—primary forest still in parts. Now halfway up those hills there
were the huts and shacks of illegal immigrants from the other islands.
Small islands surrounded by sea: plantation barracoons, slavery and
Africa quarantined and festering together for two centuries: immigrants from those islands had altered our landscape, our population,
our mood.

Where there had been swamp at the foot of the Northern Range,
with mud huts with earthen walls that showed the damp halfway up,
there was now a landscape of Holland: acres upon acres of vegetable
plots, the ridges and furrows and irrigation canals straight. Sugarcane
as a crop had ceased to be important. None of the Indian villages were
like villages I had known. No narrow roads; no dark, overhanging
trees; no huts; no earth yards with hibiscus hedges; no ceremonial
lighting of lamps, no play of shadows on the wall; no cooking of food
in half-walled verandas, no leaping firelight; no flowers along gutters
or ditches where frogs croaked the night away. But highways and
clover-shaped exits and direction boards: a wooded land laid bare, its
secrets opened up.

We had made ourselves anew. The world we found ourselves in
—the suburban houses, with gardens, where my sister's farewell ceremony had taken place—was one we had partly made ourselves, and
had longed for, when we had longed for money and the end of distress; we couldn't go back. There was no ship of antique shape now
to take us back. We had come out of the nightmare; and there was
nowhere else to go.

The pundit gave his last instructions. One brass plate with consecrated food was to be placed somewhere; another plate of food was
to be cast into the river that had borne away her ashes: a final offering.
Then, a big man dressed in cream-colored silk, the silk showing the
heaviness above his waist, the pundit got in his car and drove away.
(Such memories I had of Sunday visits, holiday excursions, with my
father to his family house—my father's brother's house—forty years
and more before: flat sugarcane fields all around, grass tracks between
the fields, scattered huts and houses on stilts and tall pillars, dimly

lit at night, animals in some yards, bonfires of grass to keep away mosquitoes, grocery shops with pitched corrugated-iron roofs, and silence.)

A visitor, an old man, a distant relation of my sister's husband, began—perhaps because of the ceremonies that had taken place—to talk of our past, and of the difference between us, originally from the Gangetic plain, immigrants to the New World since 1845, and the other Indians in other parts of the island, especially in the villages to the northwest of Port of Spain.

This man said, "Those other people haven't been here since 1845, you know. They've been here long, long before. You've heard about Columbus? Well, Queen Isabella opened this place up to everybody, provided they was Catholics. And that was when the French came in. They was Catholics, you see. Now, you hear about a place in India called Pondicherry? That was the French place in India, and that was where they bring over those Indians near Port of Spain from. So those Indian people up in Boissière and places like that, they not like us—they've been here four, five hundred years."

History! He had run together the events of 1498, when Columbus had discovered the island for Queen Isabella on his third voyage; 1784, when the Spanish authorities, after three hundred years of neglect, and out of a wish to protect their empire, opened up the island to Catholic immigration, giving preference and free land to people who could bring in slaves; and 1845, when the British, ten years after slavery had been abolished in the British Empire, began to bring in Indians from India to work the land. He had created a composite history. But it was enough for him. Men need history; it helps them to have an idea of who they are. But history, like sanctity, can reside in the heart; it is enough that there is something there.

Our sacred world—the sanctities that had been handed down to us as children by our families, the sacred places of our childhood, sacred because we had seen them as children and had filled them with wonder, places doubly and trebly sacred to me because far away in England I had lived in them imaginatively over many books and had in my fantasy set in those places the very beginning of things, had constructed out of them a fantasy of home, though I was to learn that the ground was bloody, that there had been aboriginal people there once, who had been killed or made to die away—our sacred world had vanished. Every generation now was to take us further away from those sanctities. But we remade the world for ourselves; every generation does that, as we found when we came together for the death of this sister and felt the need to honor and remember. It forced us to look on death. It forced me to face the death I had been contemplating at night, in my sleep; it fitted a real grief where melancholy had created a vacancy, as if to prepare me for the moment. It showed me life and man as the mystery, the true religion of men, the grief and the glory. And that was when, faced with a real death, and with this new wonder about men, I laid aside my drafts and hesitations and began to write very fast about Jack and his garden.

October 1984–April 1986

A Note on the Type

THIS BOOK WAS SET VIA COMPUTER-DRIVEN CATHODE-RAY TUBE IN FOURNIER, A TYPEFACE NAMED FOR PIERRE SIMON FOURNIER, A CELEBRATED TYPE DESIGNER IN EIGHTEENTH-CENTURY FRANCE. FOURNIER'S TYPE IS CONSIDERED TRANSITIONAL IN THAT IT DREW ITS INSPIRATION FROM THE OLD STYLE YET WAS INGENIOUSLY INNOVATIONAL IN ITS NARROW ELEGANCE AND ANGLING OF THE SERIFS. FOR SOME TIME AFTER HIS DEATH IN 1768, FOURNIER WAS REMEMBERED PRIMARILY AS THE AUTHOR OF A FAMOUS MANUAL OF TYPOGRAPHY AND AS A PIONEER OF THE POINT SYSTEM. SIGNIFICANT MODERN APPRECIATION OF HIS TYPEFACE BEGAN WITH D. B. UPDIKE'S *PRINTING TYPES* IN 1922, FOLLOWED SOON AFTER BY THE MONOTYPE CORPORATION'S REVIVAL OF FOURNIER'S ROMAN AND ITALIC TYPES.

COMPOSED BY CRANE TYPESETTING
BARNSTABLE, MASSACHUSETTS
PRINTED AND BOUND BY THE HADDON CRAFTSMEN, INC.,
SCRANTON, PENNSYLVANIA

DESIGNED BY PETER A. ANDERSEN